QUEST FOR THE
DRAGON STAR

An Oral History of WMAC Masters

Kristopher Landis

This book is dedicated to the men and women who made WMAC Masters possible, which in turn inspired future generations.

In memory of Richard Branden.

FORWARD BY **HERB PEREZ**

There are times when the Universe and all its energy come together to allow an extraordinary, life-changing event to occur. In these times, those of us affected simply need to realize this and walk through the door of opportunity that has been opened for us through the good fortune of chance. Luckily for all of us involved, we all saw the potential and took the path for what would be an amazing ride as the characters of *WMAC Masters*. Little did we know the impact it would leave on us and others but perhaps more importantly, all the amazing lifelong fans.

For a short time, the Quest for the Dragon Star held children and martial arts enthusiasts in weekly anticipation of what new developments would be revealed every Saturday morning. Who would take a step closer to becoming the next champion, who would reveal the truth behind JuKiDo, and how many lines would Tiger Claw lose at the next script reading? (inside joke)

For a moment, a small group of gifted martial artists, and an incredibly talented creative team led by Dan Hubp entertained America with good old-fashioned wholesome storylines and action. As a result, a new generation of martial artists was inspired to enter schools around the world and study martial arts so they too could join the Quest to be their Best.

In closing, we must thank Kristopher Landis, Victoria Spahn, and Jenny Leidecker for their endless passion and perseverance in creating this book. Without them, the story behind our show would have been untold and lost forever. It is genuinely humbling for all of us involved to have this team create and complete this Sisyphean task. If I may be so bold, on behalf of the *WMAC Masters*, we are eternally thankful. May this book serve as a constant reminder that we are blessed to have taken this journey to become martial artists and are better for it. I hope this book will continue the legacy and inspire future generations to train and become Champions in Life and whatever passion they choose to pursue.

Long Live the Dragon Star!

TABLE OF **CONTENTS**

CHAPTER 01
Introduction

I wish I could tell you I had some fantastic story about the first time I watched *WMAC Masters*. It'd be the perfect beginning to this book. How seven year old me sat on the couch in our living room, cereal bowl in hand, enraptured, watching Superstar and Olympus and The Machine all kick the stuffing out of ninjas, and then each other; or staring, dumbfounded as Great Wolf shattered a massive block of ice with one blow.

Unfortunately, I can't do that. The simple answer is I just don't remember. When I think about loving *WMAC Masters* as a kid, it was just... always there. I owned the action figures and VHS tapes. I took a year of Tae Kwon Do because I wanted to be Olympus. My elementary school principal even scolded me once for organizing our own "Battle Dome" matches inside a dome-shaped jungle gym, but the origin of my love of the show eludes me. *WMAC Masters* feels like it was just always there, a building block of my childhood.

I will, however, offer you an origin story of the making of this book instead.

It all began in the spring of 2021. It wasn't supposed to be a book at all. At that time, I planned to make it into just another blog, or maybe a series of pieces on the platform Medium, if I could drum up enough interest. I was pondering my next project in the wake of my debut novel, *Murder at Daybreak*, blowing up in my face. Long story short, the publisher, a fly-by-night charlatan who popped up in the midst of the pandemic to prey on writers, decided to simply not honor the contracts of his writers and staff, absconding with all the money instead. I wasn't prepared mentally or emotionally to attempt to re-edit and republish that book or consider writing another work of fiction. I needed something different. Something I felt passionate about that I could lose myself in for a while. It's weird how things happen sometimes.

As many people do, I retreated into the comfort of nostalgia to cheer myself up and began watching old episodes of *WMAC Masters* on YouTube. When I finished, I found myself, once again, for the umpteenth time in my life, at the show's cliffhanger ending. I was frustrated, a familiar feeling watching the end of that last episode. Surely there was someone out there who knew where the story was going. I started to wonder, as one does, if anyone had ever written anything about it or if anyone had told the story of what was to happen next before the show's cancellation. A deep Google dive later revealed that no one had written about the show much at all. There was definitely no in-depth piece I could find anywhere. Trust me; I looked everywhere.

I decided I needed to know more. Specifically, I wanted to know if anyone involved with the show remembered where the story was heading, and more importantly, would someone tell me. So, really, this book started because I needed to solve a mystery. My writing background (one novel and some time spent covering the Columbus Crew, my hometown Major League Soccer team) gave me just enough juice to seem legitimate, or at least I hoped it would. So I did some digging and found email addresses for several cast members. I told them that I was a writer working on something about the show. Which was true. However, I wasn't about to tell them I had no real idea what form that something was going to take.

Chris Casamassa was the first to respond and say yes to talking with me. I don't know if you'd be reading this book if he hadn't been so kind, outgoing, and open in sharing his stories and memories with me about the show. Someone the caliber of Red Dragon (or Scorpion, if you're a *Mortal Kombat* fan) treating me like a legitimate writer not only gave me the confidence to take things on with aplomb but also helped to boost the legitimacy of me and this project in the eyes of the other cast members. Being able to toss out that, "I've already spoken with Chris" was a huge help in getting some of the others to agree to an interview with me.

It all grew from there. Each interview opened another door for me. "You should talk to..." and "let me get you in touch with..." became phrases I heard repeatedly. I was then and still remain overwhelmed with the openness and support the cast and crew showed me. As an outsider with no connection to the show other than being a fan, they had no reason to be as helpful as they were. It has been one of the most humbling experiences of my life.

All those stories and meetings finally led to the moment I had hoped for and set out to achieve. I was on a Zoom call with Norman Grossfeld, the show's Executive Producer, where he laid out the plans and storyline of the show and where it was heading in the future. It was surreal. Even as the cast and crew welcomed me into their world and trusted me to tell their story, I never truly believed I'd find out what was going to happen in Season Three. I've gone back dozens of times and watched the video of that call with him, and it's clear on my face how those revelations of what was to come affected me- I even get a little misty-eyed during the interview. No shame in my game, to steal a phrase from Bridgett Riley.

That moment wasn't the end of my journey by a long shot. By this time in the process, I knew I was writing a book, this book, an oral history of the show itself and what it meant to those who created it and the cast members. I wanted to speak to everyone, and I definitely tried, but I didn't quite hit that lofty goal, some of the cast and crew remained unreachable, while others were not interested. I came damn close, though.

The book grew, then grew some more, and then it kept growing. A simple social media push led to starting a Patreon where I post behind-the-scenes info, book updates, and stories that didn't quite make the cut. The book continued to grow, not just in word count either. It was on a call one day with Master Willie "The Bam" Johnson that it grew beyond anything I expected when he asked me if I wanted to help him put together a cast reunion in conjunction with the US Capitol Classics martial arts tournament.

As if there was an answer I'd ever give other than "yes." As of this writing, that reunion is still a couple of months away. I'm sure I'll cover it extensively on my Patreon account, and you'll be able to find plenty of exclusive posts on there if you're interested. If it goes even half as well as writing this book has, it will be an amazing experience, to say the least.

Amazing experience doesn't begin to do justice to what writing this book has meant to me. To interview and connect with the men and women who were literally heroes (and, in one notable case, a crush) to my seven-year-old self has been surreal in the best way possible. Being treated as just one of the gang has impacted me even more. To sit under the learning tree of Master Bam and work with him on the reunion has been one of the best learning experiences of my life so far.

This whole process has restored my confidence as a writer and opened up new worlds of possibility to me, both personally and professionally. I hope that this book offers you some small window into the minds and hearts of the amazing men and women who made the show possible. Even though Bandai, the show's primary financiers, may have treated the show as little more than a vehicle for selling toys, the people involved in making it cared deeply about the project and the message they were spreading to the youth of America (and, for that matter, the world).

It has been the greatest honor of my professional career to get to share this story and perhaps add my own small piece to it. I hope you all enjoy this book as much as I have enjoyed writing it.

How the Show Works

If you're new to the *WMAC Masters* universe and are using this book as a guide to your first viewing, here's what you need to know before you dive in:

The World Martial Arts Council (WMAC) is a fictional organization that brought together the top competitors in eleven disciplines to crown the World's Greatest Martial Artist. It takes the form of a tournament, which is a continuing competition in which fighters vie to become the Dragon Star Champion. Each episode of the show is one week's installment of the competition.

The majority of the episodes follow the same basic structure. There are three matches in each episode, two preliminary fights at Battle Zones, the winners of which meet in that week's Battle Dome final. Whoever wins the Battle Dome adds their defeated opponent's Ki Symbol to their Dragon Belt. When you get to ten Ki Symbols, you can challenge for the Dragon Star.

In the preliminary fights, two Masters square off, trying to drain each other's power bars in a very video game-like fashion. Then, ninja warriors are added to the mix, attacking both Masters to up the action ante and difficulty level. The winner is the first fighter to completely drain their opponent's power bar.

In the Battle Dome, the participants earn and accumulate their points differently than in the other rounds. A fighter scores a point every time their opponent is knocked into the cage, either by themselves or by one of the ninjas. After two minutes, whoever has the most points wins. If there's a tie, things go into SUDDEN DEATH!

Dragon Star Championship matches are another animal entirely. They take place on a rotating platform that towers some eight to ten feet above the arena floor. These fights are what the show is all about- winner-take-all brawls to determine the World's Greatest Martial Artist. As the fighters battle on the giant, spinning platform and ninjas jump into the mix when called into action once a "violation" occurs. To win the fight, a Master has to be the last man or woman on the platform, eliminating all ninjas as well as their opponent. There are no time limits, no points, and there must be a winner!

There are other, less common fight and episode types, but we'll get to those.

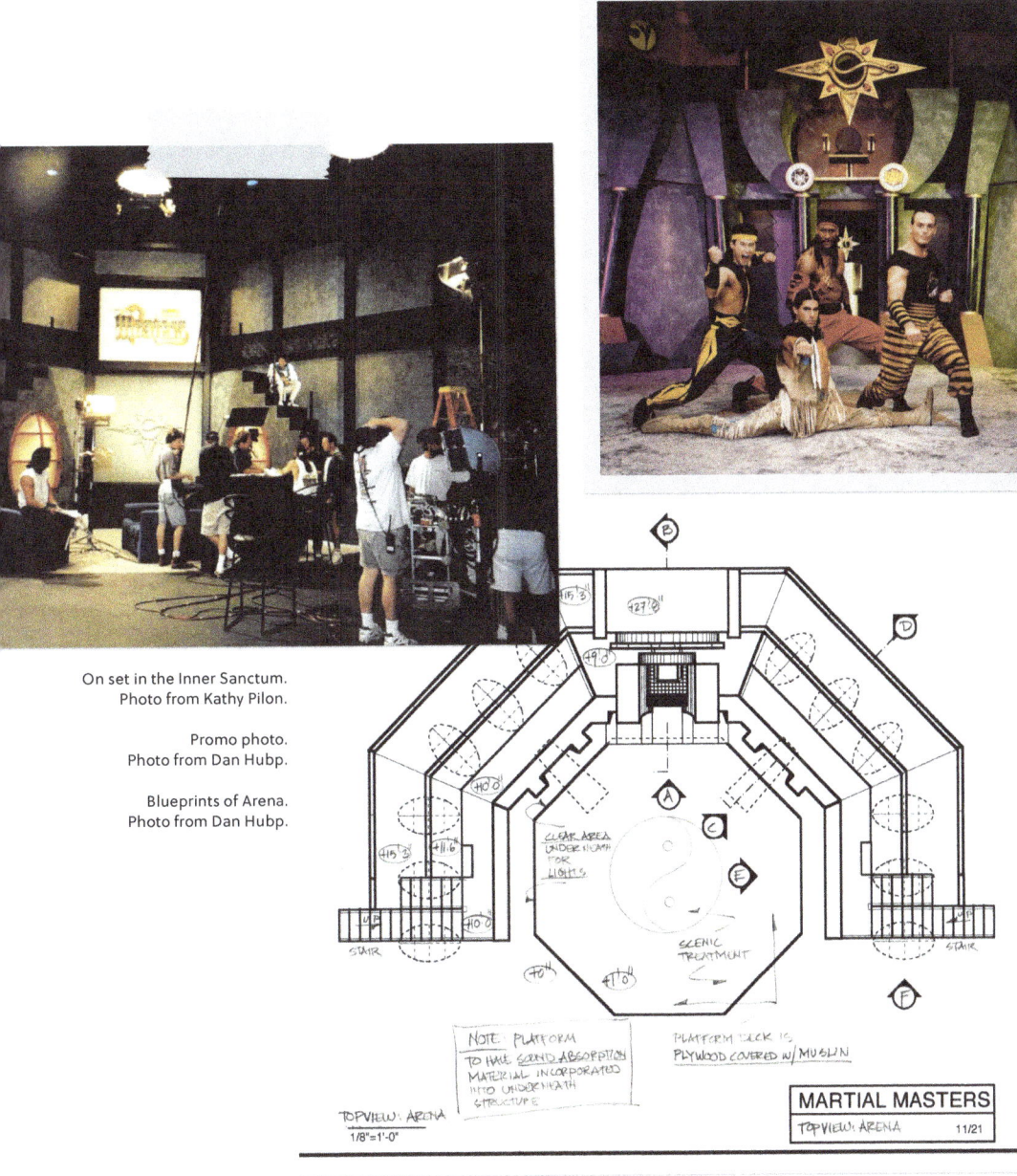

On set in the Inner Sanctum.
Photo from Kathy Pilon.

Promo photo.
Photo from Dan Hubp.

Blueprints of Arena.
Photo from Dan Hubp.

CHAPTER 02

Making the Masters

Origins of the Show

"I know that martial arts did wonders for me"

As much as *WMAC Masters* has always seemed to be a part of my personal universe, it is not some primordial force that has existed for all time. Neither did it spring fully formed into being. The show's debut was instead the culmination of a long process that involved several creative forces, bringing to life a vision that had grown and evolved through several iterations. As a result, there were highs and lows, false starts and near misses, and even moments where it looked like the show may not happen.

It began with monster trucks. No, really. Monster trucks. A struggling show called *Monster Wars* was in need of assistance in trying to achieve its goals of setting the world ablaze with its strange blend of monster-trucks-meets-pro-wrestling. So they reached out to a man named Norman Grossfeld, who had experience helping intellectual properties (IPs) with merchandising and licensing deals. They had a vision for the show but didn't know how to execute it, and thought Norman would be the man for the job. Unfortunately, despite the young New Yorker's prodigious talents, *Monster Wars* was not able to take over the kid's TV world. However, his efforts to salvage the show were enough to get Norman on the radar of Al Kahn, one of the biggest names in children's television and head of 4Kids Entertainment. There was a concept Al had high hopes for, and he thought Norman would be the right man to make it happen.

That concept? In Norman's words, "What if we did the WWF, but for martial artists?"

Al Kahn had experience in that world. He was a longtime confidant of Vince McMahon, the CEO of the World Wrestling Federation (now WWE), having worked on merchandising with the titan of sports

Thundercats, Teenage Mutant Ninja Turtles, Pokémon, Yu-Gi-Oh!

Sound like a timeline of your childhood? If so, you have one man to thank for it- Al Kahn.

Starting in the 70s and 80s Al Kahn worked in licensing for properties ranging from *Thundercats* to the World Wrestling Federation. Throughout the 1990s he would guide 4Kids Entertainment to the pinnacle of the entertainment industry by importing mega-hits *Pokémon* and *Yu-Gi-Oh!* to America.

entertainment for years. Al Kahn, however, does not claim credit for the show's original concept. Instead, that credit belongs to his protegee Carlin West.

Carlin brought me the idea. I don't know where she got the idea. But I instantly saw the potential.

Al Kahn
Executive Producer

Carlin West had already made her first million dollars licensing IPs and was looking for an idea of her own to nurture into the next big thing. Despite those ambitions, the idea that would become *WMAC Masters* was born out of a dark period for her.

I was going through a very hard time in my life. I had just come out of a bad breakup and started taking martial arts classes to try to center myself. In researching which classes to take, I discovered just how many different forms of martial arts there were.

Carlin West
Show Creator

The world of martial arts is wide and varied. In the 90s, with the internet far less ubiquitous than it is today, it could be hard to find reliable information on what schools, teachers, and styles were best suited for a particular need and which were most reputable. The idea struck Carlin, what if there was one governing body for martial arts? Soccer has FIFA, and football has the NFL. Why isn't there a World Martial Arts Organization? The name that stuck with her was the World Martial Arts Council or WMAC.

WMAC Masters would go through several different names before ending up back where it began in Carlin's original vision—marketing the show as the *World Martial Arts Federation, Martial Masters,* and *Quest for the Dragon Star* before finally landing on *WMAC Masters.* Therefore, we will refer to the show as *WMAC Masters* throughout the book unless referencing a specific iteration or event that occurred under one of the other names.

What would be the target audience, though? With shows like *American Gladiators* already a part of the public consciousness by the mid-90s there was obviously a demand for the athletics-meets-entertainment genre, but Carlin felt as if she should go in another direction.

I've always felt very strongly about doing children's programming. I knew that if I had questions about martial arts, then parents would as well. I know that martial arts did wonders for me, personally, and I thought there would be a way to share those values with kids if presented correctly.

Carlin West
Show Creator

The concept had immediate and obvious appeal to "Big Al," and the pair quickly brought Norman Grossfeld and his future wife, Kathy Borland (now Kathy Pilon), into the fold as producers. Norman and Kathy would spend over a year working on the show bible for the fledgling program, establishing the rules for the fights, the Battle Zones, and even beginning character sketches as casting got underway.

While this early behind-the-scenes work was taking place, Al and Carlin worked on another equally crucial task, finding a partner to finance the show. 4Kids was not yet the behemoth it would become with the advent of *Pokémon*. In fact, *WMAC Masters* would be its debut production.

Making a show is expensive. We knew we'd need partners. Licensing was really our bread and butter. We knew how to sell IP.

Norman Grossfeld
Executive Producer

The early partners they had their sights set on were Al Kahn's old friends— the WWF. There were several conversations between the two sides, initiated by Carlin West, about partnering to make the show. The talks advanced far enough that several trade papers carried articles about the forthcoming World Martial Arts Federation. Still, ultimately the WWF pulled out of the show due to the disastrous reception for its first spin-off, the *World Bodybuilding Federation*.

Norman Grossfeld described this period as preliminary conversations, adding there was "no real developmental work being done" to the show. No footage was shot, and the collaboration, if it could even be called that, ended quickly.

This would end up being a minor setback for the show, but the production team continued, undaunted. After work on the series bible concluded, the next step was to shoot a Proof of Concept (POC) video, a small slice of test footage to show to potential partners. The concept footage, dubbed *Martial Masters*, was shot at Universal Studios in California and featured a cast entirely different from the one that would populate the show. Derron McBee, best known as Malibu from the original *American Gladiators*, played Jaguar.

> *It was a lot of fun. We did some really cool stuff. It was at the Water World set at Universal. I fought Michael Jai White.*

Derron McBee
Jaguar

McBee recalled the video was almost all action, with little to no character development. Grossfeld told me that the video, shot very quickly, demonstrated the show's concept quite well, but the "fighting wasn't very good," at least compared to what was to come. Unfortunately, the *Martial Masters* proof of concept video has been lost to the ages but was instrumental in helping what was to be *WMAC Masters* take shape.

NATPE

The NATPE (National Association of Television Program Executives) convention is an annual gathering of TV execs, producers, and other creators. It is one of the key dates on any fledging TV show's calendar. If a show is looking to find a production partner, NATPE is where it will happen. It was at the 1993 iteration of this convention, held in Miami, where several key events in the formation of *WMAC Masters* took place.

The first and most significant is that the American division of Bandai, a Japanese toy company, signed on as both merchandiser and primary financier of the show through sister-company Renaissance Atlantic.

> *The point of the POC video was to get a company like Bandai on board. It was two separate deals, one for the licensing to make*

toys and stuff and one to produce the show (through Renaissance Atlantic). That was for the first season only. So they had a say in everything from casting to design to music.

Norman Grossfeld
Executive Producer

Bandai seemed to be an ideal partner. They had experience in all the aspects of creating a hit kid's TV show and seemed enthusiastic about the concept. While the relationship between the producers and Bandai would eventually sour, both sides began the partnership with high hopes.

There was one other show-changing event that took place at the NATPE convention. While not quite on the level of finding a financing partner, the meeting between Norman Grossfeld and director Isaac Florentine was a key moment in the show's trajectory.

We were there for Power Rangers, a lot of us. Erik (Betts) and Hien (Nguyen) were out on the convention floor in their (Power Ranger) outfits, and they came across this booth that had this pilot they saw. (NOTE: Isaac is referring to the POC video. In our conversation, he called it a pilot.) They thought it was cool and that it would be something I'd be interested in. So they told me to go over and see it. I thought it was interesting, but the fighting was... not very good. :laughs: I told Norman, "You've got to fix this. I can tell you how to fix it." It was my first time meeting him. He said, "Sure, I'd love to hear your ideas," and took my number, and I figured that was it. :laughs:

Isaac Florentine
Director

However, that initial conversation was far from it for Isaac and the show. According to Isaac's recollections, a few weeks later, he was in Los Angeles having lunch with Norman and laying out his ideas of how martial arts action should be shot. After a couple of meetings, Norman ended up offering Isaac a job on the show.

Isaac would bring several cast members with him from *Mighty Morphin Power Rangers*, namely Betts, Riley, and Nguyen. They, however, would come later, after the first wave of cast members were brought on.

Casting the Masters

One of, if not the single most important parts of launching a new TV show is casting. No matter how strong the concept or how amazing the writing, a bad cast can sink a show faster than an iceberg in the Atlantic. This was even more vital for a show like *WMAC Masters*, which was to lean so heavily on the legitimacy of its stars. Casting the show was a long, drawn-out process, but one that eventually produced results, forming the most impressive cast of martial artists ever assembled on TV.

The majority of the cast was head-hunted from the North American Sport Karate Association (NASKA) circuit. NASKA was, at the time, the premier stage for martial artists to showcase their skills, featuring a wide variety of disciplines and competitions, making it the perfect place for the producers to scout talent.

At the start, I just traveled around the country to the different tournaments on my own dime, filming and scouting. There was a different tournament every weekend.

Carlin West
Show Creator

She would later be joined by Grossfeld, Pilon, and eventually Pat Johnson, the legendary director and fight choreographer behind films such as *The Karate Kid*, *Teenage Mutant Ninja Turtles*, and *Mortal Kombat*. Johnson, a well-known and revered figure on the circuit, acted not only as a talent scout but as an intermediary. He would go on to be one of the two directors, along with Isaac Florentine, during season one, but his early contributions in shaping the show are perhaps even of greater impact.

Many of the cast members, including Chris Casamassa, Willie Johnson, and Christine Rodrigues, all recall the producers approaching them after The Battle of Atlanta in 1994.

I remember they brought us all into this big conference room. There were probably close to a hundred of us. They presented us with a contract, the rights, and whatnot. I don't know how many of us signed, but I think it was a lot. I remember they said they planned on introducing more characters as the show went on.

Willie Johnson
The Bam

Pat Johnson with cast.
Photo from Carmichael Simon.

While both Carlin West and Norman Grossfeld told me they felt 75-100 was a bit high as far as offered contracts, they did tell me they cast a wide net when looking for talent. As a result, there is no doubt several martial artists signed contracts who did not appear on the show, at least as "face characters" (the cast's preferred terminology for the main characters of the show, the Masters). Two such martial artists signed contracts at The Battle of Atlanta, Pedro Xaiver and Alberto Montrond. Both ended up playing ninjas but were in line to become face characters in the future.

The plan was for Xavier to play Axeman, supposedly debuting in season three. Montrond was going to develop into Superfoot. Still, the development of his character ceased when he informed the producers he would have to drop out to return to his recently-opened martial arts school shortly into filming. So, there seems to be no Ki Symbol art for those characters. It seems they were lost forever, if they ever existed at all. Additionally, Clayton Barber, who also worked on the series as a ninja, was slated to play Hollywood, possibly in season three.

Pat Johnson is best known as the fight choreographer (and referee) from *The Karate Kid*, and was the choreographer for *Teenage Mutant Ninja Turtles*, *The Last Dragon*, *Mortal Kombat*, and dozens of other films. In addition to his cinematic work he was an accomplished martial artist, training with Chuck Norris, as well as one of the top karate referees in the United States.

"The creative, the cast and names and symbols, was in flux right up until filming," Dan Hubp told me. Dan worked as a production designer, editor, and even second unit director for the show. An early sizzle reel exists from when the show was still *Martial Masters* and demonstrates just how dramatically the characters and combatants would change between conception and execution.

The video showcased everyone cast in the show at that point. They designed it to appeal to potential TV carriers (as the show was sold direct to channels in local markets, not to major networks) and other licensing partners. Several big name martial artists are on the list of cast members as part of the fledgling show but ultimately didn't participate.

Perhaps the most well-known name is Benny "The Jet" Urquidez. The video claims he is "the most famous martial artist in America," which is a questionable assertion in 1994. What isn't debatable is the impact The Jet had on American kickboxing, where he was one of the most successful fighters of the era. He was, undoubtedly, a name in the martial arts world, and his involvement would have been a boost for the show. Benny's sister managed Bridgett "Babydoll" Riley at the time, but his would-be involvement never came up.

I had no idea he was going to be on the show. That's so wild.

Bridgett Riley
Babydoll

Mr. Urquidez's agent declined requests for an interview on behalf of his client.

Another big name featured in the tape, albeit one from a different corner of the martial arts community, was Jason Morris. They wanted Morris, a silver medalist in Judo at the 1992 Olympic Games, to play the character All American, a fact confirmed by Dan Hubp. All Americans' Ki Symbol would later be used in the Dragon Belt toy as a bonus symbol, as was Hollywood's.

When I reached out to Morris for his memories, his response shocked me. He had no recollection of being a part of the show! So despite being featured and advertised (and his character turning into a bit of a legacy character), the man behind All American was never actually consulted about playing the part, at least to his recollection.

He was not the only one featured in the *Martial Masters'* sales tape, who didn't recall someone asking them to be on the show. Sayuri Kelly was a martial artist at the time, and while there is very little information online about her, I was able to make contact with her. She told me my email was the first time she had heard of the show!

Other would-be cast members did recall their involvement, Thunderwolf, a towering Native American who worked with several of the cast members on *Shootfighter*, told me that his participation didn't extend much beyond the *Martial Masters* sales tape.

Also listed on the sales tape which didn't make the final show was James Lew, whom I could not reach for comment for this book.

The sales tape also features early iterations of characters the fans of the show would come to know and love, and several spot dramatic differences from how they would end up looking in the series. For example, Hakim Alston was The Dream, not The Machine, Ho-Young Pak was Ninja, and Larry Lam was Mantis. These early iterations were all tweaked to become the characters they would play in the show.

> *I saw the art, the costume, for what they were working on (The Dream), and I just wasn't feeling it. So we played around with a few more ideas, and I saw what they had in mind for "The Machine", and I knew instantly. I was like, "This is it."*

Hakim Alston
The Machine

Other Masters featured in the video had radically different costumes, despite the name of their characters being the same as the final show. One example is how Olympus started in a brightly colored outfit that made him resemble a cyborg. And in Tarantula's original concepts, she was wearing what was essentially a dominatrix outfit, a far cry from fare fit for kid's TV.

> *I never saw that (concept art) before. I definitely would have been a little hesitant to wear something like that!*

Lynette Love
Tarantula

| Yin Yang Man | Superstar | Gold |

| Turbo | Red Dragon | Striking Eagle |

| Hollywood | Han "Bruce" Lee | Lady Lightning |

| Tomahawk | All American | Blade Master |

Unused Ki Symbol art from early production. Photo from Dan Hubp.

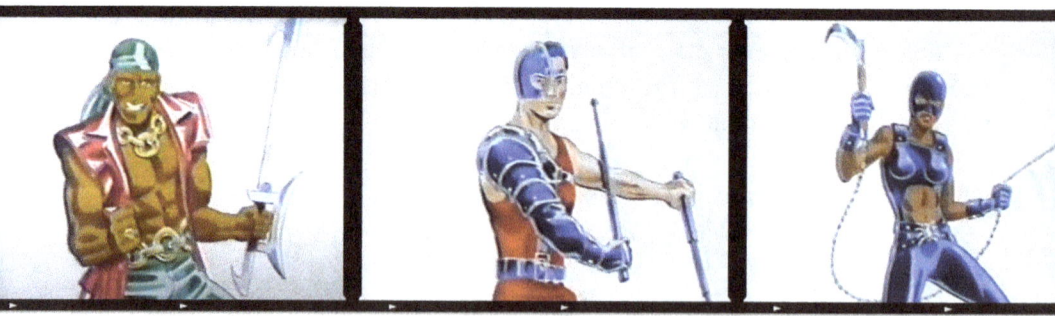

Early character designs for The Dream, Olympus, and Tarantula from the *Martial Masters* sales tape.

There were also several concepts for characters created that didn't end up getting used. Dan Hubp provided a Ki Symbol sheet that shows several of them, in addition to art for Hollywood and All American.

Live from New York (For One Night Only)

The NATPE convention wasn't the only event the production attended to try to drum up interest for the show. Carmichael Simon recalled an event in New York City before the show went to air.

It was a stage show. It was me, Hakim (Alston), and at least one other cast member that I can't recall. We didn't have our full uniforms, but kind of like casual versions of them. We'd each go up on stage and do a kata. I got sick after rehearsal and couldn't perform!

Carmichael Simon
Kid Carmichael

Kathy Pilon added:

It was held at Town Hall in New York City. I don't remember who all performed, but they came out one by one and walked down the aisle with a music video playing, then did an individual kata on stage. It was pretty dramatic and exciting. (We) produced (it) like a concert. It was for a licensing show to pick up interest in making the toys before the pilot went to air.

Kathy Pilon
Executive Producer

It worked. Bandai would come on board as toy makers, leading to another appearance for the show in public before it made it to air. At the 1995 edition of the New York Toy Fair, there was a presentation on the show to prospective toy store purchasers. A man in a traditional martial arts gi (uniform) explains the in-universe back-story for the show and the it's premise before showing a sizzle reel. At this point, the name had shifted to *Quest for the Dragon Star*, which it will keep for the pilot but change before hitting airwaves.

The sizzle reel is all footage we will ultimately see in the series, with the possible exception of one incredibly quick shot of the Turbo/Yin Yang Man Dragon Star match that shows them battling with their weapons. After the sizzle reel, the presenter describes the toys on offer. Everything that he speaks of eventually came out. However, one interesting note is a strange Ki Symbol on the Dragon Belt display. Unfortunately, I have not been able to identify it, even as one of the unused characters.

There was still one piece of the puzzle to figure out, where would they shoot the show?

"They gave us the world."

The initial proof of concept video for *Martial Masters* was shot at Universal Studios in Hollywood. This relationship would prove vital for the show that would become *WMAC Masters*. When it came time to shoot the pilot Grossfeld and his team reached out to Universal Studios Orlando. At the time it was one of the epicenters for children's television, home to Nickelodeon Studios, as well as the world-renowned theme park. They were met with a positive response, and the show was produced almost entirely at Universal.

> *Everything we asked for they gave us. We asked to shoot our fights on their sets in off-hours. They said yes. We asked for sound-stage space. They said yes. We even asked for money to buy equipment, and they said yes. We asked for the world, and they gave us the world. It was a wonderful partnership.*

Norman Grossfeld
Executive Producer

The partnership would last the whole life of the show, with the vast majority of the series being produced almost entirely on location at Universal, with a few fights filmed at nearby Splendid China theme park, now defunct, and several vignettes filmed around the Central Florida area.

Shooting at Universal was, undeniably, one of the highlights of the *WMAC Masters* experience for everyone involved.

The partnership even went so far as to lend the burgeoning production the use of an on-site editing studio while filming the pilot, a huge bonus for the small, self-contained shoot.

> *We all were holed up (in Orlando) together. It was like our own little army, all working together to make it happen. It was quite an experience.*

Norman Grossfeld
Executive Producer

That experience would continue for the series, most of the cast would stay in Orlando for filming. However, before that adventure could begin, they had a pilot to shoot.

A look inside the Inner Sanctum.
Photos from Kathy Pilon.

Shannon "Irish" Stewart behind the scenes and on the Wild West Stunt Show set on one of the coldest nights ever. Photo from Shannon "Irish" Stewart.

CHAPTER 03

Quest for the Dragon Star

The "Lost" Pilot

"I really thought we had something special"

Many TV series will have two separate first episodes, the pilot, made to attract a TV deal, and the actual first episode that airs. *WMAC Masters* is no exception. The original first episode ended up being different from the first broadcasted episode (S1E01: "Meet the Masters") in several ways, despite sharing nearly 50% of the footage ultimately used in the final product.

The differences are apparent from the very beginning. The show wasn't *WMAC Masters* at the time. Instead, it's called *Quest for the Dragon Star*. This name was the way-station between the original name of *Martial Masters* and the final title of *WMAC Masters*, but it was one that at least one cast member preferred.

I told Norman, the name (WMAC Masters) is garbage. You've got the perfect name right there, Quest for the Dragon Star.

Erik Betts
Panther

Panther is not in the pilot. In fact, most of the cast doesn't feature in it. There are no scenes in the WMAC Inner Sanctum that become a vital part of the show as it developed either. Those scenes would become where we, as viewers, get to know the Masters, where the storylines would advance, and where the Masters would bridge into their vignettes. This is where the lessons and tenets of martial arts would be taught to young, impressionable viewers.

Instead, *Quest for the Dragon Star* is presented as a straightforward sporting program. Shannon Lee serves as host, as she would in season one of *WMAC Masters*, but unlike the show proper, she is not alone. Billy Zabka, of *The Karate Kid* (and now *Cobra Kai*) fame, joins her as co-host. They present the program as if they were ESPN anchors, explaining the rules of the tournament, the battles, as well as introducing the episode's "Meet the Masters" segment (More on that to come). The hosts are also joined by the unseen Joe Richards, who serves as a typical sports play-by-play man, narrating the fights.

The flow of the show is roughly the same as the episodes that would later be produced, two preliminary fights followed by a Battle Dome final. In between the fights, Lee and Zabka offer commentary on the events unfolding in lieu of the backstage shots, as mentioned above.

However, the preliminary fights are very different from what viewers of

WMAC Masters would come to know.

They are still a one versus one affair, with a period of battling shadow warriors (later simply called ninjas) before the Masters square off against each other. (In this universe, these ninjas are WMAC Academy recruits. In reality, they are usually played by other cast members under hoods, with a few stunt men and women brought in to flesh out the ranks) This goes on for the first minute of the two-minute fight (in the series proper, there is no stated time limit on either the ninja portion or the fight as a whole).

After the ninja segment, the Masters fight one-on-one. In the pilot, the fights work slightly differently. In the series, the Masters aim to drain their opponent's power bar, a video game-like health bar projected on the side of the screen during the fight. Once they extinguish their opponent's power bar, that Master wins the battle. In the pilot, however, securing hits on your opponent and exhibiting great technique would raise a Master's own power bar. Once a Master's power bar is full, they can unlock their Ki Symbol from a replica Dragon Star on site of each battle, the first Master to unlock their symbol wins the match.

The giant Dragon Star was a real beast. It took two people to carry and a third to bring the base it sat in.

Nick Farrell
Prop Master

These modified preliminary bouts are far from the only differences from the series as fans would come to know it, though they are possibly the most drastic. Another minor difference is that the Council, the upper ring of silhouettes in the Arena, is played by real people, unlike in the show. All these people were Universal Studio's park-goers, as were the fans in the Arena for the Battle Dome and fighter entrances.

The pilot for the show had people standing at the top of the arena dressed as the Council members. They were Universal Studios Florida attendees who stood in line to get a chance to 'dress up and be on TV.' But the shoots were so long that they got tired and bored and needed bathroom breaks (several actually peed in a bottle while we were shooting). We couldn't just rotate new people in because of continuity concerns - so - when we got the green light to shoot the first season back in Orlando, one of the first decisions was to replace all the people with dressed-up mannequins. It is actually pretty obvious when you watch the show, and none of the Council ever moves. The fans in attendance were dropped for a similar reason, boredom between shots and bathroom breaks were more trouble than they were worth.

Dan Hubp
Production Designer, Editor

The people were miserable. They didn't want to be spending part of their vacation in a hot studio pretending to be faceless council people.

Shannon "Irish" Stewart
Production Assistant for the Pilot

The energy the crowd provides, particularly during the Battle Dome, is uniquely intense. It's evident that the fans are excited to see something new and different. (The Battle Dome match from the pilot would be reused in S1E01: "Meet the Masters", as was the "Meet the Masters" segment)

Billy Zabka acting as co-host is a curiosity. Unfortunately, he and Shannon don't have enough screen time to really exhibit any real chemistry one way or the other, and what lines he has to himself are relatively mundane.

Billy was just another attempt to have a name associated with the show. Karate

The replica, over-sized Dragon Star would later make an appearance in the second episode of season two, where The Machine and Superstar must battle through an underground area and be the first to put their Ki Symbol IN the Dragon Star to win the match.

Kid was a big deal. He wasn't bad or anything. We just realized that the more time we devoted to those kind of peripheral pieces (such as commentators) it was less time we could devote to the characters of the show who were going to be selling the merchandise.

Norman Grossfeld
Executive Producer

Joe Richards as play-by-play man serves the same function Shannon Lee did during season one, narrating the action as it unfolds. However, his delivery is much more traditional sportscaster than Shannon Lee's in season one. He does a good job of balancing narrating the action with explaining the show's concept (the Council, how things are scored, etc.).

Joe was a sports play-by-play guy. Again, he did a fine job, but we knew that Shannon could do the job perfectly well, and she had the name recognition we needed, so when it came time to do the series, she was our pick.

Norman Grossfeld
Executive Producer

The opening credits are also vastly different from the series. A narrator describes the history of martial arts, how the various disciplines would constantly vie for superiority, and how the World Martial Arts Council founded the Quest for the Dragon Star Tournament to establish who was the World's Greatest Martial Artist. This narration is set over shots of the cast performing their kata forms, usually with weapons, in front of the Asian-themed sets, which they would later use for the exterior shots of the WMAC Headquarters in the series. Superstar, Turbo, and Striking Eagle are featured heavily in the opening. Parts of this title sequence would be used in season two as the footage shown on the *WMAC Masters* computer. (See S2E06: "Battle of the Brothers")

Preliminary Match One
Competitors:
The Machine ⬡⬡⬡⬡⬡⬡⬡⬡ vs. Red Dragon ● ● ● ● ●
Battle Zone: Jungle
Ninjas: Shadow Warriors

The first of the two preliminary matches pits Hakim "The Machine" Alston vs. Chris "Red Dragon" Casamassa from the Jungle Battle Zone. The main storyline presented in this episode is The Machine going for full Dragon Belt in order to challenge for the Dragon Star, so the focus is on him in this fight.

Before the fight, we see the two enter the Arena and do a short demonstration of their skills, as would become common in the series. However, the lighting of the demonstrations is different, more warm than cold and sterile.

> *I don't know about the pilot, but in the series, the gel we used most often (to color the lights) was Kongo Blue.*

Robert Tuscani
Lighting Department

Compared to the rest of the first half of the pilot, this preliminary fight looks the most like the series that would follow. The only notable difference not already mentioned being some of the shadow warriors sport weapons, something not seen in the series.

Both Red Dragon and The Machine were considered "major" characters for the show, and both are made to look very strong in this fight, taking on the shadow warriors with ease. Highlights are The Machine lifting one of the ninjas onto his shoulders and using it to kick several others, and Red Dragon kicking one of the shadow warriors plunging them into the water below, beginning the series' recurring theme of water stunts.

After the first minute, the shadow warriors clear out, and it becomes the traditional one-on-one fight, Joe Richards aptly stating, "It's time to see how Red Dragon's karate can handle The Machine's kickboxing and vice versa!" They are evenly matched here, as well, with The Machine maintaining a slight advantage through most of the fight. As the minute winds down, The Machine scores a direct hit, filling his power bar and activating the unlock mechanism on the

Dragon Star, but he is unable to open it and retrieve his Ki Symbol before Red Dragon scores a hit, lowering his power bar and closing the Dragon Star again. He manages to score another strike, opening the Dragon Star and securing the win just as time expires.

This way of ending the match did add a little drama with the false finish but lacked the literal and metaphorical bang of the series' use of blowing up the CGI Ki Symbol of the loser. In the end, the lower the power bar method was considered more straightforward and easier for kids to understand due to it being the standard in fighting video games.

After the match, our hosts show some highlights of the action we've just seen and put a spotlight on Mike "Turbo" Bernardo, the incumbent Dragon Star champion. We get short clips of him defeating Richard "Yin Yang Man" Branden and standing triumphant with the Dragon Star, all of which we'd see later in the series, nothing new for fans here.

> *They never really told me why I was chosen as the first champion or gave me any real back story on how I won it. Pat (Johnson, one of the original show directors) was a big proponent of mine, so I wasn't about to argue with them.*

Mike Bernardo
Turbo

> *We had too much going on to write out any sort of "prehistory" for the show. Especially at that point.*

Norman Grossfeld
Executive Producer

The show then moves on to the second preliminary match.

Preliminary Match Two
Competitors:
Superstar ⬡⬡⬡⬡⬡⬡⬡⬡ vs.
Striking Eagle ⬡⬡
Battle Zone: Dark Alley
Ninjas: Shadow Warriors

Perhaps the most intriguing aspect of the pilot, at least as far as fans of the series are concerned, is the involvement of Taimak, who plays Striking Eagle. The star of the cult classic film *The Last Dragon*, where he played Bruce Leroy, Taimak had made the jump to mainstream pop culture name by appearing in Janet Jackson's "Let's Wait Awhile" music video. He appears just once, briefly, in season two of the series proper but is a major player in the pilot. According to producer Norman Grossfeld, Taimak was envisioned as a key part of the series.

At the very beginning, we had Taimak, he was in a big movie, and he was going to be one of the main guys, one of the toys we used.

Norman Grossfeld
Executive Producer

Taimak is known on the show as Striking Eagle, which the show says is the translation of Taimak from Aztec to English, and he faces Ho-Sung Pak, better known as Superstar. Ho-Sung, while not as big of a mainstream name, came into the show with quite the reputation, having starred in The *Drunken Master II* with Jackie Chan. He was also a highly ranked martial artist, competing for the prestigious Team Paul Mitchell, where he was known for his weapons forms.

Team Paul Mitchell remains active in the NASKA circuit to this day, billing themselves as the "Oldest and most prestigious team in martial arts." Several *WMAC Masters* came from Team Paul Mitchell, including Richard Branden, Christine Bannon-Rodrigues, and ninja Pedro Xavier.

According to the pilot, the eleven martial arts disciplines that comprise the WMAC are Karate, Kung Fu, Wushu, Chinese Gojou, Tae Kwon Do, Kempo, Judo, Kickboxing, Shorin Ryu, Capoeira, and Hapkido.

QUEST FOR THE DRAGON STAR

DAY:

...DING 22, ORLANDO, FL..
... 354-6486

...ND UNIT

DAY
CREW
SHOO...
SUNR...
SUNS...

...SMERE, ORLANDO...

...:	N/D	P...	
	D	3...	
	D	3-6/8	CHRIS AND HAKIM MEET

Chris "Red Dragon" Casamassa and
Hakim "The Machine" Alston face off in the
unaired pilot. Photo from Chris Casamassa.

Mike "Turbo" Bernardo and Richard "Yin Yang Man"
Branden fight for the Dragon Star in the pilot.
Photos from Dan Hubp.

This match, like the first, pits two characters who were envisioned as being central to the series against each other. However, the show was always meant to be an ensemble cast, with different characters getting the spotlight at different times. So how did they determine who would get the focus in these early episodes?

Bandai had their say, but it was really kind of a group effort. We wanted guys and girls who had some name recognition with some people, who could somewhat act, have a level of charisma, and that had the moves we thought would make the show look good.

Norman Grossfeld
Executive Producer

Striking Eagle, however, did not work out, despite his name value and acting experience. Several people on the production noted that he "wasn't a good fit."

We all got down there (to Orlando) for early days, rehearsals, figuring out the show, and everything. We were a couple of weeks in, and it just wasn't working out. It was key, crucial time to establish a team spirit because it was this huge, taxing production- all these huge fight scenes. It became clear early on that Taimak's contribution wasn't going to match what the others were going to be doing. From a mental, attitudinal, even just what he was willing to put into the fight scenes.

Norman Grossfeld
Executive Producer

While the producers had the most to say about him, his fellow fighters also noticed a difference in approach.

Taimak and I were rehearsing for a fight (that didn't end up making air), and I noticed he was a little stiff. Just the way he carried himself, probably as a product of how he was trained (on The Last Dragon). He wasn't bad to work with; it was just a different challenge. I remember having some dialogue with Pat Johnson and the producers about it.

Hakim Alston
The Machine

While Taimak's relationship with the producers was rocky, several of the cast noted he was entirely professional during filming.

I think I probably took most of the hits from Taimak in the pilot. I didn't really interact with him at all when we weren't shooting, but he was very professional.

Carmichael Simon
Kid Carmichael, played ninja in pilot

Another ninja, Alberto Montrond, agreed.

I had no negative interactions with Taimak. Whatever the issue was with him was between him and the producers.

Alberto Montrond
Ninja

This fight has achieved legendary status amongst *WMAC Masters* fans, due in no small part to the stature of both fighters and the tantalizing clips shown in season two. Upon seeing the pilot, however, I discovered a sad reality. The fight does not live up to the lofty status it has achieved as a "lost" fight. The action in the fight is not what you would expect from two competitors the caliber of Ho-Sung Pak and Taimak, and ultimately the best pieces of the fight were used in season two.

While it could be easy to assign blame to Taimak based solely on the producer's comments, it is not only his performance that keeps this fight from being up to snuff. Everything from the shooting to the acting was below what you would expect from the two fighters, and the fight features several puzzling moments.

There is an unintentionally hilarious spot in the match where three ninja warriors try side kicks at Superstar, who is standing too far away to be hit. He doesn't move out of the way, he's just out of range. Superstar stares at them for a beat, they lower their legs as if embarrassed, and then he nails them with one single spin kick, taking them all out. In other circumstances, it could have been humorous, but in the context of this fight, it's just confusing.

There's another "What was he trying to do!?" moment slightly later in the ninja sequence, as one of the warriors tries to clobber Striking Eagle with a crate. Striking Eagle simply kicks straight through the crate, taking the shadow warrior out. The shot is far closer to a traditional martial arts film than something we'd see later in the series, which can be said for much of this battle. Even the flashiest moment in the fight, a move where Superstar runs up a wall, springs off, and nails a kick, seems less visceral than the action in the series to come.

Following shortly after the wall kick, Taimak lies prone on the ground, and Superstar elects to let him to his feet rather than attack while he's grounded, possibly an early iteration of him forfeiting his fight with Star Warrior in season one. However, this comes back to bite him, as he can't reach the full power bar before time runs out, sending the battle to a judge's decision!

This event never happens in the series, as all fights must go to a finish, so its occurrence here is a unique footnote in the show's history. The judge's decision functions just as it would in boxing or mixed martial arts. A referee stands between Striking Eagle and Superstar as the results are read off, each Council member (of which there are eleven, one for each discipline represented by the WMAC) getting one vote. They are read off one by one, each discipline getting their symbol (which adorns the top of the WMAC Arena and the fighters' info cards before fights) flashed on the screen as their vote is announced.

The judges scored it fairly evenly, it would seem, with Superstar pulling out a 6-5 win. This ending, however, was never revisited in the series, as the producers didn't think it worked.

We decided that kids would rather see a clear-cut and obvious outcome to each match that they can easily understand and that a "judges' decision" was unsatisfying and not intuitive. Not only did we believe that kids would prefer it that way, but as a viewer, I felt that way too!

Norman Grossfeld
Executive Producer

In all, the Striking Eagle vs. Superstar match is a curiosity. It is far and away, the most interesting part of the unaired pilot, a capsule look at what could have been had *WMAC Masters* gone other directions. Ultimately, however, neither Taimak's involvement nor the fight itself lives up to the unrealistic expectations fans have formed of it over the years.

The remainder of the episode is almost exactly the same as the final parts of the first episode of the series as it aired, with only one significant difference. Hakim "The Machine" Alston's vignette is presented differently in the pilot. It is the first of a "Meet the Masters" series rather than a flashback as part of an Inner Sanctum shot (more on this later). Hakim narrates his story to the camera as if being interviewed, but the actual footage is the same as in the coming episode

The Battle Dome final (which we will look at in the next chapter in detail) is largely identical, the only difference being the commentary.

Quest for the Dragon Star ended up being enough to get the show picked up on several networks across the US, but due to the departure of Taimak, it would have to be re-shot. As the crew was finishing it, however, the feeling was very optimistic about the show's direction.

When we finished it, I remember being very excited. I really thought we had something special.

Norman Grossfeld
Executive Producer

The cast also recalled a real positive, communal spirit during filming.

During filming, everyone was very excited. It was such a new opportunity; no one had done anything like this. The feeling on the set was one of excitement and camaraderie. We couldn't wait for the series.

Alberto Montrond
Ninja

Ultimately, despite its allure for longtime fans as a "lost" episode, the *Quest for the Dragon Star* pilot is little more than a curiosity. It is inferior to the first episode of the series that actually aired, and the main drawing point, Taimak's involvement, doesn't live up to the hype the years have generated. Due to the complicated ownership issue, it's unlikely that this pilot will ever see the light of day. It is no real loss. It is not a lost classic but rather a rough draft for the show that was to come.

The cast poses during shooting of the pilot. One of the few photos of Taimak as part of the *WMAC Masters* cast. Photo from Christine Bannon-Rodrigues.

Taimak and Carmichael during filming of the pilot. Photo from Carmichael Simon.

Carmichael and Barbara Bernhardt behind the scenes. Photo from Carmichael Simon.

Promo material for unaired pilot. Photo from Dan Hubp.

CHAPTER 04

S1E01:
Meet the Masters

The Machine vs. Great Wolf

Red Dragon vs. Superstar

"We definitely knew we were setting the tone"

What fans of the series would come to know as the first episode was called "Meet The Masters" and remains one of the highest rated (according to IMDB) and most remembered installments of the program. It serves as a set-up for the show, the World Martial Arts Council, the Dragon Star and its tournament, the rules of the matches, and the Masters themselves are all introduced. The Masters explain how they got their nicknames, giving the episode a clear through line.

The episode begins, as every episode will, with the opening title sequence. This simple component of the show was vital and could easily have gone wrong. It had to set the stage for the show and immediately explain the concept to the young audience who would be watching while also hooking viewers. The *WMAC Masters* title sequence is particularly effective, with its dramatic opening narration, "The World's Greatest Martial Artists, competing for the ultimate prize," as well as showing (and naming) all of the principal cast with abbreviated versions of their Arena entrance shots.

The Arena shots would be used throughout the series to introduce characters before their matches and are among the best of the show, dramatic and effective at conveying the essence of the character entering the Arena without words. In a few seconds, you immediately get a feeling of who these Masters are, based solely on their walk, costumes, and expressions: The Machine is the intense, focused monster, Superstar the cocky but talented artist, Yin Yang Man a quiet, unassuming assassin.

We shot (the Arena entrances) at the back of the ET ride at Universal. They were some of my favorite shots we did, probably because I got to shoot them

A through-line refers to a concept or storyline that runs through an episode or season, forming its backbone.

myself! :laughs: I am very proud of them.

Tom Laskowski
Camera Crew

Following the title sequence, the series proper begins with an exterior shot of the WMAC Headquarters. In reality, it was an exterior shot of the now defunct Splendid China amusement park in Orlando. This is before heading inside for our first Inner Sanctum segment of the series, where Jamie "Great Wolf" Webster is teaching Hien "Tsunami" Nguyen how to say his name in Cherokee. He explains that he was the grandson of a chief known as Great Wolf.

The producers told me to come up with some name ideas, and they came up with some name ideas. Great Wolf was the one they liked the best. My favorite was actually Chief Crazylegs, kind of a take on Chief Crazyhorse, who was a real-life chief. But they thought it was too silly, so we settled on Great Wolf.

Jamie Webster
Great Wolf

According to Webster, the Cherokee Great Wolf is attempting to teach Tsunami is actually accurate.

So when I came up with the name, I asked my dad, who was very involved with (Native American) affairs, to see if he could figure out how to say it. He contacted a friend of his at the University of Oklahoma, and a few days later, they came back with what we used in the show. A few years ago, though, my son Greyson was actually doing some research, and it turns out a more accurate translation would be "the greater wolf" or "larger wolf." But we didn't know that then.

Jamie Webster
Great Wolf

Johnny Lee Smith, Tiger Claw (who we will later learn is Great Wolf's best friend), joins the conversation and says he wants to know why Hakeem Alston took the nickname The Machine. The Machine gives the trio an icy stare and growls, "You're about to find out."

We were all martial artists, not actors. They definitely tried to keep it simple for us, at least at first, when it came to dialogue and stuff like that.

Chris Casamassa
Red Dragon

The Machine and Great Wolf then enter the arena to the roar of fans. Great Wolf does a kata while The Machine poses as the fans chant "Ma-CHINE!".

A form or kata is a set routine a martial artist enacts, usually for competition. It showcases their skills, agility, and creativity.

Preliminary Match One
Competitors:
The Machine ⬡⬡⬡⬡⬡⬡⬡⬡ vs.
Great Wolf ⬡⬡⬡⬡⬡⬡
Battle Zone: Stone Valley
Ninjas: Kabuki Warriors

Shannon Lee, the program's host, tells us that this is the first match ever between Great Wolf and The Machine. She serves as the play-by-play analyst for the fights in season one, explaining the rules and scoring system and occasionally offering small factoids about the fighters. However, her involvement in the show ran much deeper than simply being Bruce Lee's daughter.

Shannon was very important to the show early on. Not just because of how good she was on camera, explaining things, but because it gave us that legitimacy in the eyes of the martial arts community. When we approached her, when she saw that we were about the same things her father was teaching, she got it right away. She wanted to be a part of it.

Norman Grossfeld
Executive Producer

Shannon was well-liked by the crew, who noted her humbleness and work ethic.

Shannon was a joy to work with. Just a total pro.

Dan Hubp
Production Designer, Editor

This fight features the Kabuki Warriors, the most iconic of the several different styles of ninjas the show would offer. Their most memorable feature, their unique, double-sided masks, were a last-minute decision.

I remember staying up most of the night before the first shoot with (the Kabuki warriors) painting masks. It was a decision we made as a team last minute to enhance the look of them.

Kathy Pilon
Executive Producer

Kabuki Ninjas from Season 1 Episode 1.

This fight, while not the first to be shot in the series as a whole, was the first for several members of the team, including Great Wolf Jamie Webster.

That fight (with Hakim) was my first night shooting. It was all new to me- getting my hair and makeup done, stuff like that. They had my hair in these Little House on the Prairie pigtails. There was so much product in it I would hear it crack when I went to sleep at night. But my first night shooting, I get there and get through hair and makeup and all that, and then I have to go fight Hakim!

Jamie Webster
Great Wolf

The biggest move of the fight, at least according to Great Wolf, is hard to make out in the final cut.

So it's my first night, and I'm fighting Hakim, and he clips me with this axe kick right in the head. All this is choreographed, of course, but he got me a little more than we meant to, and I just remember thinking, "if this guy had a go at me for real, I'd be out!"

Jamie Webster
Great Wolf

Alston remembered:

I have to take some of the blame (for things like that). I remember being told when I was learning how to fight for the camera that for someone my size, I have to really bring it. If I try to tweak anything or pull anything, it will be very obvious. So I always warned the guys when we were rehearsing- "I'm bringing it."

Hakim Alston
The Machine

After an exciting, close-run fight, The Machine picks up the victory to advance to the Battle Dome!

Back in the Inner Sanctum. Herb "Olympus" Perez explains how the WMAC approached him just after the 92 Olympics, where he won gold in Tae Kwon Do, so his nickname was a no-brainer. In real life, it was much the same story.

> *It was the only name picked for me. We just wanted something that sounded close to Olympics. We picked the torch symbol (for his Ki Symbol) for the same reason. The Olympic Rings are trademarked. We couldn't use them, so the torch was the best symbol we could use.*

Herb Perez
Olympus

Hakim still won't explain his nickname, so the crew moves on to Superstar Ho-Sung Pak. Superstar is the transliteration of his name from Chinese into English, making it another easy one. (We also learn, in the next episode, that there's a little more to it than that.) We then head into our second preliminary match.

Dan Hubp's original sketch of the Inner Sanctum.

Preliminary Match Two

Competitors:

Red Dragon ● ● ● ● ● vs. Superstar ○ ○ ○ ○ ○ ○ ○ ○

Battle Zone: Doom City

Ninjas: Black

Shannon Lee explains the Battle Zones to the fans at home as we see shots of the Masters warming up. The Masters are taken by underground transport to a random location for their match, not knowing where they will be fighting until they arrive. The Council does this to add difficulty to the fights, making the Battle Zone a part of the action.

In reality, the zones were various rides and attractions at Universal Studios (as well as occasionally at Splendid China, a nearby Asian-themed park).

It was really wild. We'd be shooting most of the time, from seven at night to seven in the morning. We'd break for 'lunch' at three-thirty. We'd all be so exhausted by the end of the day, we'd go back to the hotel and just crash.

Jamie Webster
Great Wolf

Doom City is the Battle Zone where the second preliminary match of the episode takes place and is part of the King Kong attraction at Universal.

The King Kong set was so cool. We were out there doing our moves, and there's Kong just towering over us.

Jamie Webster
Great Wolf

This second fight of the episode features a greater number of long, unbroken shots than the previous battle, which was an almost ideological point for Isaac Florentine, one of the directors.

I told Norman (after I saw the proof of concept video at NATPE) that he was shooting it all wrong. All the cuts (the traditional way of shooting things) just takes the audience out, makes it hard to follow the action. What he needed was long takes, unbroken shots. It keeps the viewer engaged. It's dynamic.

Isaac Florentine
Director

The difference in opinion of how to shoot the show, the more naturalistic presentation favored by Johnson or the more cinematic vision of Florentine, would end up being a major point of contention within the production. It would ultimately have a large impact on the future of the show.

This battle, however, is a mix of the two styles and is an effective, dramatic contest. In the end, Superstar picks up the victory, setting the stage for the first installment of what will become one of the show's most intense (and best) rivalries.

Shannon then previews the Battle Dome final, explaining both men are on 8 Ki Symbols, meaning a win will put them one step away from challenging for the Dragon Star. This sort of sequence of educating the fans can be dull and boring but is vital in a first episode, and Shannon handles it perfectly. Again, these scenes emphasize how essential she was to the show's early success.

Before the Dome can begin, we are treated to a few more backstory explanations. Richard Branden loves drawing, specializing in Yin Yang symbols, making him Yin Yang Man. Bridgett Riley's father called her Babydoll growing up, so the name stuck. Tsunami and Panther bicker back and forth, with Tsunami saying Betts claims to be as fast as a Panther. To show him up, Betts casually back flips and does what we will come to know as Tsunami's signature taunt, giving the audience a small preview of what they will get to see from him as the series progresses.

If you needed a back flip, you called Erik.

Isaac Florentine
Director

Betts recalled the origins of his character:

So I had friends growing up, and we all said we wanted to be superheroes. I said I wanted to be Spider-Man, but they all said, "Man, Spider-Man's not black!" so I became Black Panther instead. When I got to the show, they asked what I wanted my nickname to be. It was easy, Panther. My original ideas for costumes ended up being too close to the comic, so we ended up with the black pants and paw painted on my chest. I didn't realize that I'd have to have it painted on every day. I ended up hating it!

Erik Betts
Panther

Tsunami then chimes in, explaining that he was studying Bruce Lee (making sure to point out for the suburban kids who don't know that he was Shannon Lee's father) and that Lee taught that water was the most powerful force in nature. So he chose Tsunami, one of the most powerful water events.

They had the name already, but the character, the details, they were all me. I am a huge Bruce Lee fan, so that's where it came from.

Hien Nguyen
Tsunami

In an early draft of the script, Tsunami says he wanted to actually take the nickname of Bruce Lee, but the Council wouldn't let him. It's possible the unused Ki Symbol (see Chapter 1: Making the Masters) for Han "Bruce" Lee was intended for this use. This line was axed from the show in favor of a less fanboy-ish explanation.

After preparing for his final against Superstar, The Machine finally spills as to why he is called the The Machine. The vignette is the same as in the pilot, with some slight changes in the overdub that don't impact the story at all.

The Origin of The Machine

Hakim narrates the story, explaining that shortly after gaining his black belt in Tae Kwon Do, he began kickboxing, but no one was willing to spar with him. Finally, his sensei Master Do brings in another large man, Steve, to try to push him and improve his skills. Hakim, full of confidence, believes he will wipe the floor with the newcomer, but it does not go as he plans.

Like many of the flashback vignettes, this one had a kernel of truth.

I drew on some similar situations I found myself in as a very young man. It was kind of several situations stitched together (for the show). Basically, it boiled down to me being a very young man and being very cocky. I knew I was good. I was big and strong and asserted myself. At one point, they brought in this fighter, a very good fighter, and they told him not to hold back against me even though I was only seventeen or so at the time. So he laid a little in, so I laid a little in, and so on. Basically, they let it go on way longer than maybe they would have if I didn't need that reality check. I needed to be humbled, to know I wasn't always going to assert my will.

Hakim Alston
The Machine

As the story ends, The Machine assures his fellow competitors he wants to win just as bad as each of them, but only for the love of competition, not for selfish reasons. Then, as he walks away to prepare for the Battle Dome, his fellow Masters debate whether or not he actually destroyed the heavy bag. All this while their own heavy bag, which The Machine kicked before leaving, swings ominously in the background, one of the more fun shots of this debut episode.

This first vignette sets the mold for future ones. It uses one of the Masters' not-quite-real-life stories to teach a valuable lesson to kids, in this case, to be humble about your own abilities. While the quality of the flashbacks in future episodes will vary, this one effectively sets the standard.

It is worth noting that before he was listed as The Machine, Hakim was going to be The Dream, featuring a brightly colored outfit and no discernible character to speak of.

That was (the producers) original idea. It wasn't so much an Olajuwon (NOTE: Hakeem "The Dream" Olajuwon was a star basketball player in the 1990s) thing as a marketing thing. They just thought it sounded catchy. But I didn't really like it. As things kept going, I kind of had conversations with them, with Pat

(Johnson), and decided to go another direction. The Machine was actually my idea, and they ran with it and made the armor and stuff.

Hakim Alston
The Machine

We then head to the Battle Dome final for the episode's conclusion.

Battle Dome Final
Competitors:
The Machine ⦿⦿⦿⦿⦿⦿⦿⦿ vs.
Superstar ⦿⦿⦿⦿⦿⦿⦿⦿

Like the vignette we just saw, the Battle Dome final for this episode is reused from the unaired Pilot. Shannon explains the rules, whichever Master forces their opponent into the cage the most times in two minutes will win. If it's tied, we go to sudden death. Unlike future Battle Domes, there are no ninja warriors in this one. It's a straight-up one-on-one contest.

Like all of the bigger sets, the Dome itself was created by a company called Cinnabar, a prominent California-based fabrication company. They made all the main sets, including the Battle Dome, Dragon Star throne, and the rotating platform that hosted the Dragon Star battles. Unfortunately, no one currently employed there was working for the company in the 90s, so they had nothing to offer for this book regarding the creation of the Dome.

Considering this was the first Battle Dome of the series, it had to set the tone for future fights, delivering action and excitement while still telling

Hakim Alston
The Machine
Discipline: Kickboxing

Without a doubt the most imposing presence in the *WMAC Masters* cast, Hakim "The Machine" Alston stands a legitimate (not Hollywood) 6'4", and sports an impressive resume: He is a 4 time NASKA Heavyweight champion, ISKA amatuer and professional kickboxing champion, USA WKO Gold Medal winner, and winner of three successive gold medals for overall fighting champion (1988-1991). Possessing a unique, laid back charisma, Hakim would feature in several feature films, most famously the first *Mortal Kombat* film.

Fun Fact:
Hakim Alston fought for a world Kickboxing Championship in the same gym in which this vignette was shot. He took on Ernest "The Cat" Miller of WCW pro wrestling fame.

a coherent story.

We definitely knew we were setting the tone for the show with the first (Dome fight). Everyone did. We definitely approached it with that in mind. We wanted to really get the best out of each other and put on the best fight possible.

Hakim Alston
The Machine

The pair definitely deliver on that goal, demonstrating great chemistry as combatants, something we will see further as the season progresses. There is a clever bit of storytelling in the match, as early on The Machine tries two roundhouse kicks, which Superstar ducks. He spins a third time without kicking, measuring Superstar for a clean hit that scores him a point. (We are treated to a fantastic reaction shot of Superstar in the post-fight recap) Later on, in the fight, Superstar gets him back by throwing high kicks followed by low kicks, forcing The Machine to duck and jump in succession. He does this twice before changing it up, going high when The Machine expects him to go low.

This back-and-forth, pointed out by Shannon in the post-match, emphasizes that martial arts are not simply a physical battle but a mental one. The producers, directors, and fighters were very aware that they would be presenting martial arts to a much wider audience than they had before, many of whom had no previous exposure to it. Therefore, they were all intent on showcasing not just the physical aspects but the mental and emotional sides of martial arts training and competition.

To that end, this fight also demonstrates another principle of martial arts, it's not all about size. The Machine has the power advantage, but Superstar is more agile. It's important to remember that at this time, the UFC was in its infancy and was very much an underground cult phenomenon. It was yet to bring MMA to the mainstream. Most average viewers would not be familiar with Gracie Jiu-Jitsu and its ability to be the great equalizer despite size and strength disparities. To most viewers, the bigger, stronger guy was likely to win.

The fight goes down to the wire, tied at two points each. Superstar scores the winning point by executing a twisting, flipping kick with four seconds left, giving him the win and his ninth Ki Symbol.

We then see the ceremony of the Dragon Belt, where the Battle Dome loser presents the victor with his Ki Symbol to put on his belt. This gives Superstar his ninth symbol and takes him one step closer to the Dragon Star. Shannon mentions that Herb "Olympus" Perez is going for full Dragon Belt status next week, setting the stage for our next episode!

"Meet the Masters" does everything a debut episode needs to do. It introduces the world and the characters, giving each of them time to showcase their unique personalities. We are instantly aware that The Machine is a cool bad-ass, Superstar is a flashy but full of himself star, and Tsunami is a bit of an every-man sort of character. The fights, Battle Dome, and flashbacks all work marvelously, and this is a HUGE step up from the unaired *Quest for the Dragon Star* pilot. It also ends on a note that built interest for next week's show, sometimes the most challenging thing for a first episode to do.

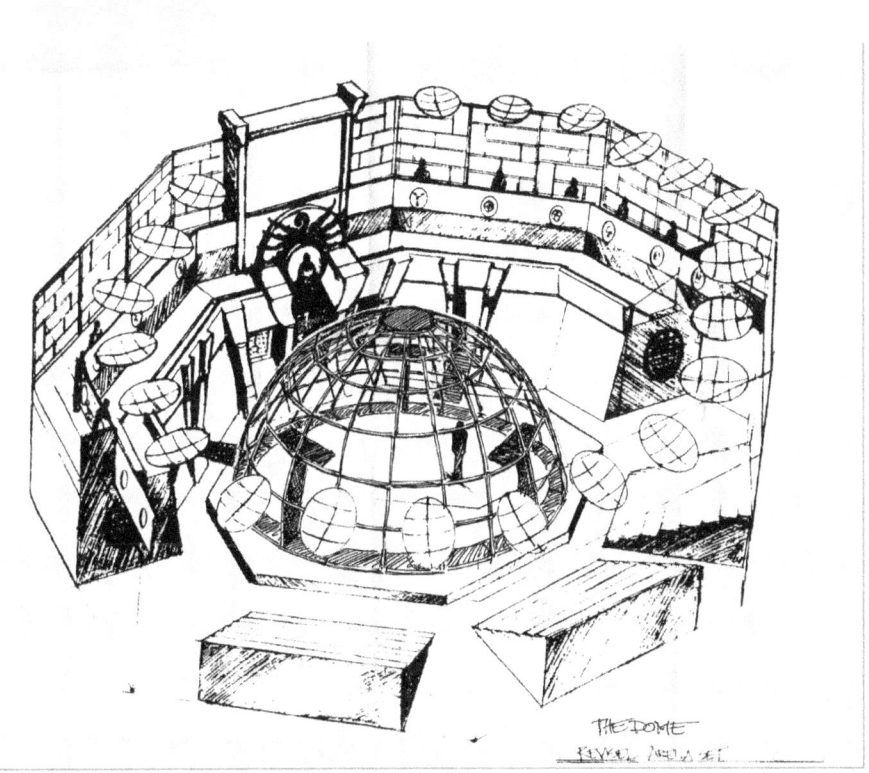

Dan Hubp's original sketch of the Battle Dome.

CHAPTER 05

S1E02: Brothers in Arms

Superstar vs. Star Warrior

Olympus vs. Tsunami

"We wanted to show kids there was more to martial arts"

Second episodes of TV shows can suffer from a unique problem. Often they have to re-tread the pilot for new viewers who missed the first installment. This can lead to dull, repetitive second efforts, but *WMAC Masters* avoids this pitfall through its clever use of its large cast. "Brothers in Arms" repeats some tropes from the debut, namely the competition structure, which will run throughout the series, and the "how the Masters got their names" story. But instead, they focus on other fighters, namely Ho-Sung Pak, who did not reveal their entire backstory in episode one. As a result, it feels fresh, despite being similar.

After the opening sequences, Shannon Lee sets viewers up for the episode. Olympus is going for full Dragon Belt, and there's a unique match-up on first, and it's Brother vs. Brother! The Masters debate the difficulties of squaring off against family, leading to The Machine beginning this episode's flashback sequence. It's a story about Superstar (Ho-Sung Pak) and Star Warrior (Ho-Young Pak).

Flashback Part I

The vignette takes us back an unspecified number of years to a time when Superstar was, somehow, even more arrogant than he is in the series. He is quite literally a Superstar, The Machine explains, making Kung Fu films, often earning the ire of co-stars and directors alike for changing the choreography to showcase his best moves, with no regard for anyone else on set.

> *Ho-Sung was definitely a star, and he wasn't shy about it. He loved to tell us about working with Jackie Chan (In Drunken Master II).*

Jamie Webster
Great Wolf

David Morizot played a ninja during the series' run and played John Oh in the vignette.

> *That shoot was a lot of fun. I was a regular as one of the ninjas, and they asked me on very short notice to do the speaking role. Of course, I said yes. Originally the character was supposed to*

be Asian, so they had to re-write some dialogue on set because it was sounding very... inappropriate for me to be saying it.

David Morizot
John Oh, Ninja

According to the script, John Oh was to follow his "What do you have to say for yourself now, Superstar?" line with "How about SAYONARA?"

The name John Oh was an inside joke, according to Morizot.

I don't remember what the character was originally called (NOTE: according to a script revision, the name of the character was originally "Yimou"), but when I was cast instead (of an Asian actor), they asked me what I wanted the name to be. Our AD (Assistant Director) was a guy named John O'Rourke, we called him John O. I knew I didn't want it to be my own name because the character was a jerk, so I looked around and saw him and told them I want to be John Oh. He loved it!

David Morizot
John Oh, Ninja

Also of note is the cameo appearance of Al Kahn, known affectionately on set as "Big Al," playing the Director of the action movie Ho-Sung is acting in. One crew member noted that "energy and work ethic really picked up" when Al was on set, as you would expect from the big boss showing up.

Unrelated but important: Hakim Alston would not take blame or credit for the awful (or awesome, if you're into that sort of thing) pun he delivers to pause his telling of the flashback: "This fight will be action Pak'd." The script confirms it was, indeed, written that way.

HO AND HO VIGNETTE -- EPISODE #2   script revision #2 -- <u>PINK</u>

HO YOUNG and HOSUNG are walking home after the shoot.

> HO YOUNG
> Making movies isn't a competitive sport,
> HoSung. You should have used a kick like
> this
> (DEMONSTRATES).
> Then you won't accidentally kick the other
> actors so often.

> HOSUNG
> (Cutting off HoYoung)
> (sarcastically)
> I don't need to learn any new moves!
> Thanks for the advice but I think I know a
> little more about martial arts than you do.

HOSUNG walks away from HO YOUNG, angry. HO YOUNG looks after him, sadly.

CUT TO:

HOSUNG walks from around a corner and hears...

> YIMOU (O.S.)
> HOSUNG PAK!!!

HOSUNG freezes. Turns. Yimou approaches. Trailing behind him, the 5 MEMBERS OF YIMOU'S GANG.

> YIMOU
> You think you're the greatest?
> You think you're unbeatable---

A major fight breaks out. HOSUNG is pinned down and it looks like he is about to get beaten up very badly.

> MACHINE (V.O.)
> HoSung yelled for his brother, but no one
> came.

> YIMOU
> What do you have to say for yourself now,
> <u>SUPERSTAR!</u> How about... SAYO-NARA!

> CUT TO:

Script excerpt showing original name and dialogue for John Oh. Script from Jamie Webster.

Preliminary Match One
Competitors:
Superstar ⬡ ⬡ ⬡ ⬡ ⬡ ⬡ ⬡ ⬡ ⬡ vs. Star Warrior ⬡ ⬡ ⬡ ⬡ ⬡ ⬡ ⬡
Battle Zone: Unnamed Asian Themed Zone
Ninjas: Black

We don't get entrances into the WMAC Arena for this one, as we cut straight to the brothers warming up beforehand. The fight takes place at Splendid China, lit up pagodas in the background in what looks like a Chinese garden.

Splendid China was absolutely beautiful. Serene and peaceful. Walking through there when we had breaks was surreal. It was like being there (in China) for real.

Tom Laskowski
Camera Crew

This fight served as Ho-Young's introduction to the series, and his vast array of impressive moves was displayed against his brother.

Ho-Young was chosen (for the show) on his own merits, not because he was Ho-Sung's brother. He was amazing on the competition circuit.

Norman Grossfeld
Executive Producer

This fight is an interesting example of the storytelling abilities of the show. Star Warrior retains a one-hit lead, but Superstar starts gaining momentum, forcing Star Warrior to switch to a drunken Kung Fu style that visibly shakes Superstar.

Superstar tries to continue the attack, but the drunken Kung Fu has him off his game. Finally, after a couple of tries to break Star Warrior's defenses, he bows and concedes the match. This is much to the surprise of Shannon Lee, and the other Masters, who all act like Superstar, just gave up a sure win when he was behind on the power bars and very close to losing the old-fashioned way.

The point of this fight wasn't so much the action as it was advancing the story being told in the vignette. Which is a shame as an all-out match between the two would undoubtedly be an all-time classic.

Back in the Inner Sanctum, The Machine says he might be able to explain what happened out there by finishing his story from earlier in the episode.

Flashback Part II

The flashback elaborates on what just happened in the fight, showing Ho-Young saving his younger brother from an impending beat down with that same drunken Kung-Fu style he used.

As Ho-Young (dressed like a bum) goes to town on John Oh and his thugs, we get a very cartoon-like sound effect that wouldn't be used often in the series. Morizot also played to the balcony with his acting, hamming it up in his one face role in the show.

> *When I get knocked out, I go cross-eyed, but only one eye. It's something I knew how to do, and Isaac (Florentine, Director) asked me to do something to add to the effect, so I crossed one eye. It's a little subtle. Maybe I should have crossed both!*

David Morizot
John Oh, Ninja

Ho-Sung Pak
Superstar
Discipline: Kung Fu

A certified Hong Kong action movie star and best known as the original sprite for Liu Kang in *Mortal Kombat*, Ho-Sung Pak was billed as a Superstar and carried himself as one. Cocky but charismatic, fans of the show either loved or hated him. After Masters ended Ho-Sung would continue to work in the industry as a stunt performer, actor, and coordinator, as well as earning his MBA and starting a production company.

Fun Fact:
A scene that was scripted but never filmed was originally included here. Great Wolf wants to show Tiger Claw a new technique, a double inside crescent kick! This would have served to set up their storyline in episode four. Interestingly their roles were reversed before filming, making Tiger Claw the teacher.

We get the full Arena entrances for this one, including Tsunami doing a back-flip kick demonstration and getting the fans to do the Tsunami Tidal Wave, known simply as The Wave in American sports or the Mexican Wave abroad. Tsunami also has a very fancy bow, unique amongst the cast.

It was a character bit I came up with. All his movements were meant to evoke a feeling of water since he was a Tsunami. So the bow was part of that, like a wave.

Hien Nguyen
Tsunami

Before the fight begins, Shannon says that Superstar declined to explain his reasons for forfeiting the fight. Saying only that seeing his brother use drunken Kung Fu "brought back painful memories." This is an interesting touch. Superstar did not publicly tell his reasons, and in fact, he did not tell them at all. The Machine did. This close-to-the-vest nature, or a desire to project a heroic star image, is some subtle character work, a relative rarity for the show.

As the match begins, Shannon explains that Tsunami was recently promoted from the WMAC Academy to the rank of full Master, explaining his empty Dragon Belt. Then, the fight starts with the ninjas, as usual. Shannon points out that Tsunami is now fighting the same recruits he trained with.

In reality, the ninjas were often cast members who were not scheduled to film their own fights that night, supplemented with other professional martial artists and stuntmen and women.

We'd get in there and mix it up with the boys. Under the hoods, you couldn't tell who was a guy or who was a girl, so sometimes they'd get us good. :laughs:

Christine Rodrigues
Lady Lightning

Morizot, who in addition to playing John Oh in this episode's flashback was a regular ninja and recalled it fondly.

It was so much fun being a ninja. It was hard work, but getting to work with so much world-class talent, it was unbelievable.

David Morizot
John Oh, Ninja

The ghost town battle zone was actually the Wild West Stunt Show set at Universal, and it was one of the more fun zones to shoot on, according to the cast.

The Old West set was a lot of fun. It was where they did a stunt show, so there were lots of gags already set up.

Jamie Webster
Great Wolf

Often it would fall to the directors to plot out which gags or stunts would go in what fight.

We used everything we could. Anything to make the fights interesting!

Isaac Florentine
Director

Tsunami shows considerable flair in this fight, showcasing some fancy moves. He dispatches one ninja with what professional wrestling fans recognize as a huracanrana, jumping onto the ninja's shoulders and using his legs to drive it head first into the ground.

I trained some pro wrestlers in the martial arts, so as I got to know them, I'd see some of their videos, and I'd see their moves, and I'd go, "yeah, I can do that," and work it into the show.

Hien Nguyen
Tsunami

He one-ups that by nailing a beautiful back-flip kick, which is one of the coolest looking techniques in the episode, which is quite the feat. He credits this to his previous TV work.

> *So we all had a lot of freedom (to come up with moves for the fights). They would lay out kind of the architecture of the fight and let us fill in the details. Both Pat (Johnson) and Isaac (Florentine) were great like that. For my fights, I wanted to stand out, do moves that would drive the kids wild and make them want to do them, too. So I brought a lot of the techniques from my work on Power Rangers.*

Hien Nguyen
Tsunami

Mighty Morphin Power Rangers, the original US iteration of the mega-popular franchise, was a fully-fledged cultural phenomenon by the time *WMAC Masters* made its debut. As a result, there are many connections between the two shows. Most tie back to Isaac Florentine, who directed on both series and was instrumental in bringing several cast members to the Masters fold. In addition to Hien "Tsunami" Nguyen and Erik "Panther" Betts, Richard "Yin Yang Man" Branden, "Princess" Mer Mer Chen, and Bridgett "Babydoll" Riley were all performers on both shows. As were later series additions Sophia "Chameleon" Crawford, Yuji "Cyclone" Noguchi, and "Wizard" Mike Chaturantabut.

The show was created and distributed by Saban Entertainment, a partner of Bandai, financiers, and toy distributors for *WMAC Masters*. The parallels were obvious. Both live-action martial arts shows are aimed at kids with massive toy selling potential. Those similarities, however, ultimately became a disadvantage, even a burden to the show.

> *It became an issue. Bandai didn't want to be competing with itself, and Power Rangers was their cash cow. I think we suffered for it.*

Carlin West
Series Creator

This fight is Tsunami's first in the series, and despite his loss, it helped solidify his status as a fan favorite. He is the first two episodes situate him as an everyman sort of character. The newest of the Masters, yet to get a win, but full of excitement and inquisitiveness, not to mention a dazzling array of flashy moves. Both children and adult fans would rally around Tsunami, especially as season one would play out. This would come into play later, with devastating effect, but we'll get there...

In a totally shocking, never saw that coming moment, Olympus wins easily, sending him to the Battle Dome final!

Before the finals, however, we get a look back at the previous Dragon Star match, as Turbo successfully defended his title against Richard Branden, the Yin Yang Man. Shannon explains that with Olympus potentially filling his Dragon Belt and challenging for the title, the Council wanted to look back at the last match. However, in reality, the show needed to introduce the concept of the title fights.

The battle was filmed at the same time as the unaired *Quest for the Dragon Star* pilot. In recent years the clips of the fight used in the series have led to internet speculation that a full unreleased Dragon Star match may still be in the WMAC Archives, but that is wishful thinking.

We didn't shoot a whole fight for that, just pieces they used (in the show).

Mike Bernardo
Turbo

This was because the show did not have a budget for extra footage.

There was very little if any footage that we shot that wasn't used. Hardly any. Definitely no full fights. We didn't have the budget to be that wasteful!

Isaac Florentine
Director

The clips from the fight show Turbo winning by using his trademark Turbo-Staff to sweep the legs out from under Yin Yang man, sending him spiraling to the mats below. The only time in the series that weapons are used in any fight.

I don't remember using the weapons in the fight, honestly, but weapons were kind of what I was known for (on the circuit), and Richie (Branden) could use any weapon you gave him. So it makes sense.

Mike Bernardo
Turbo

These clips are followed by a kata from Yin Yang Man. This serves as an introduction to the Master Blaster concept, where the Masters will have the chance to demonstrate their kata forms in the arena. This concept was essential to the show for a number of reasons.

We didn't want it to be all fighting. We wanted to show kids there was more to martial arts.

Norman Grossfeld
Executive Producer

It also served to amplify the cool factor of the Masters. After all, the show was financed by a merchandising company, and moving toys was never far from the producers' minds. The Master Blaster segments were a way to get kids buzzing, especially when they were done by Masters, featured in the first toy line. (More on that later).

After this demonstration, the Battle Dome comes down, and it's Olympus's time to go for full Dragon Belt!

Battle Dome Final
Competitors:
Star Warrior ◗ ◗ ◗ ◗ ◗ ◗ ◗ vs. Olympus ◎ ◎ ◎ ◎ ◎ ◎ ◎ ◎ ◎ ◎

This was a very even match, both men looking like legitimate threats to win it. It was very much the power of Tae Kwon Do against the grace and agility of Kung Fu type of story, and it was highly effective. Even though the through-line of the episode was Olympus's quest for full Dragon Belt status, there was still enough action to put the result in some doubt, if only for a moment. This fight is also the first in the series to go to sudden death over time, something that will become almost cliche.

We get the Dragon Belt ceremony, then Olympus poses, staring down Turbo. Shannon comments that Turbo has defended the title TWICE already, meaning there is one more defense besides Yin Yang Man that we don't know about!

We didn't really come up with stuff like that. We wrote it for Shannon to say, but we didn't have an intricate title history or anything. It just wasn't what we were concerned about.

Norman Grossfeld
Executive Producer

Considering the fact that only Yin Yang Man comes into season one working on his second Dragon Belt, it's safe to assume that whoever lost to Turbo in the previous Dragon Star match either retired or took a sabbatical from the competition. Perhaps paving the way for Tsunami to be promoted. This is, of course, speculation, but considering the writers never wrote anything to fill this gap, I feel it's as good an answer as any, and this is my book, so we are running with it!

In the end, "Brothers in Arms" is an effective second episode, establishing the concept of the series for viewers who missed the first episode while not feeling like a total rehash. By focusing on Superstar and Olympus, two of the major characters who we didn't see much of in episode one, as well as introducing the Master Blaster concept, this episode adds to the show's arsenal, not just reiterate it. While the fights featured in this episode won't go down among the show's best, there are no clunkers here, making "Brothers in Arms" another early-series favorite.

Photos from Bruce Heinsius Photography.

CHAPTER 06

Interlude: The Legend of the Stupid Ninja

"WHO IS THAT STUPID NINJA!?"

While researching and interviewing for this book, I heard countless stories from cast and crew members. Sad stories, exciting stories, funny stories- I heard them all. But the one I'd heard most often, from the most people, is what I have dubbed The Legend of the Stupid Ninja.

I call it a legend because, like most legends, it has grown in the telling (and retelling), and no two versions of it were quite the same, but everyone who told me their iteration assured me their version was the "real" one. I have questioned and poked and prodded the storytellers in an attempt to sift through the various layers and strata of the legend. I believe I have come as close as possible to the answer, but only those who were there know for sure.

Most, in fact, almost all of the stories have the same basic set-up: Director Isaac Florentine is in the midst of one of his trademark long playing shots. Complicated and intricate, with lots of moving parts (namely ninjas), it unfolds without a hitch until suddenly, seemingly out of nowhere, a ninja is massively out of position, ruining the shot. Isaac, known for his booming voice and passionate outbursts, bellows out, "WHO IS THAT STUPID NINJA!?"

Hilarity ensued, the cast and crew cracking up except, of course, for Isaac, whose shot was ruined entirely by this impetuous ninja. It would quickly become a rallying cry for the show, particularly any time a ninja put a foot wrong or ended up in the wrong place while filming with the legendary Israeli director. As part of the ongoing joke, someone made t-shirts and distributed them only to the cast and crew.

The question remained, however, who was the original Stupid Ninja?

Erik Betts and Hien Nguyen were the two face characters who played ninjas most often and were the likely suspects.

:laughs: I mean, everyone who played (a) ninja long enough ended up as a stupid ninja eventually, but I wasn't the first one, though. I was there, for sure, but it wasn't me. I remember looking around and wondering who screwed up.

Erik Betts
Panther

I want to make sure I point out here that there is some confusion about when and where the first Stupid Ninja sighting occurred. Most recollections place it as happening at the Doom City Battle Zone, though not all remember it that way. Also, they didn't shoot the episodes in order, so even though it happened early in filming (this point is almost universally agreed upon), it did not necessarily occur in one of the first aired episodes, though it could have.

Dan Hubp, a swiss-army knife of a crew member who served as art department, editor, and second unit director at various times, was the first to tell me the story.

It was a great shot, this big sweeping shot, and right at the very end, this ninja crosses in front of the camera and is just up against the car. We all hear (Isaac) boom, "CUT! WHO IS THAT STUPID F**KING NINJA!?" We all lost it.

Dan Hubp
Production Designer, Editor

However, Florentine remembers it a little differently.

I never said that word (the F Word). It was "Who's that stupid ninja!"

Isaac Florentine
Director

More from the man himself in a bit, but first, we have to look at the other most likely candidate, Hien Nguyen.

I was there, but it wasn't me. :laughs: It was one of the first shoots, and it was a big complicated shot. Isaac loved those shots, and we go through it, and everyone hits their spots right to the end, and then someone is out of position, and Isaac just loses it. "Who is that STUPID NINJA!?"

Hien Nguyen
Tsunami

So it was neither of the two most likely suspects, but they were far from the only face characters to play the role of a ninja. Most of the cast did, at least on some occasions.

I played a ninja lot. It was always fun. That first night though, I don't think I was there. I had a fight that episode, and generally, I didn't play ninja when I had a fight since you had choreography to layout, things like that.

Jamie Webster
Great Wolf

Who, then, was the original stupid ninja? In the end, one of the cast did admit to me that they were the perpetrator, and it was someone I never expected.

It was me! I was the stupid ninja! :laughs:

Herb Perez
Olympus

How did it happen that mighty Olympus, the all-American good guy, the shining hero of season one, could be the original stupid ninja?

It was one of the first nights of shooting. It was my first time as a ninja. I had no background in it, in stunt work or working on TV, I came from Olympic Tae Kwon Do, so I had no idea what I was doing. So when the camera panned over or whatever, I was out of position, so it was just my butt right in the camera's face! :laughs: Then Isaac lost it, and I had to sheepishly admit it was me.

Herb Perez
Olympus

Sheepish as his initial admittance was, the Legend of the Stupid Ninja became one of the stories I often heard while putting together this book, and Perez proudly owned up to it.

It just became a thing. It took on a life of its own, really. I ended up making t-shirts with the phrase on them and giving them to the cast and crew.

Herb Perez
Olympus

The only trace of these shirts I have found was a social media post from Hien "Tsunami" Nguyen. However, one crew member did see one "in the wild" years after the show.

A few years after the show, I took my son to a local martial arts school, and one of the instructors was talking about how he worked on a martial arts show here locally (in Orlando). Naturally, I asked which one. It turns out he had been on the show! He still had his stupid ninja shirt and everything!

Shannon "Irish" Stewart
Script Supervisor

It seems that everyone on the show had a story of the stupid ninja, either playing it or having one of their otherwise pristine takes ruined by one. It became a rallying cry for the cast during the long, difficult nights of shooting.

I was a very demanding director. I know this. I'm sure everyone has a story about how I worked them to the bone. I wanted perfection.

Isaac Florentine
Director

The cast agreed.

It was kind of a way for us to let off steam. Keep us from going crazy.

Erik Betts
Panther

In the end, the story of the Stupid Ninja became much more than a simple blooper, even more than a rallying cry for the cast. It became a legend.

Shirt printed for cast by Herb Perez.
Photo from Hien Nguyen.

Promo photo of Hien Nguyen.
Photo from Dan Hubp.

Willie Johnson in ninja garb.
Photo from Willie Johnson.

Carmichael Simon in ninja garb with Shannon
Lee. Photo from Carmichael Simon.

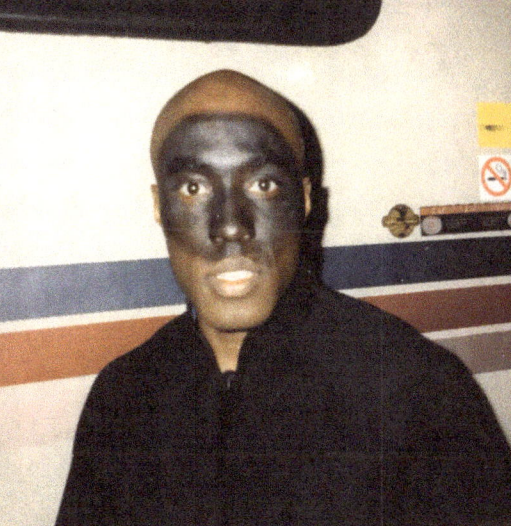

CHAPTER 07

S1E03:
Going for the Gold

Lady Lightning vs. Princess

Babydoll vs. Mouse

Turbo vs. Olympus

"I ended up in the hospital..."

It's three episodes in, and it's time for the first major deviation in show structure. Today we get our first Dragon Star match. Similar to a world title match in other combat sports, this fight will be the big one to decide who is the World's Greatest Martial Artist. This episode does a good job of feeling different and special and sets the stage for future Dragon Star fights.

"Going for the Gold" opens with a shot of the raised Dragon Star platform as Shannon Lee welcomes us to the show and informs us today we will see the Dragon Star match between Turbo and Olympus. The audience is full of WMAC ninja recruits, not fans, and the platform has been raised to meet the throne at the top of the arena. It's a marvelous sight. It was completely different from anything else on TV at the time, be it pro wrestling, combat sports, or other mainstream sports.

In the Inner Sanctum, Red Dragon, The Machine, and Tsunami all talk about the pressure of fighting for the Dragon Star and how Olympus should be able to handle it, being an Olympic gold medalist. This leads to Olympus telling a story of going back to his old high school and a crazy event that ended up changing his life and someone else's.

Flashback: Jake's Story

Olympus narrates the story of returning to his old high school, Panther in tow, to put on a seminar about staying away from drugs and how to use the martial arts to improve your life.

Their seminar begins with Panther doing a kata for the gathered teens. One of the kids watches, unimpressed, then tries to fight another student, only to be stopped by Olympus. "Something about the kid reminded me of myself at his age," Olympus explains in the voiceover. Adding it was "this very school that helped me turn it all around."

He wants to show his appreciation for the school and its principal, who was one of his teachers and decides to donate his Olympic gold medal to the school. We see the ceremony, where he gives a short speech to kids gathered around the school's trophy case in a hallway.

As he gives the speech, Panther produces a handkerchief from his pocket and pretends to cry into it, a great piece of comedy, lightening up an otherwise serious flashback.

That was a Norman Grossfeld idea. He pulled out a tissue and said, 'when Herb is talking, use this and pretend to cry.' Herb wasn't expecting it.

Erik Betts
Panther

After donating the medal, we cut to the Masters back outside as Panther warms up the crowd for the duo's main demonstration. The young man from before and his gang of friends clown around while Panther performs. Before Olympus joins the demo, the principal approaches him and informs him that his gold medal has been stolen. Olympus asks how it happened, but the principal doesn't know. Probably had something to do with leaving it in a run-of-the-mill trophy case that didn't even appear to be locked, but I digress. Olympus narrates that "the show must go on" and joins the demonstration.

I ended up in the hospital for those vignettes. There's a point where I say 'I am Panther' and go into the demonstration, I damn near passed out. There were record highs in Orlando at the time, so the medic had to come put salt on my tongue. I was severely dehydrated.

Erik Betts
Panther

The young man and his group mock the WMAC catchphrase they are hammering home. "Do what's right, don't fight" (possibly the most 1990s catchphrase ever), and Panther says if they don't like it, they should leave. The young man who has been causing all the trouble says Panther should make him leave. Olympus says that's a good idea and invites the young man down, but he begs off, only to be goaded into it by his friends.

Olympus asks the young man's name and he replies, "Turbo, loser," drawing "ooohs" from the crowd. He places an unlit cigarette in his mouth, which Olympus promptly kicks in half before telling the group, "Let's hear it for Turbo!"

This, naturally, embarrasses and enrages the teen, who tries to attack Olympus. He throws some jumping kicks that the gold medalist easily dodges. Olympus narrates, "The kid knew some martial arts moves, but he was no martial artist." The demo ends with Turbo on his butt on the ground, refusing the Master's help to get up, running off embarrassed as the whole school laughs at him.

Neil (the actor who played Jake) was actually a pretty good martial artist. He had some moves.

Herb Perez
Olympus

Neil Brown, Jr, who played Jake, would go on to achieve fame as DJ Yella in *Straight Outta Compton* as well as starring in the TV drama *Seal Team Six*. Everyone involved could tell he was a special talent during their shoot, even at his age.

I found Neil at a dojo here locally (in Orlando). He was a good kid, very bright, from a good home. Good grades and structured life. I never cast a child unless they're doing well in school. But from the second I met him, I knew he was special.

Pati Robinson
Casting Director

Betts agreed, instantly taking a shine to the young martial artist.

He was very smart. He asked a lot of questions, and I was happy to answer how to save money, invest, things like that. We stayed in touch over the years. I'm so proud of his success and was really happy to get to work with him again (on Seal Team Six). On my first day of shooting (STS), he introduced me to everyone and publicly thanked me. It was very humbling.

Erik Betts
Panther

This vignette was special for Herb Perez, as well.

I loved doing things like that. I visited a lot of schools and gave a lot of speeches. It still is very near and dear to my heart, speaking with students, trying to guide them.

Herb Perez
Olympus

Brown remembered the casting process well, his first experience in the world of acting.

(The Producers) came to my dojo, where I would hang out after school and train and everything. My sensei called me over. I thought I was in trouble. He asked me to do a couple of moves. I was like, "okay." So I did them and just walked away. I had no idea. Later they told me who they were and asked me to come to an audition.

Neil Brown Jr.
Jake

The audition was what is known in the entertainment industry as a cattle call.

I got there, and there were like, a hundred kids there. Most had their parents with them or whatever, but I was there by myself. I took the bus. They handed me a script and explained that I'd need to read lines. I'd never acted before. I had no idea what I was doing. So I took a nap. I was one of the last to go, and when I woke up, they asked if I needed a minute to look it over again, and I was like, "Nah, I got it," and I did it. Then they told everyone we were done. So I left to go try to find a cab home, but they pulled me aside and kind of half-whispered, "you got the part." I was like, "cool, can someone give me a ride home?"

Neil Brown Jr.
Jake

For the producers, there was no real option.

He was my first and only choice. I just knew he was special. He had that quality.

Pati Robinson
Casting Director

Olympus, in voiceover, laments that he hit it off with the young man "about as well as the real Turbo and I did." We then see Panther and Olympus walking the school hall. Panther says there's a better chance of finding a second Dragon Star than finding Olympus's medal, which isn't really what Olympus needs to hear at that moment. As they pass the principal's office, they overhear the young man from earlier getting an earful before being told to sit down and wait for his parents.

Olympus pulls up a chair and tries to have a heart-to-heart with him like a good comic book hero would. The kid says his name is Jake. Olympus tells him they have a lot in common. Olympus was a young wild child too, but "this very school" helped him sort it out and become an Olympic champion. We get a time-lapse shot of them spending a few hours together, talking, practicing martial arts, and bonding.

It's funny. I had no clue about acting, like at all. One of the crew, after one of the first shots, joked with me, "Don't worry, Segall can't act either," and I was worried I'd screwed up. But then later, after the scenes with the principal, he came over and apologized, "I had no idea you were an actor. I'm so sorry." It was funny. That was the day the acting bug bit me.

Neil Brown Jr.
Jake

We then cut to Olympus and Panther playing basketball, with Panther dogging him for his hoops skills. Olympus says the barbs sting as he's just getting over losing his gold medal (that was quick), but Panther points out that he at least got through to Jake. They finish up, and Olympus goes back inside the school to get his bag while Panther retrieves the car. Olympus stealthily watches Jake return the gold medal to the trophy case, smiling.

Back in the Inner Sanctum, Red Dragon, Tsunami, and The Machine agree that Jake was just looking for respect, but doing it in the wrong way, hammering home that respect is a key point of the Dragon Star and one of the cornerstones of martial arts.

Women's Tournament Update

We then see Turbo enter the arena and pose with the Dragon Star before we get a segment with Shannon, an update on the women's tournament! This is the first time we've seen the ladies of the WMAC get in on the action, and unfortunately, it's only clips of fights.

Preliminary Match One
Competitors:
Lady Lightning ⬡⬡⬡⬡⬡⬡⬡⬡ vs. **Princess** ⬡⬡⬡
Battle Zone: Doom City
Ninjas: Black

Shannon describes the fight as "very even," which it appears to be from the few seconds we get to see it. Lady Lightning picks up the win.

> *Our matches didn't get as much screen time, ya know, as the men's, but we put just as much work into them. Everybody did. From the directors to the guys playing the ninjas, everyone wanted them to be as good as they could be, even if it wasn't going to get featured.*

Christine Rodrigues
Lady Lightning

The lack of time for the women's matches is something the producers lamented but was a sad reality.

> *We definitely wanted to feature the ladies more. Diversity was very important to us, as you can see (from the cast). It was just a matter of screen time. We had our main characters we featured, the ones who were the toys, and we could only go so long without*

featuring them. So sadly, it became a victim of screen time.

Norman Grossfeld
Executive Producer

Michelle Krasnoo
Mouse
Discipline: Karate

Preliminary Match Two
Competitors:
Babydoll ⬡⬡⬡⬡⬡⬡⬡ vs. **Mouse** ⬡⬡⬡
Battle Zone: Doom City
Ninjas: Black

"Tiny but mighty" would be the perfect descriptor for Mouse, an early cast member who unfortunately didn't feature in the finished show as much as others. Born into a martial arts practicing family, her father operating the famed Sherman Oaks Karate Studio originally founded by Chuck Norris. After her brief run on the show Mouse starred in several fitness and martial arts workout DVDs and raised a family.

Another clip-job, as we see very little. Babydoll dominates the fight, with Shannon saying Mouse "struggled against the ninjas." Babydoll picks up an easy win.

Michele "Mouse" Krasnoo did not respond to requests to be interviewed for this book, but her fellow fighters spoke highly of her.

Michele (Krasnoo, Mouse) was one of those people I only knew by reputation coming in. But we got there, and I was like, "I like this chic." It was a shame we didn't get to work together more.

Bridgett Riley
Babydoll

We then follow this with clips from the Battle Dome final.

Battle Dome Final
Competitors:
Lady Lightning ⬣⬣⬣⬣⬣⬣⬣⬣ vs. Babydoll ⬣⬣⬣⬣⬣⬣⬣

We don't really get anything of note from this Battle Dome. Lady Lightning wins 4-2, claiming her ninth Ki Symbol and her first win over Babydoll, who will become her biggest rival on the show. We don't even get a good shot of Tarantula on the Dragon Star throne.

Despite the disappointingly short duration, this segment offers a tantalizing glimpse at the immensely talented women of the WMAC. Luckily for fans, there is much more of them to come, though it must be said that it's not nearly as much as the athletes themselves deserve.

We go back to live action and see Turbo do a kata with his trademark Turbo Staff. Bernardo, known in real life for his weapons forms, oozes intensity here, his biker-style gear the perfect foil for the literal golden boy, Olympus.

> *I liked (being the villain). It suited me. I'm kind of a quiet guy, so it meant I didn't have to talk much.*

Michael Bernardo
Turbo

To cap off his kata, Turbo lights a giant Olympus Ki Symbol on fire and poses as it burns, an ominous sight that reinforces the bad guy dynamic. Next, we cut to the Inner Sanctum and the Masters' reactions. They all seem to take it as an affront towards Olympus (which it is), but the man himself isn't phased. He has something of his own planned.

In the script for this episode dated 7/6/95, there is a scene that follows where Tsunami says he hopes Olympus wins. Red Dragon mockingly asks if it's because Turbo has already beaten Tsunami three times. The other Masters then debate the relative toughness of Turbo and Olympus, culminating in Superstar saying, "this isn't some rinky-dink Olympics. We're talking a fight for the Dragon Star."

This was likely cut due to the timeline not making sense. Turbo couldn't have fought Tsunami three times, as he has been Dragon Star champion for quite a while (long enough to defend it three times), and Tsunami recently graduated to full Master status from the WMAC Academy. It is unknown if this was filmed or cut before being filmed.

That something he has in store is his own form demonstration, this one featuring Turbo's trademark staffs. Turbo doesn't look pleased with his signature weapon being bandied about and is even less so when Olympus begins to break them with a series of kicks. He follows that by breaking some boards, traditional martial arts fare, and then finishes by breaking a balloon, a seeming favorite of the *WMAC Masters* series, as viewers will come to see. Why balloons?

> *Balloons just looked great on camera. We'd spend hours trying different things, seeing what worked best. We tried all different combinations of materials and fillings to find the best 'pop' on camera.*

Nick Ferrell
Prop Master

Before he began his form, Olympus relinquished his Dragon Belt, the last requirement to challenge for the Dragon Star. So now all that is left is for Turbo to place the Star in the "Tri-Chamber Cyber-Cell" (remember that mouthful of a name, dear reader, it becomes important later) for the match to begin!

Dragon Star Championship
Competitors: Turbo (Champion) vs. Olympus (Challenger)

The first Dragon Star match of the series is also one of the most remembered, probably due to it being featured on one of the three VHS releases. Much like The Machine and Superstar had to set the tone for all future Battle Dome finals, this match had to set the tone for the Dragon Star championship matches.

Shannon explains the rules as the fight begins. The winner will be the last Master standing. He must eject not only his opponent but all ninjas from the spinning platform. Ninjas are called in when a Master is knocked onto one of the areas off the platform, but not all the way to the mats at the bottom of the arena.

This fight effectively showcases both fighters while telling a fun little story. Turbo is the more aggressive fighter, while Olympus is calmer and more calculating. The fight features a nice spot of drama as it looks like Olympus has fallen from one of the rings hanging around the platform, losing the match, but it's all tricky camera work as he rises back to the platform to call out the villainous Turbo. After that feat, the result is never in doubt, as Olympus ends up winning the Dragon Star!

We cut to the Inner Sanctum where the Masters clap, happy Olympus won, reinforcing Turbo's status as a villain, or at the very least, a pariah. In reality, however, Mike Bernardo was very well-liked.

Mike was a nice guy. Very quiet. Super talented.

Jamie Webster
Great Wolf

Many of the cast commented on Bernardo's quiet demeanor, but the Canadian also hid some secret talents.

One of my favorite behind-the-scenes memories is playing basketball during the day when we weren't shooting. Out of everybody, Mike (Bernardo) had the most surprising game. The guy could play.

Willie Johnson
The Bam

As Olympus poses with his newly won prize, Shannon informs us he dedicated the victory to a young man named Jake, tying the episode together. We then see Turbo return to the Inner Sanctum and give his fellow Masters the ol' stink-eye. He asks what everyone is looking at. Red Dragon (replacing Panther from the original script draft) replies, "oh, just the ex-champion" in what passes for a sick burn in 1995. Turbo responds, "Don't worry, I'll be back."

The show wraps up, and The Machine gives us our post-credits scene, explaining to the kids at home the importance of setting goals and persevering through adversity, something this show would exemplify during its run, continuing to push on despite severe budgetary cuts between seasons. More on that to come.

This episode would set the standard for Dragon Star matches for the show. While several (maybe even most) of the future title fights would surpass this one in terms of the actual quality of action, Going for the Gold remains a classic for its combination of setting the tone and memorable flashback sequence.

Herb Perez
Olympus
Discipline: Tae Kwon Do

The 1992 Olympic Gold Medalist in Tae Kwon Do Herb Perez became one of the main characters of season one. Clad in a shining gold outfit that would be released as a Halloween costume, the stately, almost stoic Olympian took on the role of comic book hero. Having graduated from Rutgers University with a law degree, Perez served with both the World Tae Kwon Do Federation and the International Olympic Committee, while also entering politics in California.

Fun Fact:
Olympus's yell of, "It's not over yet, Bernardo!" is the only instance of any of the Masters smack-talking during a fight.

CHAPTER 08

S1E04: Broken Promise

Tiger Claw vs. Great Wolf

Tsunami vs. Red Dragon

"A chord of fear rang through me"

One of the major strengths of *WMAC Masters* was the deep cast it had to draw on. "Broken Promise" is the first episode of the series to dip into that depth, giving a storyline to two characters who aren't at the top of the food chain, at least in terms of the show's on-screen pecking order. The story of Tiger Claw and Great Wolf is one of the most memorable ones in the show. It remains a fan favorite to this day, showing that it's not just about the Dragon Star Champion and challenger. It's important for as many characters as possible to have their own exciting stories going on.

The show opens with host Shannon Lee informing viewers that a major injury has occurred in a preliminary battle.

Preliminary Match One
Competitors:
Tiger Claw ⬢⬢⬢⬢⬢⬢ vs. Great Wolf ⬡⬡⬡⬡⬡⬡
Battle Zone: Dark City
Ninjas: Unknown

We don't have an opportunity to see this entire battle. Instead, we listen as Shannon narrates events over clips from the fight, saying it "went on for a long time." According to her, the big moment of the match comes at the twenty-three minute forty-six second mark. Great Wolf leaps in the air and nails Tiger Claw with what Shannon calls a double inside crescent kick, knocking him out cold.

Great Wolf immediately regrets the move, and it's plain to see on his face. Medics attend to Tiger Claw while Great Wolf looks on, concerned. Shannon declares Great Wolf's win by knockout, and he will move on to the Battle Dome f'inals.

> *The kick is a real kick. It could really knock you out. It'd be a one in a million thing, you'd have to be standing perfectly still, and the guy would have to hit it perfectly, but yeah, it could happen.*

Jamie Webster
Great Wolf

The man taking the kick, however, didn't enjoy the move.

I wasn't a fan of the kick (they used in the episode). It's a real move, but it's not one you'd ever use in a real fight. It looks good on camera, though, and it wasn't my place to second guess that kind of stuff.

Johnny Lee Smith
Tiger Claw

After that brief clip of the opening match, Shannon is in the studio and teases the second preliminary match, Red Dragon vs. Tsunami, and a Master Blaster performance from Panther.

In the Inner Sanctum, Great Wolf is visibly worried sick about his best friend. The Machine tries to give him a pep talk, saying it was a good technique, nothing dirty, and pointing out that Great Wolf didn't mean to hurt him. Great Wolf says, "it all happened so fast" and that he didn't mean to throw that kick. The Machine tells Great Wolf it's going to be alright.This reinforces his characterization as total monster in the competition, but empathetic teacher outside of it, as we saw in episode one, continuing the show's efforts to show kids that competitiveness is only part of the martial arts.

Shannon informs us that Erik Betts is about to perform his Master Blaster routine in the WMAC Arena. He will demonstrate his core and upper body strength atop The Table of Terror, a table with 900 steel nails.

Master Blaster: Panther's Table of Terror

Panther begins by pointing at Olympus on the Dragon Star throne and cackling in his best horror movie villain's voice, "I'm coming for you, Olympus!" and booming out a sinister laugh. He then back-flips onto the hand-holds on the table.

They said it was nine hundred nails, but it was probably more like, I don't know. Four hundred. It was still a lot.

Erik Betts
Panther

According to the head of the props department, it was still a hellish proposition for Panther to take on.

They were real nails glued to the boards. No rubber nails or anything. We'd file them down slightly, so they weren't, you know, razor-sharp, but they were still definitely pointed. Definitely dangerous.

Nick Farrell
Prop Master

The table has two handles sticking up out of it with round hand-grips, which Panther uses to hold himself up, doing push-ups and other gymnastic twists on them. The mood of danger and concentration is enhanced by Shannon's voiceover. She whispers as if speaking too loudly would break Panther's concentration. Unlike other form demonstrations, this bed of nails was not gimmicked to make it safer or easier to perform. In fact, it was the opposite.

I have very bad eyesight. So bad that my Panther contact lenses are actually prescription. The medic on set was cleaning one right before this shoot and tore it, so I'm going into this half-blind. I get up into position on the table, and I realize that they forgot to apply the 77 adhesive spray to the handles, so if I slip even a little bit, I'm going to lose my grip and fall onto the nails. As I realized that a chord of fear rang through me, it almost paralyzed me. I can usually do a handstand push-up with no problems, but when that fear hit me...

Erik Betts
Panther

Erik Betts
Panther
Discipline: Wushu

With dashing looks, an innate charisma, and the ability to perform a back-flip at any given moment, Erik "Panther" Betts was the ideal cast member for the show. A practitioner of what he calls "Hollywood Kung Fu", a self-taught mixture of stunt-work, gymnastics, and martial arts, Betts cut his fangs on *Mighty Morphin Power Rangers* before being brought into *WMAC Masters*. After a decorated career in stunts, he shifted to acting in his 30's, and has passed the acting bug onto his son.

The relief and excitement he felt after completing the demonstration were palpable and led to one of the show's best and most iconic ad-libs. After completing the demonstration, he celebrates and can be seen shouting to the crowd. The audio is faint, but he shouts, "You want more!?" at them. He then runs and does a flip over the nails, posing in front of the camera as he lands.

That was all spur of the moment, all ad-libbed. I was just so relieved to be okay that I was just... fired up. The 'You want more' and stuff wasn't in the script. That was 100% real. I wasn't mic'd up at all or anything.

Erik Betts
Panther

After Panther's performance, Babydoll rushes into the Inner Sanctum to tell Great Wolf that Tiger Claw has woken up. The two take off to go check on their fallen comrade.

Preliminary Match Two
Competitors:
Tsunami vs. Red Dragon ● ● ● ● ● ● ● ●
Battle Zone: Mayan Mystery
Ninjas: Camouflage

Tsunami does a kata with his blue and white stick weapons, flinging a symbol (that could pass for a frisbee) up into the air and then kicking it, then leads the fans in his trademark Tidal Wave.

Red Dragon then makes his entrance and does a mini-form. He carries no weapon this time but shows off his karate kicks and agility.

We get a quick cutaway as the Masters head to the Battle Zone, showing Babydoll and Great Wolf returning to the Inner Sanctum, saying that Tiger Claw is okay and that the only damage was to Great Wolf and Tiger Claw's friendship. Great Wolf looks distraught, a very believable performance, especially by the standards of the show's early episodes.

This fight features shots of Red Dragon taking down the ninjas, which are re-used from the unaired pilot episode. Once again, the editing is seamless enough that the difference in new versus old footage is not obvious, a credit to the editing department.

The editing was all about creating the most action.
It was all very intentional.

Dan Hubp
Production Designer, Editor

It is also a unique moment in the series. Both Masters' power bars drop despite neither taking a hit. Shannon comments that the Council docked each man for sloppy techniques, reinforcing that it is ultimately their decision who wins or loses, much like the judges in Olympic martial arts competitions.

Despite this double points docking, Red Dragon takes a big lead on the power bars, but Tsunami fires back with a beautiful double-rotation spin kick. The gap is too much to overcome, however, as Red Dragon takes the win with a back heel kick, cementing his place in the Battle Dome final!

Shannon Lee informs the viewers that Tiger Claw is going to be okay. He's up and walking around and can compete again as early as next week. Obviously, with what we know now about concussions and their effects, there likely would be push-back on this part of the story today, though as we'll see in future episodes, the injury is not exactly shrugged off.

We cut to the Inner Sanctum, and Tiger Claw returns, irate. He says it isn't his head that hurts anymore, "Being betrayed by your best friend hurts more than any kick or losing any fight."

The Machine bristles at Johnny's attitude, which considering his origin story we heard a few episodes ago about keeping emotions in check, makes sense. He doesn't want his friend to make the same mistake and ruin a friendship.

"I NEVER WOULD HAVE DONE THAT TO HIM!" Tiger Claw snaps back. He then takes a breath and explains.

Flashback: Broken Promises

Tiger Claw narrates this flashback. He explains that he and Great Wolf grew up together, not just in martial arts but in life as well. Most of the flashback vignettes in season one have a kernel of truth in them that the writers built upon to teach a life lesson, and this one is no different. Johnny Lee Smith and Jamie Webster actually did grow up together in Decatur, Alabama, where they both studied martial arts.

> *Yeah, we grew up together, trained together under my father. We really were like brothers growing up. Most tournaments we did, the local or regional ones, ended up with us as the top two.*

Jamie Webster
Great Wolf

The flashback begins with shots of the two of them training outside. Both men remembered the shoot well.

> *It was really hot. All (the training) shots, I just remember it being really, really hot.*

Johnny Lee Smith
Tiger Claw

Webster recalled it vividly.

> *It was out by some little river or creek. It was in Florida, not on location where we grew up or anything like that. We didn't have the budget for that. Those days were fun, working with my best friend, but they were rough. I remember there was a sign that said "Warning: Watch out for gators" and had instructions for how to best run away. I was like, "...okay."*

Jamie Webster
Great Wolf

Like other flashbacks, there is a kernel of truth at the heart of this one, namely the kick at the heart of their issue. In real life, however, it was Jamie Webster who learned the kick first and then taught it to Tiger Claw.

My sensei taught it to me. So I showed it to Johnny. That's just what we'd do. I don't know why the producers decided to change it for our story. I guess they thought Johnny could play angry better than I could!

Jamie Webster
Great Wolf

Jamie Webster
Great Wolf
Discipline: Karate

Jamie Webster was a Battle of Atlanta Grand Champion, one of the dozens of titles he accumulated in his career. Of Cherokee descent, he continues the tradition started by his father of teaching martial arts in his native Alabama.

During this flashback, Tiger Claw utters one of the show's most quoted pieces of dialogue, "I was lit hotter than a dog on a grill," but as it turns out, he hated the phrase.

I hated it! I told Norman we don't say things like that in Alabama. He laughed, and we tried a few different things. Some of them I came up with, some they did, but then he didn't use any of them, and that line stayed in! :laughs:

Johnny Lee Smith
Tiger Claw

The heated exchanges between the two real-life best friends weren't the easiest for the martial artists to shoot.

I wasn't an actor. I took acting classes after, learned a lot, but at the time... I wasn't real sure what I was doing, but I always gave it my best.

Jamie Webster
Great Wolf

We then fade back to the Inner Sanctum, where Tiger Claw sums up his feelings on the matter, "The most important part of having a best friend is knowing it's someone you can trust."

The other Masters try to stick up for Great Wolf, explaining how upset he is, but Tiger Claw is having none of it.

We then get a shot of the Battle Dome coming down, Red Dragon and Great Wolf inside. Red Dragon looks confident, but Great Wolf looks downright shaken, his mind obviously elsewhere, teasing the finals to come.

Battle Dome Final
Competitors:
Great Wolf ⭕⭕⭕⭕⭕⭕ vs. Red Dragon ⚫⚫⚫⚫⚫⚫⚫⚫

This whole fight was the definition of an evenly matched, back-and-forth contest. It's the main story of the battle, alongside Great Wolf's mind not fully being in the fight.

> *Each fight had to tell a story. Sometimes they were purely physical, like power versus agility, but other times they were more mental.*
>
> Isaac Florentine
> *Director*

These two had great chemistry and put on a solid neck and neck Dome fight. The fighting added to the story being told, as opposed to being the main focus, a switch from the usual. These two would have an even better showing together in the Dome in season two.

Shannon comments on Great Wolf being distracted as we see replays from the fight, hammering the message home.

Back in the Inner Sanctum, where The Machine tries to reason with Tiger Claw, pointing out how obviously shaken up Great Wolf is, Tiger Claw is having none of it. The Machine points out that forgiveness is one of the points of the Dragon Star. Tiger Claw responds, "so is honor." There is no resolution between the two.

Having each of the points of the Dragon Star represent an ideal was my idea, actually. I was talking with Norman (Grossfeld, Producer) and mentioned it would be cool if each of the points stood for something. How it could really emphasize the message we were trying to tell.

Hien Nguyen
Tsunami

Willie Johnson elaborated on the back story of the concept.

Every martial arts discipline has a creed of some kind. It was a way to try to show that (the martial arts on the show) was about more than fighting.

Willie Johnson
The Bam

We then get the ceremony of the Dragon Belt, with Red Dragon getting his second-to-last Ki Symbol before reaching full Dragon Belt. This ties him up with Superstar and The Machine in the race to 10 symbols and the right to be Olympus' first challenger!

This week's post-credits scene was with Superstar. He talks about how to deal with conflict. He says there's not always a right answer, reminding kids to choose peace over power.

This episode launches one of the more memorable sub-plots of the series, one that will run for most of the first season. While the actual in-episode action isn't top tier, the flashback sequence and storytelling keep this one in the never skip category.

CHAPTER 09

S1E05:
A Man Can Dream

Panther vs. The Machine

Warlock vs. Tiger Claw

"Of course, I was the favorite. Why wouldn't I be?"

Every series eventually has an episode that just feels off. Some shows, like The X-Files, have these turn into cult classics and fan favorites (I'm looking at you, "Jose Chung's From Outer Space"), while others, like *LOST*, see them become the worst of the series (if I never have to think about Jack's Tattoos again I'll be happy). For *WMAC Masters*, that off episode comes in the series' fifth offering, "A Man Can Dream". Full of digressions and very 90s attempts at humor, this isn't the episode to show people to get them into the show, but it is a unique time capsule of 1995.

The show begins with a shot of ninja warriors lurking around a never-before-seen Battle Zone as Shannon teases The Machine taking on Panther in the first preliminary match!

We get the opening credits followed by Shannon welcoming viewers to the show and reminding them of the rules of the competition before teasing Tiger Claw taking on Warlock, fresh off his injury last week. We then head out for match one.

Preliminary Match One
Competitors:
Panther ⬢ ⬢ ⬢ ⬢ ⬢ ⬢ vs. The Machine ⬡ ⬡ ⬡ ⬡ ⬡ ⬡ ⬡ ⬡
Battle Zone: Nuclear Nightmare
Ninjas: Unnamed Black with White Sashes

The Nuclear Nightmare Battle Zone is supposedly in the heart of a nuclear power plant and features plenty of wreckage for the Masters and ninjas to fight in. This fight is the only time it is used in the series, being replaced by the Pressure Pit later.

The Machine makes full use of the area, flinging a ninja through a pile of boxes like it was a rag-doll, then kicking another off a stairwell into the debris below. The Machine's size truly sets him apart from his fellow Masters, and it's emphasized further in a battle like this, against a more agile guy like Panther.

Most of the guys and girls, since they were all on the same deal, when it was a night we weren't shooting their fights, they'd double as the ninja warriors, under the hoods. The only one who was really exempt from ninja duty was Hakim. He was six foot four or something like that. It would have been obvious it was him.

Norman Grossfeld
Executive Producer

The Machine isn't the only one who shines in this fight, however. Panther brings his signature array of flips and twists, including a run-up-the-wall backflip and a beautiful backflip kick. At one point, he springs off The Machine's back to nail a ninja with a big kick, one of the more creative spots of the first season. He also exhibits his trademark agility, performing a back handspring to evade a low leg sweep by The Machine.

Some of the things Erik did were like a video game come to life.

Hien Nguyen
Tsunami

In the end, The Machine's size is too much for Panther to overcome, giving The Machine the win.

We get Arena entrances for match two and see Warlock, who is making his competitive debut on the show, wearing his trademark dark blue/green costume.

I hated that costume. :laughs: The material was like this fake velour. It was so bad.

Larry Lam
Warlock

Unlike other cast members, who told me they all had a fair degree of input on their costume and character, Larry told me the Warlock character was already designed.

They knew what they wanted. The look and the character and everything. It didn't bother me or anything, I was happy to be there, but I didn't have any real say.

Larry Lam
Warlock

He's followed into the arena by Tiger Claw. Both men perform short katas with weapons and then head to the Battle Zone for match two!

Preliminary Match Two
Competitors:
Warlock ⬡ ⬡ ⬡ ⬡ vs. Tiger Claw ⬣ ⬣ ⬣ ⬣ ⬣ ⬣
Battle Zone: Ghost Town
Ninjas: Ghost

As the match begins, Shannon speculates that it may be too early for Tiger Claw. He might not be recovered from last week. She also states that he and Great Wolf are no longer speaking.

Compared to the previous fight, this one lacks in flashy moves. Both guys showcasing their techniques, but nothing overly flippy like Panther or overwhelmingly strong like The Machine. Wizard busts out his quick multi-high-kick, which will become a signature technique, but that is really it as far as memorable moves.

> *That's the machine-gun kick. We all wanted to have a signature move, something cool only we did.*

Larry Lam
Warlock

Interestingly, these signature moves are often not the same as those listed on their pre-fight stats cards displayed before every prelim match. The moves listed on those were usually just cool-sounding moves the writers came up with, often with no resemblance to a fighter's existing arsenal.

The fight is pretty even, both men hovering near the end of their power bars as they fight each other, still surrounded by ninjas. Tiger Claw drops to his last power bar but is trying to close out the match. However, a ninja kicks sawdust (or mulch, Shannon calls it both) into his eyes, blinding him, leaving him wide open to take a kick and lose the match!

Post-match, Shannon talks about Tiger Claw's bad luck as she recaps the end of the fight, noting that he likely tried to come back too soon.

Back in the Inner Sanctum, Tsunami watches Shannon on the big screen, obviously smitten. Panther and Babydoll poke fun at him in a friendly way, Babydoll wearing the most 90s tank-top imaginable. Tsunami tries the name Hien Lee on for size, saying for her he'd break tradition and take Shannon's name.

> *The writers knew I was a big Bruce Lee fan, so that whole thing was just a play on that. He was a big influence on me, so I was happy to do it.*

Hien Nguyen
Tsunami

Panther shows up and teases knowing a secret about Shannon. Babydoll and Lady Lightning immediately assume she's entering the competition and freak out. Tsunami begs for information, but Panther says he'd have to check with her before saying anything, a subtle lesson to kids about not sharing others' secrets. He goes to leave the Inner Sanctum to check with her, and Tsunami passes him a note to give to Shannon.

Tsunami calls his crush "love at first sight," which leads to Red Dragon telling a story about a time he fell in love at first sight with a girl that was out of this world.

Red Dragon Has A Space Girlfriend (and other life lessons)

This episode's vignette is one of the all-time classics. Red Dragon and The Machine visit a NASA facility in Florida. Red Dragon spots a female astronaut while they are there and has a creepy "I've got to meet her" moment. He learns that Nicole the Astronaut jogs on a particular beach daily, so he and The Machine set up camp on the stretch of sand and wait for her.

While they wait, The Machine reminds Red Dragon of plans they made for later that week. The Machine's sister is in town, and her kids love Red Dragon. The Machine jokes he's not even the favorite Master of his own family.

> *Of course, I was the favorite. Why wouldn't I be? :laughs:*

Chris Casamassa
Red Dragon

The Machine catches some rays while Red Dragon waits, falling asleep. What follows is perhaps the zaniest scene in the entirety of the show.

After an undisclosed amount of time, Nicole the Astronaut makes her way down the beach. Red Dragon attempts to wake The Machine up, but he is out cold. Not wanting to miss his chance, Red Dragon chases after her, giving us a stereotypical running down the beach in slow-motion scene anyone around at the time would instantly recognize from *Baywatch*.

They cut back and forth between Red Dragon and Nicole the Astronaut, with Nicole suddenly wearing her spacesuit as they finally meet on the sand and embrace. Red Dragon goes to remove her helmet to kiss her, only to find it's The Machine!

Red Dragon, asleep this whole time, is roused awake by The Machine, who tells him his Astronaut is running towards them now! He jogs over to her and straight up hits on her, saying he just had to meet her and asking her out for dinner. Sadly (for him), she declines with what he (in narration) would call the most creative rejection I'd ever gotten. She's going into orbit!

She starts to jog away, leaving him dejected, only to double back and ask, "You're Chris Casamassa, right?" Apparently, she is a fan of both the show and Red Dragon's suave ways. Despite their false start, they hit it off, getting a big, cheesy thumbs up from The Machine.

We are then treated to a montage of Nicole showing Red Dragon around, including Red Dragon puking after taking a ride on the zero-gravity

Fun Fact:
In early drafts of the script for this episode, it is Superstar accompanying Red Dragon. This was changed due to Casamassa and Alston's real-life friendship and on-screen chemistry.

The actress who played Nicole the Astronaut was Sheri Cook, who would go on to play roles in *Sealab 2032*, amongst other shows.

simulator, the two of them splashing in the water together, and even sharing a milkshake. It is completely unlike any other vignette in the show.

> *I guess (the producers) thought I had a little more charisma, could act a little better, so they gave me the more performance-based stuff. We were all martial artists pretending to be actors (on season one), a lot of the guys weren't comfortable with it.*

Chris Casamassa
Red Dragon

After the montage, we see Nicole invite Red Dragon to be her special guest at mission control for the space shuttle launch that Friday. It is, she explains, a rare honor and one she wants to share with him. This conflicts with the plans he had made with The Machine earlier, leaving him in a quandary. There was only one thing to do.

We see an angelic Red Dragon appear on one shoulder, telling him to honor his previous commitment to his friend. A devilish Red Dragon appears on the other, telling him The Machine will understand and that this is a special circumstance. For some reason (likely budgetary), the Angel and Devil Red Dragon are dressed exactly like Red Dragon, but this does nothing to diminish the sheer 90s hilarity of the scene.

Eventually, he chooses to take the once in a lifetime opportunity. After all, The Machine is his friend. So, he'll understand, right?

We see some stock footage of a shuttle liftoff, then pull back to see Red Dragon and Nicole the Astronaut are watching it with The Machine and his family on TV! What a totally unexpected and shocking twist for a kid's show! It turns out it was Nicole's idea, and she ends up loving The Machine's niece and nephew. Nicole ends up dunking Red Dragon in the pool, much to everyone's amusement. Red Dragon, not one to get dunked on his own, pulls The Machine in after him!

> *That shoot was just a lot of fun. Our normal shoots were very intense, physically and mentally, so to get to go to Cocoa Beach and just hang out and laugh... it was a good time.*

Hakim Alston
The Machine

Red Dragon enjoyed them too, though perhaps for other reasons.

The whole shoot was a lot of fun. The actress who played the astronaut, I feel bad I can't remember her name, was great to work with. And, I just want this on the record, I was the only Master in the whole series who gets the girl! :laughs: Even to this day, when I talk to Hakim or Mike, I tell them, "Your vignette had a bunch of dudes. I had a girlfriend!" :laughs:

Chris Casamassa
Red Dragon

Back in the Inner Sanctum, the Masters ask Red Dragon what happened with Nicole. He says she's in orbit right now, a fitting way to end "The Saga of Red Dragon's Space Girlfriend."

Original sketch of WMAC Arena by Dan Hubp. Photo from Dan Hubp.

4 KIDS PRODUCTIONS, INC.	DAY: 9	OUT OF: 12

1000 UNIVERSAL STUDIOS PLAZA BUILDING 22, ORLANDO, FL 32819

PHONE: (407) 354-6480   FAX: (407) 354-6486

"WMAC MASTERS"

CALL SHEET   2ND UNIT   EPISODE 5

Exec. Producer:	Norman Grossfeld		DAY /	WEDNESDAY 7-19-95
Producer:	Michael Attanasio		CREW CALL:	8:00AM
Producer:	Kathy Borland		SHOOTING	8:45AM
Director:	Dan Hubp		SUNRISE:	6:40AM
Asst. Director:			SUNSET:	8:23PM

LOCATION   HAZZARD   RESIDENCE   8550   LANDSMERE,   ORLANDO   407-298-3088

	SCENE:	CAST:	N/D	PAGES	DESCRIPTION:
EXT-SUBURBAN PATIO SC-34	10	1,5,	D	3/8	EVERYONE WATCHES SPACE
					SHUTTLE LAUNCH ON TV.
COMPANY MOVE TO:					
OCEAN LANDINGS RESORT					
900 NO. ATLANTIC AVE					
COCOA BEACH, FL.					
407-783-9430					
EXT- COCOA BEACH SC-34	1,2,3,4,5,6,8	1,5	D	3-6/8	CHRIS AND HAKIM MEET
					ASTRONAUT BABE ON BEACH

CAST	NAME	CHARACTER	LEAVE	MAKE	SET	REMARKS
1	HAKIM ALSTON	MACHINE	7:30AM	8:00AM	8:30AM	P/U @ RESIDENCE INN
14	JAMIE WEBSTER	GREATWOLF	7:30AM	8:00AM	8:30AM	P/U @ RESIDENCE INN
22	SHERI COOK	ASTRO BABE	7:30AM	8:00AM	8:30AM	REPORT TO RESIDENCE INN P/U
23	BRUCE JARMAN	FATHER	---	8:00AM	8:30AM	SELF REPORT TO LOCATION
24	J. DEAN MCCLAIN	MOTHER	---	8:00AM	8:30AM	SELF REPORT TO LOCATION
25	KENNETH MCCLAIN	SON	---	8:00AM	8:30AM	SELF REPORT TO LOCATION
26	ARISYN OWENS	DAUGHTER	---	8:00AM	8:30AM	SELF REPORT TO LOCATION

NOTES

DEPARTMENT INSTRUCTIONS:

RADO'S PROPS: BBQ, TV FOR PLAYBACK,
FOOTBALL, TOWELS, BEACH ACC., BEACH STUFF, UMBRELLA
RADO'S PROD: STOCK FOOTAGE, VCR FOR PLAYBACK,
STINGERS, COOLER W/ DRINKS, AD KIT, SUN BLOCK,
TAPE STOCK, WALKIES W/ CHARGER,
WRDRB:SWIM TRUNKS, NASA TEE, SPACE SUIT SUIT/HELMET

PHONE # TO HAZZARD RESIDENCE: (407) 298-3088
PHONE# TO OCEAN LANDINGS RESORT: 407-783-9430

TRANSPORTATION

COURTESY VAN WILL PICK UP: CHRIS, HAKIM,
SHERI COOK, MEREDITH, RADO @ 7:30AM

DAN HUBP, BOB VAN DOREN, DANA CARAFAL &
GINA WILLIAMS ARE ALL SELF DRIVEN - REPORT TO
HAZZARD RESIDENCE

SEE REVERSE FOR ADVANC

Call Sheet for Red Dragon vignette.
Photo from Dan Hubp.

Set documents showing Cocoa Beach shoot location,
Space Camp guide, and an on-set Polaroid. .
Photo from Dan Hubp.

Early script draft showing Superstar in place of The
Machine. Script from Jamie Webster.

Script page showing production notes.
Photo from Dan Hubp.

Visitor's Guide
U.S. ASTRONAUT
HALL OF FAME
Home of U.S. SPACE CAMP Florida

34. VIGNETTE

34-1. EXT. PLAYALINDA BEACH @ WATER. DAY.   34-1.

    CHRIS and HOSUNG PAK, in swimming trunks with their colors,
are having fun playing paddle ball near the surf.

                CHRIS
        I can't believe we haven't seen
        her yet!

                HOSUNG
        Seen who?

                CHRIS
        Remember that astronaut we saw on TV
        the other day -- the beautiful one?

                HOSUNG
        Yeah -- you've been spaced out ever
        since.

                CHRIS
        Yeah -- well it was love at first
        sight. This is the beach where she
        runs everyday...

The camera pulls around to reveal...

    ...right past the launch pads.

Chris points to the two Shuttle launch platforms looming in
the distance.

CU on Chris's fixated stare.

                CHRIS
        Gotta meet her.

34-2. EXT.

HOSU

CHRIS CASSAMASA VIGNETTE - EPISODE #5 -- 17 JULY 95 **PINK**

34. VIGNETTE

34-A1.NASA SPACE FOOTAGE.   (SHUTTLE)   34-A1.

    A ~~Saturn VI~~ rocket launches into space, space walking
astronauts float over the "big blue marble", etc.

                HAKIM (V.O)
         (mimicing radio chatter)
        STATIC...This is Mission Control,
        you are go for lift off...STATIC

                CHRIS (V.O.)
         (mimicing radio chatter)
        Roger, Houston, we have lift off...STATIC

34-B1.INT. ~~APOLLO 13 EXHIBIT~~. NIGHT.   34-B1.

    Shakey-cam shot of CHRIS and HAKIM strapped into ~~Apollo~~ command
capsule.

34-C1.NASA SPACE FOOTAGE.   SHUTTLE   34-C1.

    Splash down footage of an ~~Apollo~~ command capsule.

                HAKIM (V.O.)
         (mimicing radio chatter)
        STATIC...Splash down! Mission accomplished,
        congradulations Commander Casamassa.

                CHRIS (V.O.)
        STATIC...Roger that, thanks for
        the ride...STATIC

34-D1.INT. ~~APOLLO 13 EXHIBIT~~. NIGHT.   34-D1.

    A hand in the foreground reaches into frame and opens the hatch
to the ~~Apollo~~ command capsule revealing CHRIS and HAKIM inside,
smiling.

34-E1.~~EXT.~~ ~~ROCKET GARDEN~~. DAY.   34-E1.

    CHRIS and HAKIM walk through the impressive NASA exhibit
looking at a photo of Shuttle astronauts. ~~Multi-stage booster~~
~~rockets tower in the background~~.

                CHRIS (V.O.)
        A few months ago, Hakim and I
        visited the NASA Space Center,
        and then it happened...

             CONTINUED

Tarantula and the Women's Dragon Star ───────────────

Shannon then gives us another ladies tournament recap where we see Christine "Lady Lightning" Rodrigues defeat Lynette "Tarantula" Love. We get approximately four seconds of the fight, which Shannon says went for twenty minutes.

Lynette Love is an interesting case in *WMAC Masters* history. A former Olympian, having won gold in Tae Kwon Do in 1988 and bronze in 1992. She was included in very early sales videos and was chosen to be the inaugural women's Dragon Star Champion. Still, she never had an entire fight featured on the show or any dialogue, disappearing entirely after this loss to Lady Lightning.

> *I wasn't really told how much I'd be doing. I was brought in for maybe ten days. The first five or so, I didn't really do anything, filming-wise. We rehearsed and choreographed for two days, then shot for a couple of days. Then I went home, and kind of forgot about it until I got paid. It was like, "Oh yeah, awesome."*

Lynette Love
Tarantula

The only person she fought on the show was Lady Lightning, who speculated that the Olympian's stature may have worked against her.

> *I think it was a size thing for the camera. There was just such a difference between us. Bridgett (Riley, Babydoll) and I just matched up better.*

Christine Rodrigues
Lady Lightning

As far as the fight, Love recalled shooting far more than what ended up being used.

> *I don't know how long the full fight would have been, but it was definitely more than thirty seconds. We rehearsed hard. I remember thinking after the two days of rehearsals, if the choreography is this tiring, I'm not sure I can do the fight!*

:laughs: Most of what I remember is the big fall off the platform. It was probably a solid hour or two of trying to psych myself up to do it.

Lynette Love
Tarantula

The strangeness around Tarantula continued even after she disappeared from the show, as a new character Black Widow, played by Tiana Noguchi, appeared in season two, with a similar name and aesthetic and an entirely different mystery.

Battle Dome Final Competitors:

The Machine ⬡⬡⬡⬡⬡⬡⬡⬡ vs.
Warlock ⬡⬡⬡⬡

As the Dome comes down, Shannon hypes up The Machine, talking about how dominant he looked in his opening contest. The Machine looks likely to live up to the hype as the match starts, manhandling (or Machinehandling, perhaps) Warlock as the fight begins.

The story of the match is The Machine's size and strength against Warlock's agility and guile, a dichotomy most of The Machine's fights on the show fall into due to his size. This one works better than most, however, a credit to both Warlock's skills and the two men's compatibility.

Larry (Lam, Warlock) is another of those guys I came to consider a brother in arms through working with him. He's small, very quick. It took some time in rehearsals to get on the same page. I'd say, "You have to go sooner" or

Lynette Love
Tarantula
Discipline: Tae Kwon Do

Lynette Love won Gold at the 1988 Olympics in Tae Kwon Do and followed it up four years later by medaling again, this time Bronze. Couple that with her three world championships she was a natural choice to be the first Women's Dragon Star Champion. An imposing presence, fans sadly only got to see snippets of her in the show. She still teaches Tae Kwon Do in Washington, DC and southern Maryland.

something, and he'd get right back at me with, "No, you have to do it this way," and after a little bit of rehearsal, we really started to gel. I love Larry.

Hakim Alston
The Machine

Larry recalled the banter being both serious but funny, both men intent on making the best fight possible.

We were like two little schoolgirls, bickering back and forth. "You do this," " No, you do this!" :laughs: I love Hakim. We worked really well together.

Larry Lam
Warlock

As you'd expect from the storyline and commentary, The Machine picks up a victory, eeking it out at the last second! This fight really established Warlock as a skilled fighter, making him look great despite his defeat. For a non-main character to go toe to toe with The Machine and almost win really made him look like a threat, giving him building blocks for his future in the series.

We then head back to the Inner Sanctum for the only segment that could possibly usurp Red Dragon Has A Space Girlfriend for the most ridiculous thing on the show, not just this episode but the entire series, The WMAC Dance Party.

You read that right, the WMAC Dance Party. Panther says he got permission from Shannon to tell her secret and puts a cassette tape in which begins to play an R&B style song about the World Martial Arts Council, supposedly sung by Ms. Lee. A music video plays, interspersed with shots of the cast dancing together in the Inner Sanctum. Nothing I write in this book could possibly do this bit justice. You just have to see it.

(A small note on the segment: it includes Willie "The Bam" Johnson's first appearance on the show, in a brief shot of him entering the arena)

We then get the Dragon Belt Ceremony and Shannon's wrap-up. Shannon notes that Superstar is the only other Master on 9 Ki Symbols, which jives with the error from the last episode, where she mentioned The Machine being on 9 when Red Dragon hit the mark. These episodes seem to be aired out of order. Except Tiger Claw was injured! No one I spoke to out of the crew remembered this particular hiccup, which indicates it was a simple continuity error.

As Shannon closes, out the show she sends words of encouragement to Tsunami, who is going for his first Ki Symbols in the special Ninja Challenge episode next week, reminding him that nothing is impossible!

In the post-credits scene, Olympus recites the Code of the Dragon Star for the viewers at home.

This episode was the strangest and most random of the series but also features such memorable (if, perhaps, for the wrong reasons) moments that it's hard to call skip-able. It's worth watching to ensure you get the full *WMAC Masters* experience, but for repeat viewers, it's probably one that you can gloss over, but you shouldn't.

CHAPTER 10

S1E06:
Ninja Challenge I

Red Dragon

Tsunami

Great Wolf

Warlock

Tiger Claw

Panther

"The hardest fight of my life was that first four-man dome"

Season one's sixth episode is the first of the Ninja Challenge (later Super Challenge) episodes, a change of pace from the typical Dragon Star competition that would be among many fans (and cast members) favorites. Called Ninja Bash episodes in the scripts. We will get three of these in the series. They are often used to showcase the techniques and skills of less featured fighters and are a way to get more fighters on screen in each episode.

The episode begins with reigning Dragon Star Champion Olympus putting on an exhibition of what today's special Ninja Challenge competition will look like. It takes place inside the WMAC Arena, and Shannon narrates the rules, calling it a one-time-only competition. Which, as we will see, is very much not the case.

Olympus puts on an excellent demonstration against the ninjas, orienting the viewers to how the fights today will work.

We then get the title sequence, and Shannon gives us a better overview of the rules of the competition. Explaining that six Masters will go against the ninjas, and the top four scorers will go to a special Battle Dome free-for-all with the chance to win three Ki Symbols!

Back in the Inner Sanctum, the Masters are warming up for the big challenge. Great Wolf is feeling confident, and Tsunami does some push-ups to get the blood flowing. Superstar comes over and mocks him for thinking he can win three Ki Symbols when he doesn't even have one. However, Tsunami doesn't let it phase him. Instead he makes a bet with Superstar, if Tsunami wins, Superstar will have to do one hundred push-ups for each Ki Symbol Tsunami has, but if Tsunami loses, he must do one hundred push-ups for every symbol Superstar has. Great Wolf reminds Tsunami that Superstar has nine symbols, which is "a lot of push-ups," but Tsunami believes in himself and takes the bet!

This episode seals Tsunami's characterization as the plucky underdog, everyman sort of character. Through the first five episodes, we've seen him be mocked, lose, and still maintain his belief in himself. This episode sees him take a bet against loudmouth, brash Superstar, thanks to that belief. Combine that spirit with his flashy moves; it was a perfect recipe for a fan favorite character.

Ninja Challenge Contestant One: Red Dragon ● ● ● ● ● ● ● ● ● ●
Battle Zone: Mayan Mystery

Each Master gets forty-five seconds to take on the ninja warriors. Each clean hit is worth two points, and a knockdown is worth five. Red Dragon, the highest profile Master, in the competition, goes first.

Several shots in this scene are reused from the *Quest for the Dragon Star* pilot episode, from the unaired fight between The Machine and Red Dragon at the same Battle Zone. As such, there are not a lot of particularly exciting elements in this fight. Instead, it's a relatively basic exhibition of Red Dragon's superb karate skills.

He ends up ending the fight with 93 points. He's the first competitor, so we have no context as to how good of a score that is!

Next, Tsunami enters the Arena, ready for his turn!

Ninja Challenge Contestant Two: Tsunami
Battle Zone: WMAC Arena

Several of the fights in this episode occur within the Arena, which begins with the lights dimming on the Master, then coming back up revealing the ninjas, a very cool visual.

Tsunami's go at the ninjas has a lot more flair and flash than Red Dragon's, as you would expect. He hits a very cool roll-through kick and his usual array of spins and flips.

This fight is also noticeably different from the Red Dragon fight in the way it's shot, featuring more long takes and fewer quick cuts. The difference is quite pronounced in a short scene such as these forty-five-second ninja battles. This difference is primarily due to the shooting styles of directors Pat Johnson and Isaac Florentine being different- a topic we will go into greater detail about in the chapter Interlude: Two Directors, Two Visions, One Choice to Shape the Show.

Time runs out as Tsunami hits 101 points, being the first to break the century mark in the ninja challenge!

Ninja Challenge Contestant Three:
Great Wolf ⬡⬡⬡⬡⬡⬡
Battle Zone: WMAC Arena

Great Wolf looks confident as this fight begins with another set of ninjas appearing from the darkness. His battle is fairly straightforward, the highlight being his execution of what wrestling fans would know as a monkey-flip on one of the ninjas. He's trending towards finishing below Tsunami but scores a flying side kick triple knockdown just as time expires to end up with 126 points!

> *I liked the ninja episodes. I think I was the only one to be in all of them. They were lots of fun to put together.*

Jamie Webster
Great Wolf

Back in the Inner Sanctum, where Tsunami is mad that his score got topped by Great Wolf, Panther uses the opportunity to mock Red Dragon for being in last place.

This leads to talk about the ninjas being trainees at the WMAC Academy, the very same Academy Tsunami graduated from. He was the first to make the jump to Master, in fact, but as of next week, he won't be alone in that regard, as Kid Carmichael will be going for full Master status.

Tsunami then pulls up his initiation ceremony on the WMAC computer, playing it for his fellow Masters. Pulling up the initiation requires, for some reason, a swipe of a keycard with his logo on it, placing his hands on light-up circles on either side of the keyboard, and saying his name into a microphone. The 90s, ladies and gentlemen.

Hien Nguyen
Tsunami
Discipline: Kung Fu

Second only to his fellow *Mighty Morphin Power Rangers* alumnus Erik Betts in the flipping department, the white and blue clad master of the wave was the up and coming character designed for kids to empathize with. Humorous but still capable of delivering in the fights- Hien also often doubled as one of the ninjas, making the other Masters look good. He now lives and teaches martial arts in the north-east.

Man Without Sight

His performance is titled Man Without Sight and features him wearing a blindfold while exhibiting his skills. He starts with some of his patented flipping kicks, following that up by breaking some boards.

Following that, he is surrounded by ninjas, who he dispatches quickly despite nominally not being able to see them (the blindfold is white to match his outfit, but that isn't commented on).

After the ninja fight, he moves to a stack of boards that had been set up by the ninjas. Shannon explains that he is channeling the power of a tsunami to break only the bottom board while striking the top one. Of course, he completes this attempt, though it is quite obvious (especially on the replay) that they used a small pyrotechnic to pull the feat off.

Another small note is that no one is sitting on the Dragon Star throne for his demonstration, meaning this is not fixed at any point in time. It could have even been pre-Turbo. Coming as early as it did in the series, it gave the writers room to establish a prehistory of the show. Sadly they never got the chance to follow up.

As the playback of his initiation ends, Tsunami faux-celebrates and the other Masters roll their eyes. Except for Superstar, who mocks Tsunami, handing him a magazine (which he just so happens to be on the cover) for him to read while doing push-ups later.

We then get a commercial break and come back to Warlock making his entrance!

Ninja Challenge Contestant Four: Warlock ⬡⬡⬡⬡⬡
Battle Zone: WMAC Arena

This battle demonstrates just how absurd the supposed scoring system for these fights is. There's relatively little action compared to previous battles, yet Warlock manages to score 102.

(The ninja challenge) episodes were fun. Especially the four-man
Domes. It was always nice to get to showcase yourself.

Larry Lam
Warlock

In the Inner Sanctum, Tsunami freaks out about his score not being good enough since Warlock just broke 100. Great Wolf and Warlock are both locked into the Battle Dome final, Tsunami still has a chance, but his score has to hold up. Superstar comes by to mock him one more time, just because.

We then head out to the Mayan Mystery Battle Zone for our next competitor.

Ninja Challenge Contestant Five: Tiger Claw ⬡⬡⬡⬡⬡⬡
Battle Zone: Mayan Mystery

Tiger Claw hasn't had much of a chance to show his skills in the series so far, his fights showing his bad luck more than his skills, so this was a nice chance for him to show what he can do.

I liked those (Ninja Challenge) episodes. They were fun. The Battle
Domes with four guys were a challenge but a lot of fun to put
together.

Johnny Lee Smith
Tiger Claw

Nothing flashy as far as techniques in this one, but it serves as a good exhibition of Tiger Claw's power and aggressiveness. Unfortunately for him, he ends up scoring 90, which isn't enough to get him into the Dome, which means Tsunami is in!

Ninja Challenge Contestant Six: Panther ⬣⬣⬣⬣⬣⬣
Battle Zone: WMAC Arena

If there is a more polar opposite Master than Tiger Claw than Panther, I can't think of them, at least as far as styles go. It's a great touch going from Tiger Claw's strength to Panther's agility, showcasing the variety of skills on the show (and in the world of martial arts at large). This was something very intentional.

> *We wanted diversity. Not just racial and gender diversity, but as far as martial arts. What disciplines, what skills they brought to the table. We wanted to show it was a wide world out there. It wasn't just karate or kung fu.*

Norman Grossfeld
Executive Producer

This is particularly important regarding Erik Betts, the man behind Panther. Unlike most other cast members, he did not have a traditional martial arts education.

> *I call it "Hollywood Kung Fu". Basically, I'd take whatever free classes were offered wherever I went. Didn't matter what form or discipline. It'd be a class here, a week there. So being around all these guys with black belts and world championships (on the show) was both very humbling and very intimidating.*

Erik Betts
Panther

Panther showcases his agility, including his trademark flips, but he seems to struggle a little more than expected to score points. At least that's what the strange, obviously artificial scoring system would lead us to believe. (Thankfully, the scoring would be less wacky in future Ninja Challenge episodes.) That's all to create drama, however, as Panther scores a last-second knockdown to send himself to the Battle Dome!

With the four top scorers set, we are ready for the Dome. We see the four Masters warming up as the Dome descends.

Battle Dome Final:
Warlock ⭕⭕⭕⭕⭕ vs. Panther ⬤⬤⬤⬤⬤⬤ vs. Tsunami vs. Great Wolf ⭕⭕⭕⭕⭕⭕

Shannon explains there will be no ninjas in the Dome today, "it's crowded enough as it is!" as we get going. The first shot is a wonderful long-playing shot, bringing each of the four men in and out of the frame, each getting a move or two in.

I will tell you, the hardest fight of my life was that first four-man dome. I've fought Jet Li, Jackie Chan, Michael Jai White, all of them, none of them compare to that first dome fight. There's a spot where Hien (Nguyen) and I both run, get kicked, throw a backflip, kick back up, run over to the other two (fighters) and fight, we swing, then get kicked and backflip again. And keep in mind there's choreography between all this. We shot that twenty-eight times. That's fifty-six backflips. I have never, to this day, I have never been that exhausted. I have never worked that hard. My entire career has been cake because of that one episode. In fact, (the producers) never did this, but the next day Hien and I got full massages at a local spa. I think Norman felt bad that we worked that hard. :laughs:

Erik Betts
Panther

Warlock opens the scoring on Panther, but Tsunami quickly scores on Warlock, tying it back up. Tsunami double-dips for a second point on Warlock, taking the lead. On the other side of the cage, Panther gets his first point on Great Wolf, who is the only one without a point in the opening salvo.

Tsunami busts out his go-to hurricanrana wrestling spot on Panther, but it doesn't score, so he kicks him into the cage to take a 1-1-3-0 lead! Great Wolf gets on the board shortly after with a point on

Tsunami, ensuring he doesn't get shut out.

We were very aware of making sure the guys felt like they weren't being made to look weak. There would be some complaints every once in a while, but it was rare.

Norman Grossfeld
Executive Producer

(NOTE: Based on the conversations I had with him, I would place Jamie Webster pretty far down the Likely to complain list, and the positioning of Norman's quote should not be read into)

Tsunami gets the point right back with a beautiful back-flip kick, making it 1-1-4-1, and that's how it finishes! Tsunami does it! Tsunami wins!

It cannot be understated how big of a moment in the show this was, at least for me and my friends who loved the show. Tsunami was definitely a fan favorite, at least in my neck of the woods, and seeing him finally get his win, and such a big one, was a touchstone of the show.

They had me win that because I kept losing! :laughs: Having me win three-in-one was their way of throwing me a bone.

Hien Nguyen
Tsunami

It is worth noting that Tsunami was one of the toy-line characters, as was Great Wolf (and Panther was supposed to be, but we'll get to that). Having him be the new-guy-punching bag wasn't going to sell many toys. The storyline of starting at zero, crushing on the host, being bullied by the more established Superstar, almost not making the finals, then ultimately winning all served to cement him as the audience's 'everyman' character. He may not have been everyone's favorite, but he was solidly in just about everyone's top three.

This would, of course, later be used to devastating effect. But we aren't there yet.

Shannon narrates the replays, highlighting Tsunami's signature Rainbow

Kick technique on Great Wolf. We then get the first ever Triple Dragon Belt Ceremony, which is a fantastic sight.

> *Those (Ki Symbols) were a type of clear laminate we put up. For the three fighter ones, we had to get them custom printed.*

Nick Farrell
Prop Master

Shannon then teases next week, the tournament resumes, and Kid Carmichael makes his debut!

Back in the Inner Sanctum, Tsunami sits on Superstar's back as the cocky kung fu star does his three-hundred push-ups, reading the magazine Superstar offered him earlier. The rest of the Masters watch, enjoying seeing Superstar get his comeuppance.

In this week's post-credits scene, Shannon talks about the importance of goal setting and giving it your all.

The first Ninja Challenge set the tone for future iterations and had the most memorable outcome. Everyman character Tsunami gets his big win. The scoring system was downright wacky, but that will be addressed in future iterations. This one is definitely one to keep in the rotation.

CHAPTER 11

S1E07: Quest for the Dragon Star (again)

Yin Yang Man vs. Kid Carmichael

Tiger Claw vs. The Bam

"I wanted to be a martial arts hero since I was a kid"

Season one's seventh episode shares a title with the unaired pilot episode (and this book) but is a very different beast than the previous iteration. Despite featuring the debut of a new fighter (technically the first time this happens in the series), this episode is one of the few I'd consider skip-able.

This episode begins with Kid Carmichael, a WMAC recruit looking to achieve Master status, making him the second to do so after Tsunami. As we saw with Tsunami, the ceremony (or test) takes the form of a kata, Kid's being known as Flight of Freedom.

The form demonstrates Kid's spectacular agility and kicking ability, showcasing his signature three-rotation spin kick, a move he is credited with innovating, being the first to hit it in competition.

That was a move I kind of became known for. It takes a lot of body control and agility. It always got a reaction out of people. Everyone tried to have a signature move, that was the obvious choice for mine.

Carmichael Simon
Kid Carmichael

The form is rated as flawless by the unseen, definitely not mannequins Council. Therefore, they bestow upon him the rank of Master, and he will enter the competition immediately!

Back in the Inner Sanctum, to see the Masters comment on his initiation. They are suitably impressed. Yin Yang Man will be his first opponent. Yin Yang shares what seems to be a strange (at the time) bromance moment with Turbo, who up until this point has been his bitter rival. As we will see, their shared battle bonded them- this is the first sign of their evolving dynamic and the first seeds of Turbo becoming less of a lone wolf, a major point in his forthcoming character arc.

This episode's flashback is simple in setup. In the Inner Sanctum, the Masters are gossiping about their newest compatriot. Panther said he offered Kid some advice before his first battle, but the youngster wasn't interested. Olympus takes the credit or blame, depending on your point of view, explaining that he told Kid a story about an event that transpired recently, and he might have taken the advice too far. This is the lead to this week's flashback.

Flashback- Searching for an Advantage

Olympus narrates how he returned to New York City before his fight with Turbo to train with his old teacher, Master Fu.

We then see them at dinner, where Master Fu tells Olympus he doesn't know why the gold medalist returned to train with him. Olympus explains he wants inside information on how to beat Turbo, who also trained with Master Fu. Master Fu looks disappointed but hands Olympus a fortune cookie, saying, "The answers you seek are within."

Printed on the paper inside the cookie is a radio station and specific time, which Olympus listens to and gets a message from Scott Shannon and Todd Pettengill. They tell him to be at a particular address at a certain time, kicking off what becomes a scavenger hunt across New York City, set to the tune of a song they play especially for him, "Quest for the Dragon Star."

I'm tempted to give *WMAC Masters* credit for putting Olympus through a proto-ARG (Alternate Reality Game) here, but that concept wasn't around in 1995, and even if it had been, it was little more than a gimmick for the flashback. That being said, if you took a straw poll of 30-somethings who are into ARGs today, I'd be willing to bet more than a few, like me, would say they were first captured by the idea with *WMAC Masters*.

The clues he finds around the city are marked with a giant version of his Ki Symbol, and he visits a wide variety of locations to find them, including a zoo, a museum, what appears to be Central Park, The World Trade Center, Times Square, the 59th Street subway station, and more. One clue is on a frisbee he intercepts. Another is held by an adorably wrinkly dog. He even rollerbladed, just in case viewers forgot in what decade this show took place.

There were, however, at least two more in-depth stops that got cut for time constraints. Todd Pettengill doesn't remember much about the shoot (it was more than twenty-five years ago and very brief), but he did remember something that didn't make much sense to me when he first told me.

I don't know why, but I vividly remember something about a gorilla. Something we said was about a gorilla.

Todd Pettengill
Radio Host

There was, of course, nothing in the episode (as it aired) about any ape, monkey, or another primate that wasn't human. So I ran Todd's remembrance by my go-to fact checker, Dan Hubp.

This definitely triggered a memory. Either Todd or his partner gave an on-air clue, "Go see the gorilla." It was the Bronx Zoo. I remember having trouble figuring out where to safely hang the Olympus logo but have it still be visible.

Dan Hubp
Production Designer, Editor

Dan also confirmed with Herb Perez that there was another cut locale, the Natural History Museum, which would have had a clue associated with them. We saw snippets of them in the montage, but the clues were cut for time constraints.

In the end, Olympus finds himself back in Chinatown, at another restaurant, seated across from Master Fu. Master Fu explains that the answer was within himself, not inside any fortune cookie. Olympus explains that self-confidence is a main point of the Dragon Star, and he lost sight of that in his desire to win. Master Fu then gives him one more fortune cookie.

Back in the Inner Sanctum, Olympus shows his fellow Masters the fortune, which he always keeps on him. It says, "Victory is not won unless it is earned." Kid Carmichael apparently took this lesson to heart and wants to win on his own merits.

Preliminary Match One
Competitors:
Yin Yang Man ⓞ ⓞ ⓞ ⓞ ⓞ ◇ vs. Kid Carmichael
Battle Zone: Danger Dock
Ninjas: Black

A couple of notes on this particular match. This is the first male fight in the entire series that does not feature a character featured in the toy line. It would be a rarity throughout the entire series, with very few instances of it occurring. The reason is simple.

Ultimately, at the end of the day, we were trying to sell licenses, sell toys. The show was really designed to push that. So we had our main or core characters, and everything was built around showcasing them. We made this matrix of fights because we didn't want to just show the same fights all the time, but we also didn't want to go too long without featuring one of the core people. It was a balance.

Norman Grossfeld
Executive Producer

Also of note is the Danger Dock Battle Zone, debuting here, which can be visited still as part of the San Fransisco area of Universal Studios. A fan-favorite Battle Zone (for reasons we will see shortly), it could be both a fun and terrible experience to perform on.

The water set was fun to work on because of all the cool stuff you could pull off, but if you were in one of the wet suits, it was hell. Hot and muggy and slimy once you were in the water.

David Morizot
Ninja

One final note is Yin Yang Man's Dragon Belt status- 5 Belt 2, meaning he's already halfway to challenging for the Dragon Star again after relinquishing his first belt to challenge Turbo!

Both men display a variety of techniques and are two of the more elegant fighters in the show.

(My style) was all about movement. Flow. I wanted to showcase that, of course. But it had to work in the story we were telling.

Carmichael Simon
Kid Carmichael

The finish to this fight is unique in the series. Kid Carmichael, losing on the power bars and near defeat in his debut, pulls off an amazing spin-kick that sends Yin Yang Man into the water!

The match is called off there, and Kid is declared the victor. Shannon explains that WMAC bylaws state that if a competitor is unable to finish the match, the win shall be given to their opponent. The finish itself was quite impressive, with Yin Yang making a huge splash.

> *Richard (Branden) had no problems with doing that. He had no problem doing anything. He was a consummate professional.*

Norman Grossfeld
Executive Producer

The ninjas drag Yin Yang out of the water, looking irate, his best acting of the series.

We then head to the Inner Sanctum, where Tiger Claw is preparing for his match. Great Wolf wishes him luck, but Tiger Claw gives him the cold shoulder.

Willie "The Bam" Johnson enters the Arena and does a kata with his self-made weapon, the Willie Whip, which is, in fact, made out of his hair. This is The Bam's debut on the show, save for the quick shot of him we saw in the *WMAC Masters* Dance Party segment in episode 5.

Like much of the cast, Willie Johnson was headhunted from the competitive martial arts circuit. Unlike the rest of the cast, however, he was coming out of a very turbulent time in his life.

Carmichael Simon
Kid Carmichael
Discipline: Wushu

The youngest of the *WMAC Masters* crew, "Kid" Carmichael would go on to have a long and influential career in not only martial arts, but also on dance and tricking. He is credited as the first person to land a 720 kick in competition, and is a multiple time NASKA Triple Crown winner.

I was just out of jail, man. I was just happy to have my life together and to be (on the show). I didn't care what they asked me to do. I was happy just to be there and do my job.

Willie Johnson
The Bam

The Bam is possibly the most memorable of the non-main characters, thanks largely to his look, bright silver pants with a faux boxing-style championship belt as part of them, and a long braid on an otherwise bald head.

That was all me. The look. The character. The "Bam!" sound. I wanted to be a martial arts hero since I was a kid. I had it all in my head, ready to go.

Willie Johnson
The Bam

Preliminary Match Two
Competitors:
Tiger Claw ⬡⬡⬡⬡⬡⬡ vs. The Bam ⬡⬡⬡⬡⬡
Battle Zone: Mayan Mystery
Ninjas: Camouflage

As the match gets rolling, Shannon explains that The Bam's nickname comes from the yell he does every time he scores a hit. The match begins, and it's immediately apparent that this one is a more traditionally shot fight, with fewer long playing shots, more cuts, and reverse shots. The lighting also appears slightly different for each of the Masters' ninja segments, but that could simply be an artifact of the transfer from video to digital. (NOTE: As of this writing, there has been no official modern release of *WMAC Masters*. So to assist in writing this book, I have used YouTube streams of various quality.)

The first big wow moment of the fight comes when The Bam crosses the Battle Zone to get closer to Tiger Claw by doing a succession of non-stop back handsprings, essentially back-flipping his way over to his opponent.

That was something I wanted to do. Showcase my agility.

Willie Johnson
The Bam

Shannon reminds the viewers that this is Tiger Claw's first win since his injury against Great Wolf, continuing that story thread.

When they told us about the story, we knew there'd be an eventual resolution, but we got the scripts kind of show to show, so we didn't know when exactly.

Jamie Webster
Great Wolf

As with most fights that feature someone in the toy line versus someone who isn't, the result of this one isn't in doubt, Tiger Claw picks up the win.

We see the Battle Dome begin to descend, and Tiger Claw is doing push-ups, looking focused and mean.

Battle Dome Final Competitors:
Kid Carmichael vs. Tiger Claw ⬡⬡⬡⬡⬡⬡

The Dome finishes descending, and the fight is on, Tiger Claw taking an early lead against the newcomer. It's a battle of strength versus speed, with Kid trying to stick and move and Tiger Claw using his power, the old adage of styles make fights ringing true even for choreographed fights.

We wanted every fight to tell a story. With so many talented fighters with

Johnny Lee Smith
Tiger Claw
Discipline: Shorin Ryu

"A country boy from Alabama" the Zubaz clad Tiger Claw had no real acting experience coming into *WMAC Masters*, but ended up portraying one of the more memorable characters in the show. The real life best-friend of Jamie "Great Wolf" Webster, Smith would go on to teach law enforcement departments across the country self-defense techniques.

such different skills, we had a lot of room to create.

Isaac Florentine
Director

This is immediately apparent as Tiger Claw overpowers Kid, scoring a quick second point to make it 0-2. He follows that up with another quick score to make it 0-3.

I felt kind of bad. I didn't want to look like a bully against this new guy, half my size.

Johnny Lee Smith
Tiger Claw

Kid tries to muster a comeback in the final minute, scoring a spin kick and sending Tiger Claw into the cage to make it 1-3. The concept of the final minute is, however, a relative one, as the timer does not stay on the screen the whole time, and the timing of the match is more than slightly suspect.

Johnny Lee Smith may not have wanted to be a bully, but that's exactly how Tiger Claw acts in the last few moments of the match, shoving Kid's attacks aside. He follows it up with one final score to make it 1-4, leaving no doubt he was the deserved victor.

Shannon recaps the fight, commenting that Tiger Claw was too strong and experienced for the newcomer to topple. This recap gives us an all-time classic reaction shot of Kid realizing he was overwhelmed.

We then get the ceremony of the Dragon Belt, with Tiger Claw becoming the first man to claim Kid's Ki Symbol, and then head to Shannon, who teases next week, where Superstar will be going for his full Dragon Belt!

This is the first real dud of the series, though it's through no fault of the athletes. Ultimately it's the lack of any story progression that fails this episode. The flashback doesn't hold as much appeal because we've already seen Olympus win the Dragon Star. The Tiger Claw and Great Wolf story continues in a small way, but it's not enough to save this episode from feeling like nothing important happened. So catch the Kid versus Yin Yang fight, and feel free to skip the rest.

Willie Johnson and Carmichael Simon behind the scenes. Photo from Willie Johnson.

Johnny Lee Smith and Shannon Lee behind the scenes. Photo from Johnny Lee Smith.

Promo photo of Johnny Lee Smith. Photo from Dan Hubp.

CHAPTER 12

Interlude: Two Directors, Two Visions, One Choice to Shape the Show

"There was definitely a divide..."

Most of the time the events that shape TV shows don't happen on screen. They happen in board rooms or writers rooms or, occasionally, on set but away from the cameras. One of the key shaping events of WMAC Masters was one, though it was not so much a lightning strike as a slow building storm, stretching back almost as far as the show's very inception.

Pat Johnson was involved in the show very early on, appearing in sales videos (back when the show was still known as *Martial Masters*) as the man who "recruited all the martial artists" for the show. While one crew member says that video "overstated Pat's involvement," several of the cast members told me they were, in fact, recruited by Pat Johnson personally.

Mr. J is like family to me. I still stay with him and his wife when I'm out there. He came to me and said he was doing a show. That's all I needed to hear.

Christine Rodrigues
Lady Lightning

It was after my win at the Battle of Atlanta. I got a phone call at home and this voice said "this is Pat Johnson". I thought it was Johnny playing a prank on me. He said they were doing a show and wanted me to audition.

Jamie Webster
Great Wolf

Everyone knew (Pat Johnson). You'd see him and his wife at tournaments, they just kind of stood out because of who they were. One night after a tournament he came up and introduced himself and said he wanted me for something he was working on.

Johnny Lee Smith
Tiger Claw

Pat Johnson was, and remains, American martial arts cinema royalty. Having him on board was a key element in giving the show early legitimacy within the martial arts community according to Norman Grossfeld. It was also hoped that his involvement would draw interest from potential partners, be they networks or production companies. How much influence his presence had on the eventual deal with Renaissance Atlantic/Bandai is impossible to calculate and ultimately irrelevant. If anyone doubts his contribution to the show, all they have to do to be remedied of that is speak to any of the cast.

Pat Johnson brought me into the game, so to speak, so I was very loyal. I was a little defensive when I would hear some of the vocal resistance or push back on his style, his way of shooting things. When there started to be a struggle with how to shoot things I was definitely affected by that.

Hakim Alston
The Machine

Make no mistake, Pat Johnson was a valued and vital part of the team. As filming began on the series in earnest, however, a problem became apparent.

Pat's episodes just weren't exciting. They weren't bad, by any means, but the action didn't... (he pauses, considering his words) Pop. The shots that were coming in from Isaac had this vigor to them, Pat's just... didn't.

Norman Grossfeld
Executive Producer

Isaac being Isaac Florentine, the other main director on the series. The two men were both highly respected, both within the industry and by the cast, and never saw each other as competition. In fact, having two main directors made things easier for the show's production, if harder on the cast at times.

Basically if it wasn't your day to shoot you were rehearsing. So while one crew was shooting, the other crew would be rehearsing. It kept things moving.

Carmichael Simon
Kid Carmichael

There was never an official segregation into "Pat's crew" and "Isaac's crew," but several cast members said there were definitely unofficial divisions.

There was definitely a divide between Isaac's crew and Pat's crew. It was just a matter of how they shot. Pat was the more traditional, kind of more basic, realistic style. Some guys were used to that. Isaac was more action-oriented, more cinematic. Some guys were better at that. It got tricky when you'd get one of Pat's crew working with Isaac's crew, or the other way around.

Erik Betts
Panther

Pat was all about presenting martial arts in the most realistic, natural way possible.

Christine Rodrigues
Lady Lightning

Some guys just felt more comfortable with Pat and his way of doing things. There were definitely Pat's guys and then the other guys. I always felt more comfortable with Isaac, but that's nothing against Pat. Just different styles. Isaac taught me a lot about what to show, how to shoot, where to be. Erik and Hien taught me how to do "Hollywood Kung Fu", it was so totally different from what I'd done.

Herb Perez
Olympus

The difference in styles was the biggest thing. Many of the cast worked with Johnson on various projects, in particular the film *Shootfighter*, and were used to his way of doing things- which was the traditional Hollywood way of shooting martial arts.

Pat was just the guy. After working with him on Shootfighter I had total faith in him, I didn't even have to think about it (when they offered me the role).

Mike Bernardo
Turbo

Essentially, in the eyes of many, Pat Jonson's way was the way. If "Mr. J" said it, it was gospel. This meant realism, the fights should be presented as if they were legitimate martial arts bouts. The fighters were world-class martial artists, after all.

His mindset was very much "this is the way it's done", and that's it. It was very traditional, very realist. The problem was it wasn't resonating with viewers as much as Isaac's way of shooting.

Norman Grossfeld
Executive Producer

Discussions were had between the producers and Johnson, but didn't lead to any major changes. Johnson was set in his ways and had years of success to back him up. No one, particularly a wet behind the ears producer with no martial arts experience, such as Grossfeld was going to change his mind.

While Mr. Johnson did not respond to interview requests for this book, one cast member told me they felt that Johnson "resented his ways being questioned."

"He was a very proud guy," another cast member (who didn't want to be named) told me. "He'd done a lot and had a bit of an ego. I don't mean that in a bad way, he deserved the recognition he got, but he definitely had a 'my way is the right way' mindset."

After much back and forth it was decided that Johnson would leave the show. It was done quietly. There were no dramatic arguments on set, no messy public statements, and above all, no efforts to derail the show.

When Pat left there was no effort for him to "taint" us, or 'take any of us with him' or anything like that. Absolutely zero. He wanted us all to stay and make the show, make it great.

Hakim Alston
The Machine

I was very loyal to Mr. J. He's family. When he left it was hard, but he was adamant that no one try to go with him.

Christine Rodrigues
Lady Lightning

Due to the nature of shooting the show in blocks, rather than episode by episode, Johnson's work would feature throughout the show's first season, despite his exit from the show before the season wrapped filming. Astute viewers can spot the differences in the shooting styles and pinpoint who directed what segment.

Some of the cast felt his departure hurt the show. Others thought it was an unfortunate situation but the right call. Nearly everyone agreed that his departure was the first step towards a bigger change away from the sports style presentation to a more dramatic, story driven approach that would dominate season two.

Director Isaac Florentine on set. Photo from Kathy Pilon.

Willie Johnson and Director Pat Johnson behind the scenes. Photo from Willie Johnson.

CHAPTER 13

S1E08:
The Joke's on You

Tsunami vs. Panther

Superstar vs. Red Dragon

"That was part of my vision from the beginning"

On the heels of the first real disappointment of the show's run, "The Joke's on You" is another episode in which I expected to be in the skip-able column when I began this project. After rewatches, however, I've come to appreciate this episode. What it lacks in storyline development, it more than makes up for in action.

The show begins with a shot of a previously unseen set of ninja warriors slinking around a Battle Zone we don't know but looks suspiciously like the backside of the *WMAC Masters* Arena set. Shannon informs us this is called The Pressure Pit and teases our first match, Tsunami taking on Panther!

We then head to the Inner Sanctum, where we see Warlock prank Babydoll with the old ink on the binoculars gag. They're spying on Panther, who is about to head to the Arena. Along with Great Wolf, they affixed a bucket above the entrance, which is supposed to dump water on Panther as he walks under. Unfortunately, it fails to happen, so Warlock sends Great Wolf to check it out, placing a sign on his back that reads, "I'm Dumber than I look" as he goes. Babydoll and Great Wolf inspect the bucket, which Warlock promptly dumps on them via remote control, soaking both.

We then get Tsunami and Panther's entrances into the WMAC Arena before jumping back to the Inner Sanctum, where The Machine tells Warlock he better not try to prank him, "Or else." The Machine, the most intimidating of the Masters, promptly sits on a well-placed whoopie cushion. He takes the pranking well, however.

We then (finally) get the opening credits and Shannon at the desk hyping the show. Superstar is going for full Dragon Belt, taking on Red Dragon in the preliminary match, but first, we have Tsunami and Panther!

Preliminary Match One
Competitors:
Tsunami ⬡⬡⬡ vs. Panther ⬢⬢⬢⬢⬢⬢
Battle Zone: Pressure Pit
Ninjas: Hazard

Shannon explains that the Pressure Pit Battle Zone is known for causing noses and ears to bleed thanks to its pressure. Then, before the fight starts, we get another classic Panther campy dialogue moment as he bares his fangs and mugs for the camera, saying, "I'm coming for you, Tsunami!"

Those (moments) were so fun. It was like being a supervillain for a minute.

Erik Betts
Panther

As discussed in previous chapters, these two men came over with Isaac Florentine from *Mighty Morphin Power Rangers*, and both regularly played ninja warriors. Naturally, both took great pride in making their fellow fighters look good, but this fight was their chance to shine.

The fight starts with ninjas swarming. The Pressure Pit is just the back of the WMAC Arena set, with a few conveniently placed obstacles scattered around to fight on. It's not the most interesting Battle Zone to look at, but it provides a decent enough environment to fight in plus the gimmick ninjas look cool in their gas masks, which is all you can ask for, right?

What commences is one of the most evenly matched and exciting preliminary fights in the series, laden with flips, kicks, and exciting techniques. To demonstrate how equal the fighters are, they bust out a double-clothesline spot, taking each other down! Both men showcase their incredible agility and array of dazzling moves, and both come out looking fantastic at the end of the battle. Panther picks up the win with a back-flip kick, but Tsunami doesn't come off looking weak at all, just unlucky on the day.

Erik was the best flipper on the show, but I was close. :laughs:

Hien Nguyen
Tsunami

Panther then celebrates his win with another classic Panther camp moment shouting, "I AM PANTHER!"

Back in the Inner Sanctum, Babydoll and Great Wolf try to get some payback on Warlock by placing itching powder in his gloves. Babydoll asks Great Wolf if he's sure they are the right gloves, and he says he is. Three guesses where THIS is going.

Shannon recaps the last meeting between Superstar and Red Dragon for the viewers at home from way back in S1E01. Superstar took the win on that occasion and will be hoping to repeat the performance tonight to secure his full Dragon Belt!

Back in the Sanctum, Great Wolf and Babydoll watch Warlock work out, confused as to why he's not itching. Great Wolf says he used more than enough itching powder. But they have a bad feeling.

Erik Betts, Chris Leps, and Hien Nguyen behind the scenes.
Photo from Erik Betts.

We then get entrances for the second match, including a weird moment where Shannon explains that Red Dragon lost a Ki Symbol on a technicality. A victory against Yin Yang Man 18 months previous (in the pre-history of the show) was overturned due to a computer error calculating the score. Red Dragon was so desperate to get it back that he said he'd give the shirt off his back to do so. That means that for some reason, he does his pre-fight Arena kata shirtless, despite this fight not being against Yin Yang Man.

> *:laughs: Yes, that was by request. On the competition circuit, I would sometimes perform with my shirt off, so someone asked me, 'why don't you do what you do in competition?'*

Chris Casamassa
Red Dragon

He declined to answer when pressed for a name, laughing the question off. (Mr. Casamassa laughed a lot in our interviews, he was a delight to talk to.)

Preliminary Match Two
Competitors:
Superstar ⭕⭕⭕⭕⭕⭕⭕⭕⭕ vs. Red Dragon 🔴🔴🔴🔴🔴🔴🔴🔴🔴

Battle Zone: Stone Valley
Ninjas: Kabuki

Red Dragon is shaking his hand in the pre-fight, so we cut to the back as Great Wolf and Babydoll realize they pranked the wrong glove, much to their horror. For some reason, Yin Yang Man has a giant Yin Yang in the background of the shot, which is never explained or seen again.

Back at the fight, Red Dragon has his shirt back on, which makes the whole deal even weirder. Red Dragon continues his (and the show's) tradition of dunking ninjas in water, kicking a ninja out of the cave into the pool below.

Red Dragon keeps adjusting his glove, due to the itching powder, but still manages to take the lead during the one on one portion of the fight. They fight by a stream, leading to a moment where Superstar gets to do his best action movie martial artist pose, and he looks every bit the, well, Superstar.

I remember that fight as a ninja. Anytime we were the lead fighters, we were always, you know, worried about looking our best on camera. Everyone wanted to look their best. But Ho-Sung was definitely always super aware of how he looked. He needed everything to be perfect. I don't say that as a knock. But I remember that fight because there's this scene where he poses at the end of a long string of action, and Isaac (Florentine, Director) yells cut, we got it, but Ho-Sung didn't like how the light caught on his muscles, and wanted to do it again. That's how much of a perfectionist he was.

Jamie Webster
Great Wolf

Crew members also recalled the event, though not necessarily in the same way.

Yeah, Ho-Sung was always very concerned with looking his best.

Tom Laskowski
Camera Crew

I remember that. He said it with humor, and we all had a good laugh.

Isaac Florentine
Director

Unfortunately, Ho-Sung declined to take part in this book, so the world will never know for sure if he was joking or not.

Superstar fires back to even the score up, then takes a slight lead. Red Dragon can't take the itching in his glove anymore, removing it to the shock of Shannon and the Masters in the back. However, he doesn't strike Superstar with his bare hand, so the fight continues. Superstar has a big lead. Red Dragon is down to his last life bar when instinct takes over, and Dragon nails him with his exposed fist, drawing the disqualification.

Shannon analyzes the fight afterward, explaining why it wasn't an instant DQ. She then goes on to tease the Battle Dome final, reminding everyone Superstar is going for his full Dragon Belt.

Back in the Sanctum, Red Dragon soaks his hand, saying it felt like it was on fire in the glove. Great Wolf and Babydoll approach and apologize, showing the kids at home that it's important to own up to your mistakes.

As the Battle Dome comes down, we get a cool over-the-shoulder shot of Superstar looking up at Olympus, something we don't typically get in the series.

Battle Dome Final
Competitors:
Panther ●●●●●● vs. Superstar ○○○○○○○○○

Superstar takes an early lead with a flying side kick that looks startlingly familiar. Almost video-game-like, you could say.

A few seconds later, Panther decides to make a tactical decision. He grabs hold of the cage, sacrificing a point (making it 2-1 to Superstar), but holds on, effectively negating the sensors until he lets go.

Two ninjas hit Superstar into the cage, but the sensors are still off because of Panther! His plan seems to have backfired. Panther drops back down to try to equalize. Still, Superstar ends up sending him into the cage to take a 3-1 lead. Effectively rendering Panther's tactical mistake little more than a footnote, as Superstar would have won anyway, as the clock runs out without further scoring.

This was a unique slightly confusing wrinkle to the fight, something the fighters injected to break up the usual flow of the matches.

Superstar celebrates, and we head straight to the Dragon Belt ceremony, which contains an interesting production error. Superstar's Dragon Belt appears to have Kid Carmichael's Ki Symbol, which is impossible, as Kid debuted the week before when Superstar was already on nine symbols.

> *Yeah, we didn't have intricate who-beat-who histories that we double-checked before each ceremony. We just knew the number of symbols we needed and put them on there.*

Nick Farrell
Prop Master

As Superstar takes his tenth symbol, we get a voiceover from Olympus, talking about how hard he worked to get the Dragon Star and how he'll work hard to keep it a total pro wrestling type of promo.

> *We never tried to be the WWF, but there were definitely influences in the way we presented things. It was impossible for there not to be, really.*

Norman Grossfeld
Executive Producer

Shannon wraps up the episode, noting that Babydoll achieved full Dragon Belt this week as well, so next week will be a DOUBLE DRAGON STAR MATCH episode. No, they won't be fighting all at the same time, just two battles.

Our last scene is The Machine chastising Warlock, Babydoll, and Great Wolf for letting their prank war get out of control. Warlock apologizes to Red Dragon as well, which is an interesting note considering what's to come for the two of them. Red Dragon accepts his apology and offers a handshake, getting his revenge on Warlock with the old hand-buzzer trick.

The post-credits scene shows The Machine talking to young viewers about the martial arts, including looking into "A WMAC School near you."

WMAC martial arts academies never materialized but were a huge part of the plan for the show.

That was part of my vision from the beginning. I pictured having WMAC dojos across the country for kids to attend, the cast traveling to teach classes like visiting professors. When we did the tie-in books (NOTE: More on those later), we included a coupon in the back for a free martial arts lesson at a WMAC dojo, but it just never materialized.

Carlin West
Series Creator

Merchandising and licensing were huge for us. They were the point of the show, really, as kind of sad as that is to say. Doing dojos was going to be a big part of what we wanted to do. Kids would watch the show and hopefully want to learn martial arts, and where better than a WMAC school? We'd license out the name, essentially let schools brand themselves as WMAC for a fee, and they'd get an increase in new students. It seemed like a no-brainer (to us). But it never happened.

Norman Grossfeld
Executive Producer

Fun Fact:
Ho-Sung Pak was the original motion-capture actor for the Mortal Kombat franchise, playing Liu Kang in the first two installments of the video game. The flying side kick was one of Kang's signature moves.

I thought that was really the way to go. Especially as we got into season two, we really wanted to push that, but it just ran into trouble. It would have been a way to help finance the show (going forward).

Herb Perez
Olympus

The problem was the people running schools. It's a very old-school, insular sort of world, at least at the time. I was one of the only cast members who ran their own school, at least that I remember. Most of them taught, of course, but I was an owner. I was in meetings. I remember it very well. It was just a non-starter for people. Even though the show was all about true martial arts values, these people (running things) were just too old-school. They couldn't see the vision.

Willie Johnson
The Bam

I have no trouble imagining how utterly awesome WMAC-branded martial arts schools would have been. Herb Perez and Norman Grossfeld both mentioned the idea of having the Masters do in-character (as much as they were characters) guest teaching at the schools, almost like a rotating professor. I took a year of Tae Kwon Do around this time, something definitely inspired by my love of the show. I can say with one hundred percent certainty that if a WMAC school had been an option, I'd have thrown the biggest of fits until that's where I got to go, and I'm sure I'm not alone in that regard. Unfortunately, this idea was just too ahead of its time and never made it to towns across America.

This episode is definitely outshone by the one that follows it, but "The Joke's on You" has more than enough quality action to warrant a re-watch. Tsunami versus Panther, in particular, is one both new fans and hardcore fans of the series should go out of their way to see.

Advertising material for WMAC Academy Program. Top photo from Willie Johnson. Bottom photo from Jamie Webster.

CHAPTER 14

S1E09: Double Dragon Star Match

Olympus vs. Superstar

Lady Lightning vs. Babydoll

"I wasn't as freaked out as some by the fall"

Episode nine of the series ups the ante by putting on two Dragon Star matches. It's the first time the women's competition gets the spotlight, as their title fight gets top billing, and they are the feature of the episode's flashback. This will be the only time in the series we see two Dragon Star fights in the same episode and one of the few times the women are given top billing over the men.

This week's massive, double-championship episode begins with a highlight package of Olympus, showing off the Dragon Star. We then get the typical opening credits before Shannon welcomes us to "A Special Dragon Star Championship Edition" of the show.

As this opening goes on, we cut to the Inner Sanctum, where Great Wolf is looking for Babydoll, who challenges Lady Lightning for the Dragon Star later that day. No one has seen her. We get a fun little quip as the Masters talk about Olympus defending his title, with Lady Lightning snapping that she's defending hers too.

They tried to give us some girl power moments when they could. It was usually me talking smack to the boys. :laughs:

Christine Rodrigues
Lady Lightning

Babydoll is nowhere to be found, putting the women's match in jeopardy, so Great Wolf and The Machine go to look for her. We get a brief shot of Babydoll, sitting on her own, outside of WMAC HQ, in reality, one of the beautiful sets at Splendid China theme park.

The second draft of the script for this episode has some added dialogue between Great Wolf and his fellow (male) Masters, with his cohorts asking Great Wolf if something is going on between him and Babydoll. He says they're just friends, which draws skepticism, leading him to ask, "can't a guy have a friend who just happens to be a girl?" The whole exchange reads like it would be hilarious- especially Red Dragon's not subtle jealousy.

We then head inside to see Superstar on the not-yet-rotating platform, relinquishing his Dragon Belt to satisfy the Council's last requirement to challenge for the Dragon Star. He then performs the (as Shannon explains) customary kata, the climax of which is a group of red ninjas forming a human

WMAC MASTERS -- EPISODE #9 script revision #1 -- <u>BLUE</u>

> RED DRAGON
> (tad jelous)
> So what is the deal between you two
> lovebirds anyway - I always see you
> hanging around together.

> GREAT WOLF
> She's just a friend, alright?

The atheletes look incredulous.

> GREAT WOLF
> What? Can't a guy have a friend who just
> happens to be a girl?

> THE MACHINE
> Relax. Theres no way she won't show up
> for a Dragon Star fight.

Great Wolf looks concerned. Hands on his face.

13. EXT. WMAC ARENA/SPLENDID CHINA - DAY

BABYDOLL is sitting cross-legged. Meditating. Out of breath GREAT WOLF pulls
up short, relieved at the sight of her....

> GREAT WOLF
> There you are?

> BABYDOLL
> Here I am.

> GREAT WOLF
> I've been all over looking for you. I thought
> you'd been abducted by aliens or ELVIS....

> BABYDOLL
> Like theres a difference.

Great Wolf CHUCKLES. Looks from her to sun overhead---

> GREAT WOLF
> So, let me guess-- you're working on your
> tan? Want to look your best for the Dragon
> Star throne?

Script page showing cut dialogue. Script from Jamie Webster.

pyramid, holding up a giant version of Olympus's Ki Symbol. Next, Superstar launches a flying side kick, Liu Kang style, through it, landing directly in front of the champion.

It's an impressive sight, befitting a Superstar. The not subtle but not overdone references to Ho-Sung's time as Liu Kang is a wonderful meta-nod and really set the stage for the clash.

We then cut back outside to Great Wolf, finding Babydoll as she waits or maybe hides. He asks what's going on, and she says she's thinking about retiring!

As earlier, there is more dialogue in the script that didn't make air, particularly a funny quip from Great Wolf saying he was worried Babydoll was abducted by aliens or had run off with Elvis, to which she replies, "like there's a difference."

It's somewhat sad that this episode wasn't a part of season two rather than season one, as these exchanges likely would have been given more time in the more character-focused of the two seasons. It would have given Babydoll and Great Wolf some depth, even if the relationship was only platonic.

There was some dialogue in the script that could have been read into, yeah. I don't know how far it would have gone.

Jamie Webster
Great Wolf

I think (the producers) wanted that element, but somewhere along the way, it got dropped.

Bridgett Riley
Babydoll

Back in the Inner Sanctum, the Masters discuss how no one has ever failed to show up for a match, let alone a Dragon Star match. While outside, Great Wolf asks Babydoll what she means about retiring. Babydoll says she's not sure if she can fight for the Dragon Star. She's got cold feet. Great Wolf says to do it for her father, but she replies, "No, that's the problem," and we head to this episode's flashback.

Babydoll Goes for the Ring

Babydoll's story shows her relationship with her father. How he coached her growing up and always encouraged her to "go for the brass ring." He was a big-time stuntman, always looking to push the boundaries, and encouraged her to always give her best (as you would expect from a kid's TV show).

> *I loved shooting that vignette. I got to work with John Medlen, who played my father, and he is one of my closest friends and mentors (in the stunt business). It was so much fun. I loved the sets. I thought it all looked really cool.*

Bridgett Riley
Babydoll

Back in reality, she explains to Great Wolf that her father grabbed his brass ring, but she is afraid of reaching for hers and failing. Great Wolf, exhibiting wisdom we haven't seen from him yet in the series, asks if she's thought about what would happen if she doesn't fight. She'll not only disappoint her father by not trying, but she'll spend the rest of her life wondering if she'd have been good enough.

According to staff member Tom Laskowski, however, the vignette had a very different ending.

> *One of my favorite shoots we did was Babydoll's story. Partially because I was on camera in it. I played the guy holding the slate :laughs:. But I just loved the story of it. Her father pushing too far and dying in a stunt, and that's why she's afraid to go too hard.*

Tom Laskowski
Camera Crew

This, of course, didn't ring right with me. Babydoll's dad didn't die. So I ran it by Bridgett Riley, who explained.

> *(What Tom said) was similar to my original pitch for the story, actually. My father died young in real life, and my idea had my father dying being my motivator. But the producers ended up*

changing it to an idea of their own.

Bridgett Riley
Babydoll

Death is not a subject that's broached in *WMAC Masters*. In the mid-90s, it likely would have been considered too intense for a kid's TV series. On the other hand, Bridgett didn't recall actually shooting her version of the scene, so it's possible Tom remembered an early idea or perhaps a feeling the scene evoked. A prospect he readily admitted when telling me the story.

As extreme as it was, the father dying version of the story would have made more sense for Babydoll's character. Her flashback shows her father being incredibly supportive, even when she fails. There's not really any incident that would realistically leave her feeling like he'd be upset that she failed if she doesn't win, save, of course, for the typical insecurity nearly every person struggles with. Perhaps that was the point.

Dragon Star Championship Competitors:
Olympus (Champion) vs. Superstar (Challenger)

We see Olympus place the Dragon Star in the Tri-Chamber Cyber-Cell, and the platform starts to rotate, signaling the beginning of the match.

People underestimate just how difficult (filming on the rotating platform) was. It was pretty high up there and constantly spinning.

Herb Perez
Olympus

Bridgett Riley
Babydoll
Discipline: Kickboxing

A multi-time World Kickboxing Champion Bridgett Riley entered the entertainment world by accident when her friend Erik Betts introduced her to Isaac Florentine, recommending her for stunt work. This led to her appearing as stunt double in the original *Mighty Morphin Power Rangers*, and later *WMAC Masters*. After the show Bridgett would continue both her entertainment and fighting careers, working on movies such as *Watchmen* and *Transformers* as well as winning boxing titles. She was also far and away the most energetic and exuberant person I talked to for this book.

This episode is the first where we see the Red Ninjas, first in Superstar's kata, then in the actual Dragon Star fight.

The fight is very even, neither man showing much of an advantage. Superstar decides, for some reason, to take a stroll through the ninja-filled audience. Olympus thinks that looks like fun and follows suit. The Masters spend a little time wailing on the ninjas in the crowd, who are, it should be remembered, lowly WMAC Academy recruits (in universe).

> *:laughs: It was just something to make the fight different. I don't think the story was supposed to be that we hated the recruits.*

Herb Perez
Olympus

The Masters manage to bash their way through the crowd and back to the platform, resuming the battle.

Olympus scores a big spin kick and looks to take command of the match. He launches a huge flying side kick, a move we've seen Superstar use several times in the past. Superstar, familiar with the move, ducks, letting Olympus fly off the platform! Superstar wins!

> *I wasn't as freaked out as some by the fall (off the platform). After you practice it a few times, you get used to it. I did have a scary moment, though. One of the practice runs, I overshot and almost missed the crash pad entirely. One of the ADs (assistant directors) named Jamin caught my head. It could have been bad.*

Herb Perez
Olympus

This match told an awesome story. Olympus and Superstar think they're the best and try to one-up each other to prove it. Superstar shows off by heading into the crowd to take out ninjas, so Olympus follows suit. Olympus takes control of the match and tries to win it with one of Superstar's own moves, but Superstar sees it coming and outsmarts the champ. Great storytelling where both guys come out looking strong, even in a loss.

I didn't have a problem (losing the Dragon Star). You know it's all scripted, you know you're going to be up and down and no one is going to be champion for long. You just want the story to be good, the fight to be good. There were guys who negotiated how they did on the show- I wasn't one of those guys. I was honored and proud to be on the show, so I wasn't worried about any of that.

Herb Perez
Olympus

Back in the Inner Sanctum, the Masters clap for Superstar, but The Machine, who is close to full Dragon Belt, says Superstar's days are numbered. Shannon, on her voiceover, says it's been five years since a Kung Fu artist was Dragon Star Champion. Another tantalizing bit of show pre-history that the writers threw in to make the show seem bigger and with a wider reach than it otherwise would. Star Warrior looks on at his brother celebrating proudly. As the crew watches, Babydoll appears at the entrance, ready to fight!

We get a commercial and return to Lady Lightning doing her pre-match kata with a Wushu weapon. We see Babydoll warming up in the Inner Sanctum as Tsunami asks Great Wolf what is happening. Great Wolf replies, "she's going for the brass ring," which doesn't really answer Tsunami's question but sounds cool.

We then cut to Babydoll on the platform, relinquishing her Dragon Belt. Star Warrior and Yin Yang Man's Ki Symbols are obviously on there, but it isn't a production error.

We just didn't have enough lady's Ki Symbols to fill out the belt. Kind of an unfortunate necessity.

Dan Hubp
Production Designer, Editor

Babydoll then performs a short kata, followed by Lady Lightning placing the Dragon Star back in the Cell!

Dragon Star Championship
Competitors: Lady Lightning (Champion) vs. Babydoll (Challenger)

Unlike the last one, this match does not start with a feeling-out process. Instead, it starts out hot and heavy with Lady Lightning jumping in and scoring some early hits, capitalizing on Babydoll's apparently lingering self-doubt.

The challenger fires back quickly, though, scoring a roundhouse kick. Bridgett Riley was a legitimate world kickboxing champion, and this fight was her best chance in the series to showcase her skills.

I just loved to fight, you know. I did the point fighting and everything, but it wasn't enough for me. I wanted to hit harder, be hit harder.

Bridgett Riley
Babydoll

The two leading ladies of the WMAC, at least in season one, both enjoyed working together immensely.

We had good chemistry, Bridgett and I. We always worked well together. Love her.

Christine Rodrigues
Lady Lightning

I knew Christine from the NASKA circuit, and I just really respected her. She's so cool and down to earth. We just totally clicked.

Bridgett Riley
Babydoll

This chemistry is undeniable. This fight is one of the best Dragon Star fights of the series, male or female, and is probably the best fight the women of the show put on, largely due to being given the big stage and not the clip treatment. Their fighting styles click well. Riley's kickboxing showcases her long, rangy frame and array of powerful distance strikes, while Lady Lightning's Kempo is graceful, flowing, and intricate.

The finish to the fight is sudden: Babydoll hits a big back-fist, but Lady Lightning pulls a beautiful cartwheel kick out of nowhere to send Babydoll plummeting to the mats below!

Babydoll looks up at Lady Lightning celebrating, heartbroken. We get a flashback to her flashback, which isn't nearly as meta as it sounds, with her dad saying all that matters is that she tried. Lady Lightning bows to Babydoll as they lock eyes, and Babydoll responds with a thumbs up.

> *It was important to show (kids at home) that losing wasn't the end of the world. Obviously, as a fighter, you want to win, but it seemed like I could do more good with the loss.*

Bridgett Riley
Babydoll

We see Lady Lightning return to her throne before throwing it to Shannon for the end of episode recap.

Our post-credits scene this week is Olympus, hammering home the point that it doesn't matter if you win or lose if you give it your best.

This episode of the show is unique for its double Dragon Star match setup, and both fights deliver. It's also the only time a female fighter gets a flashback and is one of the most women-centric episodes of the entire series. Unfortunately, the women's division never really grows past this point. This episode is its apex, but what a high point it is.

Christine Rodrigues
Lady Lightning
Discipline: Kenpo

A multiple time WAKO World Champion in Kempo and Wushu, Christine Bannon-Rodrigues was named KRZ Magazine's #1 Fighter of the 1990's. A member of the elite Team Paul Mitchell on the tournament circuit, Lady Lightning became the face of the women's division of the show. After the show she occasionally did stunt work, instead focusing on her school, molding the next generation of martial artists as well as running the Ocean State Grand Nationals tournament.

Point fighting is a style of martial arts competition where instead of looking for a knockout (as in boxing), fighters are looking to score the most points, which are given via judges. It is a less aggressive form of competition.

CHAPTER 15

S1E10: Blindsided

A Tribute to Richard Branden

This week's episode begins with Yin Yang Man entering the Arena, complete with Yin Yang-shaped paddles and a cape, and performing a kata. Tsunami then enters the Arena with his stick weapons and performs a demonstration of his own, ending with his trademark "bursting balloons with kicks" moment.

We then get a shot of ghost ninjas creeping around the Ghost Town Battle Zone before the episode's opening credits. Shannon then welcomes us back to regular competition after last week's double Dragon Star spectacular, taking us straight to the preliminary opening match!

Preliminary Match One
Competitors:
Yin Yang Man ⬡⬡⬡⬡⬡ ✦ vs. **Tsunami** ⬡⬡⬡
Battle Zone: Ghost Town
Ninjas: Ghost

As they warm up, Shannon reminds us of Yin Yang's last appearance, getting dunked into the water by Kid Carmichael. He's looking to bounce back from that here.

The fight itself starts off with a ninja clowning for the camera, then getting kicked by Yin Yang straight through one of the wagon wheels littering the set. On the other side of the Battle Zone, Tsunami fights a ninja on the balcony of one of the saloons, kicking him off in a fantastic fall!

As the fight nears its apex Tsunami, is in the lead, but Yin Yang Man fires back to close the gap. Tsunami loses his cool, grabbing one of the wagon wheels and clocking Yin Yang with it, getting himself disqualified! BUT WAIT! Yin Yang's power bar was drained before the hit, so Tsunami is the winner!?

SERIOUS CONTROVERSY! CONFUSION REIGNS!

This is a nice touch of realism, as there is usually some sort of dramatic or controversial moments in a sports league or tournament. The only thing remotely similar in the show so far was Red Dragon's bare-hand strike on Superstar, but that was very straightforward. No debate about it.

There is serious debate in the Inner Sanctum about this result. Olympus is fuming, calling Tsunami a cheater, saying he should be disqualified. Panther defends his friend, saying the match was already over.

Ultimately the Council will decide. The Machine, however, has another question: why didn't they see it coming?

We head to commercial and come back, Shannon saying that the crowd is shocked. Yin Yang wasn't injured, but the Council hasn't made any decision yet. Back in the Arena we get entrances for the second match!

Doom City will be the Battle Zone, but first, we get a peek back in the Inner Sanctum to see Yin Yang and Tsunami arrive. Yin Yang is fine. Tsunami is quiet. Olympus is still very upset, getting on Tsunami about it. Tsunami claimed it happened in the heat of the moment and wasn't intentional. Tsunami's victory will stand. The hurracanrana move apparently was enough to drain the power bar, the visuals just lagging behind the scoring of the judges.

Yin Yang Man accepts Tsunami's apology, much to the disbelief of Olympus. "He blindsided you!" the former Olympic gold medalist says. Yin Yang chuckles, saying, "something like that."

Preliminary Match Two
Competitors:
Warlock ⬡⬡⬡⬡ vs. **The Bam** ⬡⬡⬡⬡⬡
Battle Zone: Doom City
Ninjas: Black

Ninjas swarm to start, and Warlock scores the first move of the fight with a big judo throw. The Bam showcases his exceptional flipping ability and agility, easily dispatching his ninjas. Warlock, however, struggles with his and is down big on the power bars early.

Warlock then re-creates one of the worst-looking moments from the unaired pilot episode, the dreaded triple-kick! This time it's shot from a much better angle and doesn't look absolutely ridiculous, thankfully. The ninjas really do considerable damage in this fight, which is rare in the series.

Warlock is dangerously low on the power bars and unable to mount much offense. The Bam scores with a big hook kick for the win! He then celebrates like he just won the Dragon Star. The joy was real, according to The Bam, though not for what you might think.

> *:laughs: It wasn't about winning the fight. I was just so overjoyed to be a part of the show, to be doing what we were doing. Living a dream. They told me to celebrate the win, and it just came out.*

Willie Johnson
The Bam

We then see the Dome start to descend with Tsunami and The Bam inside. Shannon says that Tsunami doesn't have many fans today, thanks to his cheap shot on Yin Yang Man.

We get a commercial and then come back to the Inner Sanctum. Yin Yang Man is working out with a patch on his eye. Olympus and The Machine talk about Yin Yang being unable to see out of his right eye. This leads to our episode's flashback.

FLASHBACK: Challenges, not Handicaps.

Yin Yang Man narrates that as a kid, he was a very competitive martial artist. Maybe too competitive. Tragedy struck one night after a tournament. His parents were driving him home, and they were hit by a drunk driver. Yin Yang wasn't wearing his seat belt (Buckle up, kids!) and ended up injured, losing sight in his eye and his confidence. He became scared of doing martial arts, dropping out of it entirely.

He becomes an artist instead, a good one. He draws Yin Yang symbols, which would later give birth to his nickname in the WMAC. He spends his time at martial arts tournaments, drawing as he watches. He befriends Randy Vaughn, a wheelchair-bound martial artist who opens his eyes to the fact that a handicap doesn't have to stop you from going after your dreams when he performs a demonstration on stage.

I directed that vignette. Randy Vaughn was a legitimate martial artist. His story was real.

Dan Hubp
Production Designer, Editor

In the skit, Mr. Vaughn's performance inspires Yin Yang Man to return to Massachusetts and throw himself back into martial arts, trying to make up for lost time. He ends his narration with, "I didn't have a handicap, just a challenge to overcome."

As his flashback ends, Yin Yang is called to the Council's chambers. We see the Dome coming down in the arena, but Tsunami is nowhere to be seen. Shannon says if he doesn't make it in by the time the Dome touches down, he's disqualified!

We get a commercial and come back, and Yin Yang Man has been declared the winner of the preliminary match after further Council review. Sending him to the Battle Dome! He enters the Dome and does a mini-kata while we cut to the back, where Olympus is pumped that justice was served. Red Dragon wryly comments, "Bam's Yin is about to be Yanged." Whatever that means. Tsunami, entering the room, says he doesn't contest the decision, joking that he'd aim for Yin Yang's good eye next time, which earns him a friendly pummeling.

Tsunami's story in this episode is a very interesting piece of character development and foreshadowing. It's the first time we've seen him be anything but the clean-cut hero. It plants a seed for his future stories but in a subtle way.

Battle Dome Final Competitors:
The Bam ⬡⬡⬡⬡⬡ vs. Yin Yang Man ⬣⬣⬣⬣⬣

These two have very similar styles and are two of the more underrated fighters in the cast, and this fight really demonstrates their skills. Both men get to shine here, executing flashy Wushu techniques on each other and the ninjas. The result is in no doubt despite going down to the wire, as the character with the flashback can't lose twice in a row.

Yin Yang celebrates, and The Bam seems happy for his friend, even on the losing end. We then head to the Dragon Belt ceremony, with Yin Yang adding The Bam to his second-degree Dragon Belt.

Shannon wraps up the episode, revealing Yin Yang Man's blindness to the viewers, sharing a quote from her father, and saluting Yin Yang Man.

Remembering Richard Branden

Richard Branden tragically passed away from cancer in December of 2013, at the young age of 50. Since I was unable to speak with him for this book, I intended to sprinkle some quotes from his fellow cast members about him throughout this chapter. I was not expecting the volume and intensity of the stories I received. Everyone I spoke to had a story about Richard, or Richie as most referred to him, usually more than one. I haven't been able to tell them all here, mainly to keep this book from resembling Infinite Jest in length, but I have done my best to include as much as possible to give readers the best idea of what Richard Branden was like, not only as a cast member but as a person.

When someone passes away, there's a tendency to tilt our memories of them, to tell stories about their better qualities, to emphasize their good. With Richie, there is no tilt. He was the most genuine person you could ever meet.

Hakim Alston
The Machine

We called Richie the "Wushu Whirlwind." He was one of the guys,

Dan was kind enough to provide me a PDF of information on Randy, which was prepared for the shoot. It lists Randy as holding titles at state and national levels in non-black belt katas, and a kickboxing judge. Unfortunately, I could not find any recent information about Mr. Vaughn or his whereabouts, so I could not reach out to him for an interview.

maybe the only guy that I hated following in competitions. He was just so good at everything he did. He was hard to follow.

Chris Casamassa
Red Dragon

My stories cross because we were Power Rangers together too. He was Blue Ranger on the TV series. We have so much history together. I loved him. I'd spend the night with him, his wife, and his kids at his house studio in El Segundo. He wanted to train me. He'd say, "I'm going to get you back on that circuit." He pushed me so hard. He made a kata for me. He wanted me to come back to the circuit and clean up. I never got to do it as a kid because I didn't have the money. He said, "we're going to do it now." To this day, I still use that amazing kata he made me for auditions. He put his whole heart into me and supported me.

Bridgett Riley
Babydoll

He was just a great guy. No ego. He always came to work to do his stuff the right way. He had just perfect movement. All his techniques.

Isaac Florentine
Director

I knew him before he knew me, watching him on the tournaments. So we're on set on the show, and there's this kick called a spin-hook kick, or an outside crescent kick, and I use it on Richard Branden. Well, I kicked him, and I chipped his tooth! It's one of the perfect kicks in the show, but I chipped his tooth! I felt so bad. I had to apologize.

Hien Nguyen
Tsunami

Rich Branden was Erik Betts unleashed. :laughs: That's how I'd describe him.

Erik Betts
Panther

Richie was a great guy. I've known Richie forever. I lived down the block from him when I moved out here to California. In my personal opinion, he was one of the most talented martial artists on the show. We filmed a bunch of his instructional videos after the show. There were some funny moments in the show. He couldn't say some of the words exactly correctly because of his accent. We had a bunch of blooper reels of him trying to say 'idea.' He was the kindest, just the most sweetheart of a guy.

Herb Perez
Olympus

Richie was the most humble and one of the hardest working and most committed to his art out of anyone on the show. His Wushu abilities were amazing, especially considering his disability. Always quick to laugh, Richie was truly a good soul, so his passing was especially tragic.

Dan Hubp
Production Designer, Editor

He never caused any problems. He was always just very easygoing, and it just seemed like he was happy to be there. He wasn't a person always trying to put the attention on himself.

Shannon "Irish" Stewart
Script Supervisor

We didn't work too much together on the show since we didn't have too many scenes together. We kind of grew up together competing together in New England. We shared some instructors. I could tell stories about him all day long. We would always joke with him that because of his glass eye. He would crash into things sometimes. He'd misjudge his position on a butterfly kick and crash into a table at a tournament. :laughs: He would train so hard. I would always be saving my energy at a tournament to put on the best performance I could, but he'd be out there doing push-ups and jumping jacks and squats.

The funniest thing was we were on a team, and he'd always be on stage at the finals of a tournament, and he'd be doing his form, and he'd end up with his back to the judges and bow. So we would always try to stand behind the judges and jump up and down when he was near the end of the form to make sure he knew where the judges were and face the right direction. My husband coached him, and he'd tell Richard, "Just keep going until you see us!"

Christine Rodrigues
Lady Lightning

Me and Richie used to compete on the NASKA circuit. He did the soft style forms, and when I would get to the finals, it'd either be Richard or one of the Pak brothers I'd be competing against. Richie was just so powerful in his forms. I really respected him. I got to know him afterwards. He lived out near San Jose, and Larry Lam is a good friend of mine, and he and Richie were friends so I got to sort of meet him up there. He was such a nice guy. Richie just never said a bad word about anybody. He was so nice. He had that kind of "aww shucks" earnestness. He trained harder than anyone, and I thought I trained a lot!

Mike Bernardo
Turbo

We travailed all around the world together, we did demos, we taught seminars. Richie used to work with me, helped me run my business. He was one of my best friends. He moved up from southern California to Los Angeles, he lived with me. He had kids, I had kids and my wife, and we all lived together in my one bedroom house.

He had an eight pack no matter what- he had muscles on top of muscles. It didn't matter what he ate or didn't eat. He didn't have to diet. He just worked out that hard.

Larry Lam
Warlock

The Richard Branden diet was a burger and a beer. Heiniken. That was his thing. :laughs:

Richie was my main rival for my first few years in the adult division of NASKA. Our styles were so different, so it was a great rivalry. We would always tie in the finals, so we'd have to perform again. I think the judges liked seeing us. It seemed like every tournament, we'd be in the finals and tie. The beauty of that is Richie was such a genuinely good-hearted human being. He was the fiercest competitor, but the moment he stepped out of the ring, he was like your best bud. I learned a lot about competition from him. He made me much better. I knew I had to go up against him, outdo him. He really pushed me. My development as a world-class competitor was because of that. All this happened after the show. At the time we were doing the show, he was just another of the star competitors I looked up to. I'd always try to sneak on set if I wasn't working just to watch those guys, Richard especially.

That turned to me going to his school in El Segundo later on. He welcomed me into his world. He was just one of the hardest workers. He loved to train. He wanted to be the best at everything he did. He was competing for himself and his family. Just a great guy.

Mike Chat
Wizard

Richard Branden
Yin Yang Man
Discipline: Wushu

Richard Branden was a native of Boston, was a black belt in Tae Kwon Do, Wushu, and Kung Fu. A multi-time NASKA champion in both forms and weapons, he was named Black Belt Magazine's Kung Fu Artist of the Year in 1992.

The memories shared in this chapter by those who knew him will be a far better description of the man that this author could produce.

Anything you asked of Richard he could do. And he would do. Never had any complaints, never said a bad word about anyone.

Norman Grossfeld
Executive Producer

He was just an absolutely beautiful human being. He was a consummate martial artist. He put everything into his performances. He was the kind of person you'd go to craft services with, sit down and have a cup of coffee and a chat. He was the one who got me on the show. He brought my name up to the producers.

Sophia Crawford
Chameleon

In a follow-up, Sophia mentioned it might have been Power Rangers Richard mentioned her to producers about. I elected to leave the story in the book to showcase what type of person Branden was.

Rich knew how to party. We had a convention we went to once, all the Power Rangers, and Rich was one of the Power Rangers in costume. And everybody got pretty drunk that evening. And I remember coming down to the lobby of the hotel, and Rich had no shirt on, in Miami, 1993. And the taxi door opened- :laughs: -and Rich did a dive-roll from a seated position, out of the taxi, landed one knee up, one knee down, and went, "Tada!":laughs:

Erik Betts
Panther

I remember more about our social gatherings than anything. He was such a carefree, "what do you guys want to do? Let's have some fun," guy. He was not afraid to fail, to put himself out there. He was full of energy. I've rarely ever met someone like him. Such constant, energizer bunny-like energy. He was part of what we called The Wolfpack, our little crew. It was myself, Chris, Richard, Larry, and occasionally Herb. We'd go out and have some fun. Richard was the energizer of that crew.

Hakim Alston
The Machine

He could be a wild man, but he cares so much about his family. Rich was the depth to that man, and the training and his intensity, and his focus and determination, and then how much he gave back to the community. Rich was a force to be reckoned with. Rich was awesome. His freedom and his bravery, and his honesty, it made you want to be more like him. Richard Branden taught you how to live.

Erik Betts
Panther

"Richard Branden taught you how to live." I can't think of a better sentiment to conclude this tribute to the man.

Ultimately this episode is more memorable because it shined the spotlight on Yin Yang Man than anything else. The definition of underrated Yin Yang Man definitely deserved this chance to shine, and while it's not one of the stronger episodes of the first season, it's still worth watching to see Branden get the spotlight.

Richard Branden and Willie Johnson behind the scenes. Photo from Willie Johnson.

CHAPTER 16

S1E11: Icebreaker

Panther vs. Tiger Claw

Turbo vs. Great Wolf

"I was really going to quit the show if they said it was mandatory"

The episode begins in the Inner Sanctum with Red Dragon being filmed by Tsunami. They are creating behind the scenes footage for the show. Red Dragon notes this is "the first time cameras have been inside the WMAC Inner Sanctum." He explains that they plan to show the footage to kids at seminars they teach. The duo approach Tiger Claw and ask what's going through his mind as he warms up, but they only get a cold shoulder. Tiger Claw is on a mission. He wants a rematch with Great Wolf.

We then get the opening credits and head to Shannon at the desk, where she explains how we could see that very rematch if both Great Wolf and Tiger Claw win their preliminary fight. She recaps the storyline for viewers who might have missed it and mentions there is a severe storm on the horizon, but they're going to push through. So there will be no weather delays in the WMAC!

We then see Tiger Claw enter the Arena, looking focused as he performs his customary kata. This one with his stick weapons.

Panther then enters the Arena, his kata mainly serving as a flipping exhibition. Next, they head to the Battle Zone, and we cut back to the Inner Sanctum, where Red Dragon narrates what, exactly, the Sanctum is and describes the Masters as a *Brady Bunch*, meaning they may not always get along, but they're family.

This is, in fact, not far from the truth. There was a great camaraderie and respect amongst the cast, genuine warmth and friendship, even in the face of their natural competitiveness.

You have to remember we all knew each other from the touring circuit, or just about all of us. That was both a good and bad thing. We all respected each other. Everybody knew just how good everyone was. But we're competitors, right? Everyone wants to be the best, even on a scripted show. There was always that. Not rivalry, but competitiveness.

Chris Casamassa
Red Dragon

It just became part of it. At one point, it was like, if you don't get your shot in one take, you're doing push-ups. The whole 'I bet I can do it in one take' thing was always there. Everyone wanted to one-up each other.

Willie Johnson
The Bam

We all used it (the competitive nature) to get the best out of each other. We all wanted to look our best, and we all wanted the show to be the best it could be.

Hakim Alston
The Machine

It was something the producers were aware of and thankful they didn't have issues with.

I don't think we ever had issues with egos. I will say that early on, some of them would express concern over an upcoming battle that they saw in the script they would be losing. I think at the beginning, since they really weren't actors, it was difficult to see themselves lose to someone who, in real life, they would beat consistently. But everyone was able to get over that little bump pretty quickly and just enjoy the storylines and appreciate the show for what it was, entertainment!

Kathy Pilon
Executive Producer

The Machine and Turbo both brush Red Dragon off, but Great Wolf, one of the nicest guys in the competition, lets Dragon stick his microphone in front of him. Red Dragon asks about the possibility of going up against Tiger Claw again, but Great Wolf says it's just another match. Red Dragon decides to recap their rivalry too. In case anyone watching the show's eleventh episode somehow managed to not know it already, despite it being recapped once already. Great Wolf said he didn't mean for the rivalry to happen but won't apologize again. He says he loves Tiger Claw like a brother, adding that he misses their friendship. Red Dragon, realizing things might be getting too real, motions for Tsunami to cut the feed.

Preliminary Match One ─────────────────────────────
Competitors:
Panther ● ● ● ● ● ● vs. Tiger Claw ⬡ ⬡ ⬡ ⬡ ⬡ ⬡ ⬡
Battle Zone: Danger Dock
Ninjas: Black

The fight starts, and one of the first moves out of the gate is Panther casually lobbing a back-flip kick on a ninja like it's nothing because that's just the sort of fighter he is.

On the other side of the Battle Zone, Tiger Claw puts a life preserver around a ninja's neck before sending him splashing into the water, showing that even at his most grumpy, he's still a nice guy, deep down. He then follows that up by pushing another ninja straight through one of the walls of a dock, casting doubt on his niceness after all.

> *If I remember right, that was Carmichael (Simon). I remember feeling bad, like I was always bullying him. He was so small he was easy to throw around.*

Johnny Lee Smith
Tiger Claw

> *I don't remember that, but it definitely could have happened. I took a lot of big moves as a ninja.*

Carmichael Simon
Kid Carmichael

The match is a dead heat as the one versus one portion begins. Tiger Claw scores with a big kick which sends Panther flying through the air, flipping (of course). Panther fires back with what I can only describe as a running-jump-mule kick.

Panther tries to use his agility to his advantage, leaping around the docks, but can't avoid Tiger Claw forever. The power bars remain neck and neck, to the point where the next clean strike will win! Tiger Claw connects with a HUGE uppercut, eeking out the victory!

Shannon does her typical recap of the episode, calling it a cat fight, a pun no one I spoke to would take the blame (or credit) for. She then mentions the impending storms again.

This is followed by entrances for Great Wolf and Turbo. Great Wolf does some break-dancing as part of his kata. Turbo uses his staff.

The producers and directors were awesome. I mentioned that I could do a little break dancing, and they worked it into the show. Anything they could do to help us stand out, they did.

Jamie Webster
Great Wolf

Before we head to the second prelim match, we get another Inner Sanctum shot as Red Dragon checks his tape on the main WMAC computer. This is an incredibly 90s moment. The idea that computers could do anything you wanted them to was everywhere at the time. While watching the tape on the screen, Tiger Claw overhears Great Wolf's previous comments but doesn't seem to react to them.

Preliminary Match Two
Competitors:
Turbo ⬡ ⬡ ⬡ ✦ vs. Great Wolf ⬡ ⬡ ⬡ ⬡ ⬡ ⬡
Battle Zone: Dark Alley
Ninjas: Red

We start with some unusual camera angles (at least as far as this show goes), taking advantage of the Battle Zone. This zone screams film noir or some gritty action film, and it's a shame it wasn't used more often.

This fight is a great example of how the Masters use their fighting styles to elaborate on their characters. Turbo deals with his ninjas in a direct fashion, simple and effective. While Great Wolf uses his agility to flip and tumble away from strikes. It's an impressive feat for a man his size and a nice bit of character work. Turbo is a fighter who runs on aggression. Great Wolf relies on finesse.

The fight is tied as the one versus one portion begins. There's a fun shot of

Great Wolf coming through the fog or smoke, approaching Turbo, who looks like a film villain thanks to the Battle Zone's cinematic qualities. Shannon informs us there's been lightning sighted nearby, and the referee could call the match at any moment.

That doesn't happen, however, as Great Wolf uses his smarts and agility to pick up the win.

We see a power surge in the Arena as the dome comes down. Back in the Inner Sanctum, Red Dragon asks Lady Lightning where she got her nickname. "Lightning never strikes in the same place twice, and neither do I," she says.

Unlike several of her fellow cast members, Christine Rodrigues' character stayed consistent from the early concepts to completion, mostly. However, there was one major hurdle to overcome, her proposed hairdo.

It was Norman and Carlin, I think, and they showed me the Grace Jones haircut, and I just said I couldn't do it. It wasn't just a one episode thing, you know. I ended up having the hairstyle that we settled on for years because for three months a year, I was going down there to shoot, and we did it for a couple of years. They understood and wanted to come up with something else, so we met in the middle with the shaved sides.

Christine Rodrigues
Lady Lightning

As the show began, Lady Lightning wasn't the only one with a hair issue.

I saw some art they did for the action figures, and they had me perfect, my outfit and everything, except I was blonde. I asked them why they had me as a blonde, and they say, 'We're going to dye your hair.' I told them that absolutely wasn't going to happen. I don't know why I was so dead set against it, maybe just because I was young, but I was really going to quit the show if they said it was mandatory. Thankfully it didn't come to that.

Johnny Lee Smith
Tiger Claw

Battle Dome Final
Competitors:
Great Wolf ⬡⬡⬡⬡⬡⬡ vs. Tiger Claw ⬢⬡⬢⬡⬢⬡⬢

Tiger Claw starts the fight hot and heavy, fueled by his emotions. Shortly into the match, the lights go out entirely, and we do a quick cut to the Sanctum where Red Dragon is mugging for the camera, only to be pounced by Panther. Back in the Dome, the fight continues under ominous red lights, which Shannon calls their backup lights. Shannon says these lights and the electronic sensors on the Dome are the only things with power in the whole Arena, not mentioning how she has power to be recording all this.

The two Alabamians exhibited great chemistry in this fight, something they consider a natural extension of their friendship.

There was never any pressure working with Jamie. We knew each other so well, we knew we'd put on an awesome fight.

Johnny Lee Smith
Tiger Claw

It's cliche, but it really was like working with your brother. That's how close we were. Johnny was one of the first black belts under my dad. I was the second. He was just a year ahead of me.

Jamie Webster
Great Wolf

This fight showcases that comfortability and features lots of moves not normally seen in the show. Moves like leg scissors, take-downs, and other out of the ordinary techniques. "Not everyone was always willing to take non-traditional moves," according to one cast member who wished to remain anonymous.

Tiger Claw takes a 1-2 lead with a throw but refuses to capitalize on Great Wolf being down on the floor. Instead of letting him up to continue the fight, the first signs of the ice thawing between the two of them.

Great Wolf ties it up with a leaping kick, and time is again ticking down with the score tied, a go-to trope for these fights. The lights come on with ten seconds left, startling both men. Great Wolf reacts first, scoring the decisive point!

After time runs out, the two men hug, their issues seemingly behind them. Shannon speculates it's due to the bizarre experience they just shared, which we can assume, coupled with Tiger Claw seeing the footage of Great Wolf earlier, was enough to get through to him that he was holding a grudge that didn't help him.

Shannon recaps the fight, noting that Great Wolf actually threw the same kick that knocked Tiger Claw out and caused this rivalry. She speculates he threw it as a symbolic gesture to help heal their friendship, knowing that Tiger Claw would be ready for it and block it. As an adult, it seems like a strange way to wrap up their issue, but as a kid, I bought it whole-heartedly.

I didn't really get it, but it wasn't my job to come up with the stories. Thank God for that! Even when I didn't really agree with something or understand it. I just did my best to make it as good as possible. I was happy to have the story and the screen time. I wasn't about to complain.

Johnny Lee Smith
Tiger Claw

We then get the traditional ceremony of the Dragon Belt, where Tiger Claw clowns around with his once again best friend, pretending to withhold his Ki Symbol. Then, after handing it over, Tiger Claw and Great Wolf embrace, Tiger Claw raising Great Wolf's hand in victory.

Back in the Inner Sanctum, Red Dragon does his best to sum up the day. He starts to talk about himself, naturally, and the battery on the camera dies, cutting him off. Everyone claps, The Machine saying, "that's one power outage we needed all day." Everyone laughs.

Superstar has this week's post-credits scene talking about the power of forgiveness.

We tried to use (the story of Great Wolf and Tiger Claw) to really teach multiple lessons. We thought that sort of full cycle would resonate with kids.

Norman Grossfeld
Executive Producer

Considering the storyline is one of, if not the most remembered of the show some twenty-five years later, it's safe to say it resonated magnificently.

It's great to be remembered at all, but yeah, it's really awesome that (our story) had such an impact on kids. The fact that so many people still remember it means a lot to me.

Jamie Webster
Great Wolf

Ultimately, despite featuring the culmination of one of the biggest B-stories on the show, this episode isn't particularly memorable. The resolution between Tiger Claw and Great Wolf felt too easy, too forced, to really feel satisfying. This leaves Icebreaker as one of the more disappointing episodes of the series on rewatch- a real missed opportunity.

2.   INT. INNER SANCTUM/ - NIGHT

ANGLE - THRU TSUNAMI'S HANDHELD CAMER

MICROPHONE in hand, RED DRAGON speaks d

> RED DRAGON
> --This is the first time ever a camera
> been allowed into the inner-sanctum
> the WMAC Masters. Only those ma
> holding a Dragon Be
> the reigning Dragon
> allowed within these

UNNEL ENTRANCE.
IGER CLAW is doiing

ED DRAGON
Johnny Lee "Tiger Cl
Panther" preparing t
. Let's see if we can
Lee, can you tell us
our mind right now?
y?

Mike Bernardo, Chris Casamassa, and
Herb Perez at Producer Michael Attanasio's
laptop. Photo from Shannon "Irish" Stewart.

RA

RA. OLYMPUS walks

LYMPUS
eraldo?

> RED DRAGON
> Hien and I are making a videotape f
> kids at our seminars.

> OLYMPUS
> (drying sweat from face)
> Oh yeah?

CHAPTER 17

S1E12: Reaching the Top

The Machine vs. Red Dragon

Olympus vs. Star Warrior

"I tell you what, that was not my favorite shoot"

As *WMAC Masters* approached the end of its first season, the producers knew there would be a shifting of focus, though. At this point, they weren't aware of how drastic it would be. After the previous two episodes, the show was spinning its wheels slightly in search of a direction to move towards in advance of season two. Reaching the Top was that direction, setting the stage for one of the classic rivalries in *WMAC Masters* to return to the forefront.

This episode begins with the action already underway. Shannon narrates some clips of The Machine taking on Red Dragon in the opening contest!

Preliminary Match One
Competitors:
The Machine ⬡⬡⬡⬡⬡⬡⬡⬡⬡ vs. **Red Dragon** ●●●●●●●●●
Battle Zone: Mayan Mystery

We see clips of the one versus one segment of the fight, Shannon calling the action. According to Shannon, after five minutes of intense action, The Machine kicks Red Dragon into the water, avenging the legion of ninjas Red Dragon has dunked and taking the win!

> *I tell you what, that was not my favorite shoot. That water was cold.*

Chris Casamassa
Red Dragon

Red Dragon pulls The Machine in after him because he's a sore loser, a spot that harkens back to his unforgettable flashback in episode five, where he pulls The Machine into the pool at the end. You'd think Hakim would stop trusting him around water.

Jokes aside, this would-be match is an interesting bit of storytelling and foreshadowing. Red Dragon and The Machine are the two top contenders to Superstar's Dragon Star title, and it's fair to assume this match decided the pecking order, at least for the immediate future (speaking of in-universe terms, of course). It is also an interesting bit of foreshadowing, considering the even more high-stakes battle that awaits these two next season.

None of the crew I spoke to remembered precisely why this match was only shown in clips, but they noted the usual reason was for episode length concerns. Considering the importance (and no doubt the quality) of this fight, I find it surprising that this was what was chosen to be cut, especially considering some of the other segments in this episode.

Red Dragon and The Machine make it back into the Inner Sanctum, only to be pelted by their fellow Masters with towels. Turbo growls, "Don't want The Machine to rust," continuing his angry ex-champion characterization. Superstar, taking a break from his Dragon Throne, cracks that, "he's already rusted," showing that his title win has only inflated his already bursting-at-the-seams ego. It's a nice subtle (at least for a kid's show) piece of character work, not smashing the viewers over the head with it.

This little back and forth leads to Olympus saying he will go through Star Warrior, who he faces in the second preliminary match.

We head to the desk where Shannon introduces the episode. Olympus takes on Star Warrior in his return to competition, The Machine goes for full Dragon Belt, and Great Wolf attempts to set a record in this jam-packed episode.

Straight after that, we get the Olympus and Star Warrior entrances, complete with katas. As Olympus watches Star Warrior, we get a fun shot from above, over Superstar's shoulder, looking down at his brother and big rival. It's utterly unique in the series, both from a visual perspective and a metaphorical one. Very rarely do we get to look through a fighter's eyes, so to speak. It adds a depth of emotion to the upcoming preliminary fight.

Before the fight begins, we see Great Wolf in the Inner Sanctum, focusing on a giant ice cube. Later today, in the Master Blaster segment, he will attempt to break six hundred pounds of ice, setting a new WMAC record.

Preliminary Match Two
Competitors:
Olympus ✦ vs. Star Warrior 🜚 🜚 🜚 🜚 🜚 🜚 🜚
Battle Zone: Ghost Town
Ninjas: Ghost

The match starts, and it's immediately apparent the ghost ninjas are in for a rough go in this one, as Star Warrior launches one, sending it crashing through some set dressing. This is quickly followed up by a ninja sending him (or her-)self through a wall trying to land a flying side kick on Olympus. (This is the same move Olympus lost the Dragon Star with, just with the roles reversed, a fun little call-back)

The fight is a showcase for Olympus. He dominates, with Star Warrior doing just enough to avoid getting blown out but never threatening to win outright. Considering this is the Olympian's first match back after losing the Dragon Star, it's understandable the producers wanted to keep him looking strong.

We then head to the Inner Sanctum, where The Machine stays loose for his Battle Dome fight. He says he's sad Star Warrior didn't win. He wanted to take down both Pak brothers before claiming the Dragon Star. Turbo tells him to stay focused on Olympus, but The Machine feels confident, saying it's "His turn."

Master Blaster: Earth, Wind, and Ice

Great Wolf's Master Blaster starts with an alleged ancient Cherokee ritual, which is his typical pre-match kata. His hair is finally down, much to Jamie Webster's real-life relief.

Fun Fact:
Olympus's introduction card lists him as having one Ki Symbol on his second Dragon Belt, but this is a production error. Shannon clearly said this was his return to action after losing the Dragon Star.

I hated that hair. The pigtails. They put so much product in my hair that when my head hit the pillow at night, I'd hear a loud crack, like plastic breaking. But I was so happy to be there I wasn't about to complain.

Jamie Webster
Great Wolf

He shows off his tornado kick for the wind portion of the demonstration, following up with the Earth portion, where he breaks an Indian red stone block while holding a raw egg in his hand. The egg doesn't break, but the stone does. He then cracks the egg and eats it raw, giving us the most disgusting moment in the series.

A group of ninjas then reveal two giant blocks of ice, each weighing three-hundred pounds, which he will attempt to break. Red Dragon holds the current record, Shannon says, with one three hundred pound block of ice.

He concentrates, summoning all his strength, and breaks the ice! No visible pyrotechnics this time, either.

Webster remembered the segment well, calling it one of the high points of the show for him, though perhaps not for the reasons one would assume.

The producers had, he explained, ordered over two thousand dollars of ice for the demonstration. They were banking on the fact the combination of Florida heat and the realities of shooting the show would make a one-and-done sort of shoot impossible and ordering backups.

The break itself was difficult, but I knew I could do it.

Jamie Webster
Great Wolf

Webster completed the break on the first take, allowing the producers to return the unused ice.

I was definitely their favorite for a few days after that. :laughs:

Jamie Webster
Great Wolf

We then head to the Inner Sanctum for one of the more head-scratching segments of the series, especially considering the episode was apparently running long enough to have to cut the majority of The Machine versus Red Dragon fight.

Lady Lightning has been spending a lot of time on the WMAC computer, so her fellow Masters ask her what she's been up to. She wrote a program to set the WMAC up on the Internet! We then get another of the show's strange montage segments. This time to advertise the website?

It's a strange video, mostly reused footage from the show cut together with shots of various kids. The most bizarre part is that the video doesn't appear to actually advertise a real website. The show had an Internet presence, a very forward-thinking one, featuring behind-the-scenes interviews and web chats that were far from common in 1996, but there is no link to that website mentioned in the show.

After that diversion, it's time for the Battle Dome final and The Machine to go for full Dragon Belt!

Battle Dome Final
Competitors:
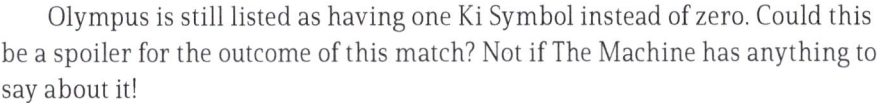
The Machine ⬡⬡⬡⬡⬡⬡⬡⬡ vs. Olympus ✦

Olympus is still listed as having one Ki Symbol instead of zero. Could this be a spoiler for the outcome of this match? Not if The Machine has anything to say about it!

This fight is exactly what you would expect from two of the best (and most featured) fighters in the series, lots of huge kicks, lots of drama, and an evenly fought contest. The only actual strike against the match is more a strike against the show at this point in its run. Many Battle Domes rely too heavily on the trope of being tied up with only a few seconds to go as their primary way of creating drama. When watching as a kid week-to-week, it wasn't particularly noticeable, but as an adult watching the episodes in quick succession, it started to feel repetitive.

In the Inner Sanctum, the Masters clap for The Machine, but both Star Warrior and Turbo look on, unimpressed.

Shannon gives us replays of the scoring moves from the match, pointing out that the kick The Machine used to tie up the fight was the same technique he missed with kicking the cage earlier in the fight. Another fun piece of storytelling, similar to the very first Battle Dome with The Machine and Superstar.

The Dragon Belt ceremony follows with The Machine completing his Dragon Belt. As he celebrates, the actual Belt looks like a toy in his hands due to his stature.

The Machine also stars in the post-credits scene, going over some of the points of the Dragon Star. For those playing at home, the eight points of the Dragon Star are:

Respect
Loyalty
Wisdom
Compassion
Forgiveness
Honor
Courage
Discipline

This was a solid episode to set up the season one finale. The Machine will get his shot at Superstar in a rematch of the series' first ever Battle Dome! This episode also stands on its own, a return to form after a couple of misses.

The Masters arrive to the 1996 New York Toy Fair in style. Photos from Jamie Webster.

CHAPTER 18

S1E13:
Showdown Part I

Babydoll vs. Princess

Superstar vs. The Machine

"The fact that I played the ninja always felt like a little Easter egg to me"

Season finales are hard. It doesn't matter the style, genre, or target demographic of a show, a good season finale is a minor miracle. What's worse is that it's a required minor miracle, as shows that fail to produce a good finale usually don't get picked up for a second season. For *WMAC Masters* this task was no small feat, but one they achieved in spades with the classic "Showdown Part I."

The final episode of season one begins in the Inner Sanctum. Superstar is meditating, looking like he is in prayer. Then, he rapidly recites the points of the Dragon Star, focusing on his upcoming Dragon Star defense against The Machine. Great Wolf, Tiger Claw, and Panther watch him, discussing how he's obsessed with keeping the Dragon Star.

This is the most serious we've seen Superstar, adding a layer of depth to his character, taking it beyond brash, cocky, but awesome, which has been his characterization so far. This slow-burn character development is surprisingly subtle for a kid's show built on over-the-top action. It also was, at least in part, not the plan.

We kind of adjusted plans as we went, as far as the writing. When we saw who viewers were reacting to, we adjusted accordingly. Sometimes that meant more screen time. Other times it meant slight changes to presentation.

Norman Grossfeld
Executive Producer

Across the room, The Machine asks Olympus for advice. "Don't fall off," the Olympian jokes before adding, more seriously, "Just be The Machine."

We then get the typical opening credits, followed by Shannon welcoming viewers to the show. She explains that the Arena is full of recruits from the WMAC Academy in their ninja attire, saying that they are ready for a battle between archrivals Superstar and The Machine.

With the possible exception of Tiger Claw and Great Wolf, it's hard to argue that The Machine versus Superstar isn't the best rivalry on the show. The two men had undeniable chemistry, both in their dialogue and in the fights. The speed and agility versus size and strength dynamic is a go-to in martial arts films and sports entertainment, and the two fighters make the most of it. The show began with The Machine and Superstar in the first Battle Dome, and season one of the show will end with the two of them fighting for the Dragon Star, quite the arc.

But first, we have highlights from the previous day's ladies' Battle Dome finals.

Battle Dome Final
Competitors:
Babydoll ⬡⬡ ✦ vs. Princess ⬡⬡⬡

We aren't given any background on how Babydoll is back to 2 Ki Symbols already, and as usual, the actors weren't given any either, so fill in your own blanks on that one.

Shannon describes this fight as, "the smooth movements and grace of Wushu against the power and speed of kickboxing," a lovely bit of narration that exemplifies what she brings to *WMAC Masters* in what ends up being Shannon's last episode (more on that later).

This fight gives Princess and Babydoll a much-needed chance to shine. Babydoll, in particular, has several incredibly impressive moves in the fight, including a huge axe kick that looks devastating. Princess takes an early lead, but Babydoll makes the come-back to win.

We get the usual replays of scoring moves followed by the Dragon Belt ceremony. The ref almost hands it to the wrong fighter, which would be a funny outtake, and the belt looks empty, but it's hard to tell. Perhaps this was initially intended to be Babydoll's return to competition and was changed in post.

Shannon then recaps The Machine versus Superstar rivalry, showing footage of their battle in the unaired pilot/episode one. She says Superstar was proudest of his victory over The Machine out of all his wins on the road to the Dragon Star. This hype makes this fight feel significant and important, even more than the usual Dragon Star match. In combat sports, commentators and fans love to talk about the big-fight feel and how it adds to the aura around a fight and even the fight itself. Small moments like this one with Shannon really add to that big-fight feel here.

Back in the Inner Sanctum, The Machine is warming up with Olympus. Panther says he can't find Star Warrior anywhere, which everyone finds strange considering his brother is about to defend the Dragon Star. They speculate where he might be, but no one knows for sure.

Also in the Inner Sanctum, old rivals Turbo and Olympus snipe back and forth at each other, remembering their Dragon Star match. Turbo says he'll be back on the Dragon Star platform "sooner than you think."

> *I liked Mike (Bernardo, Turbo) a lot. He was a real nice guy. Quiet. We had good chemistry.*

Herb Perez
Olympus

Back on the platform, Superstar does a short kata, looking amped up. Shannon points out that Superstar competed on the platform once before, recapping his fight with Olympus.

Meanwhile In the Inner Sanctum, The Machine is ready to go, decked out in his full armor, looking intense and focused. He lets out a massive scream and heads to the Arena. Shannon hypes him up, recapping his road to full Dragon Belt as he rides one of the dangling chains down from the ceiling onto the platform. From off-screen, someone drops or throws his giant staff onto the platform along with a giant Superstar Ki Symbol, which he crushes in his hand. Superstar laughs.

Quick cut to the back as the Masters clap for The Machine's display. It's pointed out that Turbo and The Bam have both gone MIA as well. Where is everyone, and why are they missing during a

Mer Mer Chen
Princess
Discipline: Wushu

Far from a damsel locked in a tower waiting for rescue, "Princess" Mer Mer Chen is a weapons expert and Wushu master, having studied under Eric Chen. Like several other cast members she cut her teeth as a stunt double and Putty Patroller on *Mighty Morphin Power Rangers* before *WMAC Masters*. In her post-acting career she graduated from UCLA and runs a non-profit ecological conservation organization.

Unfortunately Ms. Chen did not respond to interview requests for this book

Dragon Star match!?

Back on the platform, The Machine performs a kata, breaking terracotta sheets with his staff. Shannon hypes up the fight as, "The match of the year! The match of the century!" She's not usually hyperbolic, so it's particularly effective, adding even more big fight feel to the occasion.

The Machine doffs his armor as Superstar places the Dragon Star inside the Tri-Chamber Cyber-Cell, Shannon reminding us that it won't rise until there is a winner.

Dragon Star Championship
Competitors: Superstar (Champion) vs. The Machine (Challenger)

This fight is the most remembered Dragon Star contest of the series. It is full of exciting action, but the reason it's esteemed is simple, it has a shocking ending. After a long, intense battle that showcases both fighter's strengths, the Masters are on the platform with a ninja, who manages to knock both of the esteemed martial artists off the platform!

The ninja celebrates, apparently thinking he (or she?) just won the Dragon Star. They go to unmask, but we freeze-frame, getting a TO BE CONTINUED to end the season!

A shocking finish and major cliffhanger...

This was a shocking end to the season, not quite "Who shot JR?" but to an excited eight-year-old, it was close. Not knowing that it was a season finale or how long it would be until the next season, this cliffhanger left young me, and I'm sure countless other kids, twisting in the wind.

We knew a few things. We knew we wanted something to keep kids' attention during the break, and we knew we were going in a slightly different direction, a more story-focused direction. This was obviously one of the seeds of the big story of season two.

Norman Grossfeld
Executive Producer

I played the ninja (that knocked The Machine and Superstar off the platform). I know my character was in the back watching the fight, but the fact that I played the ninja always felt like a little Easter egg to me.

Hien Nguyen
Tsunami

At the time, he had no idea where his character arc would lead. The producers had an idea, if not the details.

We knew where we wanted to go, but not really all the finer points of it. We were working on it by then, but it wasn't all the way fleshed out. We always knew we wanted to do multiple seasons. We knew the numbers were good enough, so we started planning.

Norman Grossfeld
Executive Producer

I had no idea (at the time) it was going to be me.

Larry Lam
Warlock

There were some changes before season two (more on those in a bit), some of which required a shift to a more story-driven approach, away from the show's more realistic, tournament basis.

This (episode) really marked the start of that (shift).

Norman Grossfeld
Executive Producer

How did the cast members involved in the fight feel about the ending?

It was a surprise, for sure. I liked it. I knew, based on previous conversations, that sooner or later I'd be winning (the Dragon Star), so the ending of this dictated a rematch. I don't think it's what anyone expected.

Hakim Alston
The Machine

That is an understatement, to put it mildly.

A legendary rivalry

In one of the great shames of the series, the Dragon Star match itself has been overshadowed by the events surrounding it. The rivalry between The Machine and Superstar is one of the best in the series, and this fight was but one storied chapter in it.

In real life, Hakim Alston and Ho-Sung Pak were very different. Both were world-class martial artists, of course, but personality-wise, they were on opposite ends of the spectrum.

Ho-Sung was very aware of how he was portrayed. All the (cast) were, of course, but he was very invested in making sure he was presented a certain way.

Norman Grossfeld
Executive Producer

Many cast members I spoke to described Ho-Sung in similar ways, almost all of them making sure to emphasize he wasn't hard to work with. However, just very aware of his portrayal, one crew member speculated it was due to the less than pleasant experience he had as part of the original *Mortal Kombat* video game cast.

On the other hand, Alston was considerably more laid-back to use one cast member's descriptions.

I knew that if I did my job and performed the way I was supposed to, it would come across on screen, and I would be presented the right way. I focused on that.

Hakim Alston
The Machine

That dichotomy, the difference in mindset, could have been a struggle, but instead, it became a positive.

I knew how Ho-Sung's mind worked. We had a good rapport. I would kind of psych him up. Use that perfectionism to make the fight better. I tried to get inside his head, act like how my character would act. I think it brought the best out of him. I know he brought the best out of me.

Hakim Alston
The Machine

The rivalry between the two undoubtedly book-ended season one. The two were in the first-ever Battle Dome and ended the season fighting for the Dragon Star. However, as two of the most charismatic members of the cast, they remained front and center throughout the season. "They had everything you wanted," one crew member told me. "The look, the moves, that it factor. They were the natural choice."

There was, of course, one last chapter to write in their storied rivalry, but that comes later.

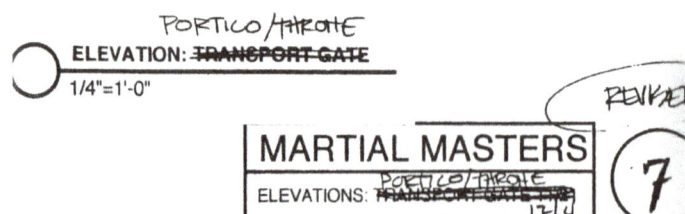

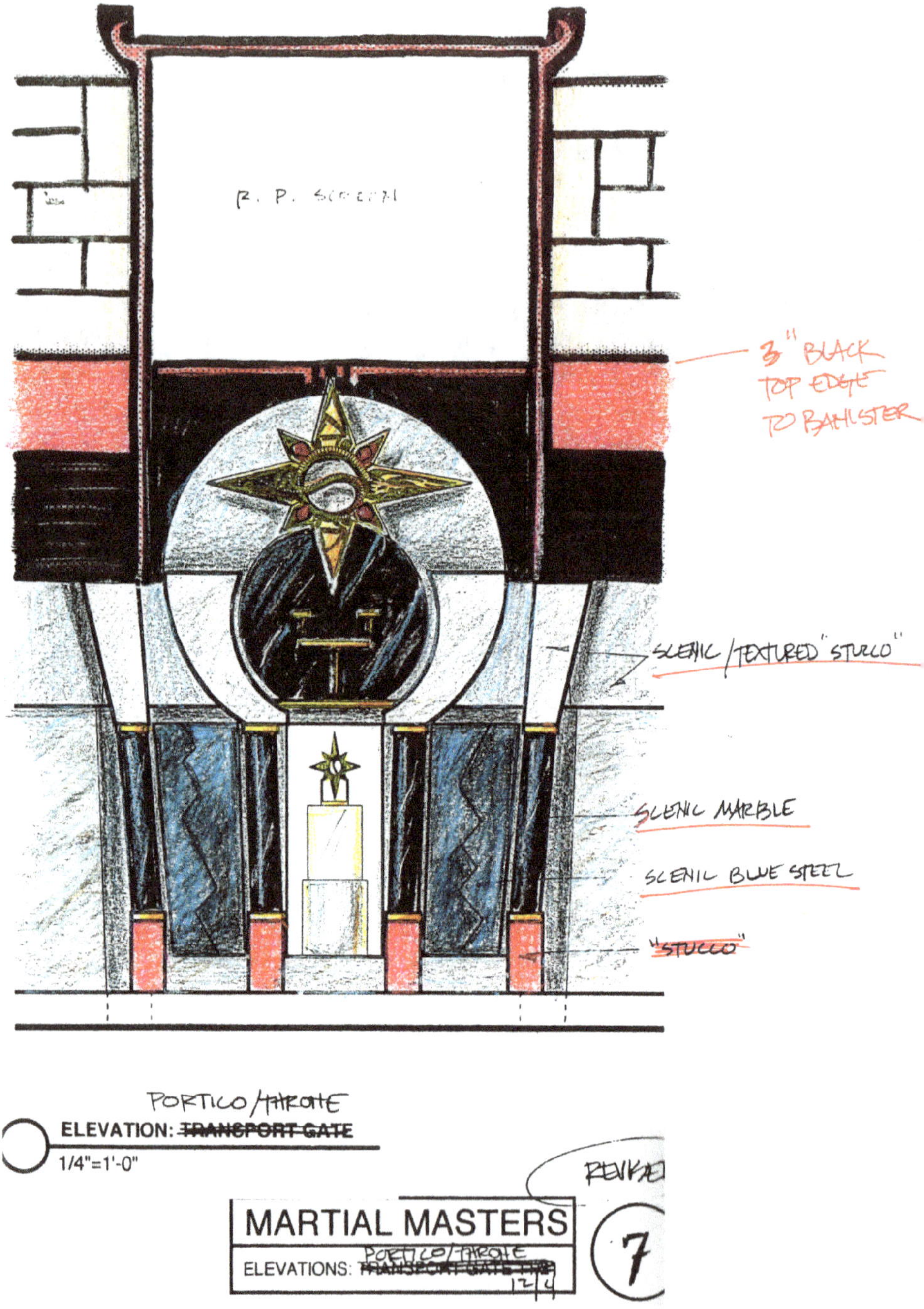

R. P. SCREEN

3" BLACK
TOP EDGE
TO BANISTER

SCENIC /TEXTURED "STUCCO"

SCENIC MARBLE

SCENIC BLUE STEEL

"STUCCO"

PORTICO /THRONE
ELECTION: ~~TRANSPORT GATE~~
1/4"=1'-0"

REVISED

MARTIAL MASTERS

ELEVATIONS: ~~TRANSPORT GATE~~ PORTICO/THRONE
12/4

7

Original sketches of WMAC Arena.
Photos from Dan Hubp.

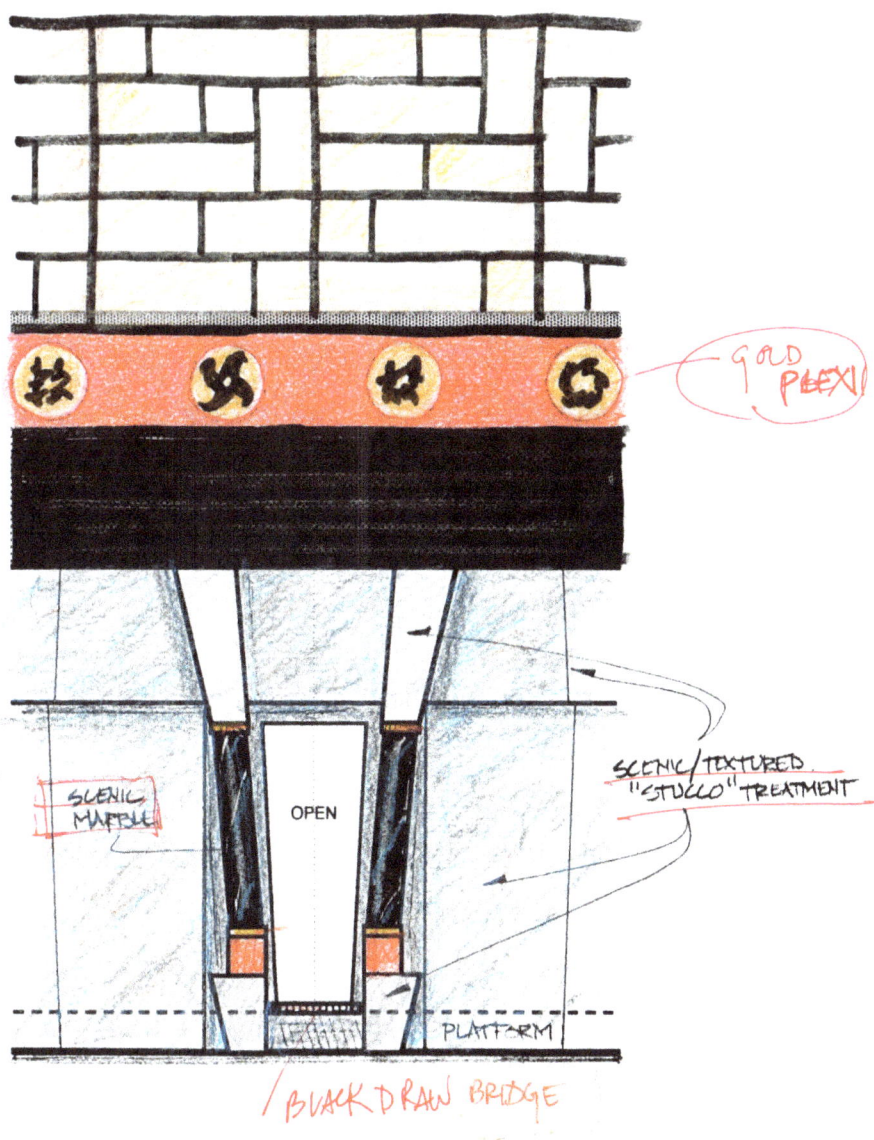

GOLD PLEXI

SCENIC/TEXTURED "STUCCO" TREATMENT

SCENIC MARBLE

OPEN

PLATFORM

/BLACK DRAW BRIDGE

ELEVATION: TALENT ENTRANCE
5/C 1/4"=1'-0"

MARTIAL MASTERS
TALENT ENTRANCE   11/21/9

CHAPTER 19

A Time of Change

Between the Seasons

"He wanted to give me time to get my affairs in order"

By the end of the first season, the cast and crew of *WMAC Masters* had settled into a groove. They had found the voice of the show, using martial arts action to teach life lessons, and had found a sports-style presentation that helped structure the show and present those themes. After some growing pains, they had embraced a more dynamic, action-movie style of shooting the fights, embracing the bombacity of the medium over a more traditional, realistic presentation. The first series of action figures, produced by their partners at Bandai, were out and selling well, and ratings were good, if not spectacular.

> **We were the number one rated program in our time slot in a lot of markets.**

Chris Casamassa
Red Dragon

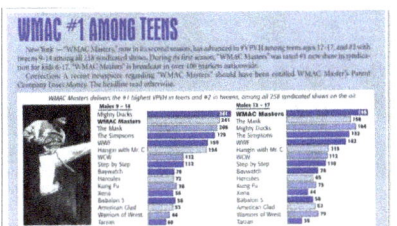

This graphic is the only corroborating evidence I could find for this information, and I was unable to determine its source. The consensus from the cast and crew I spoke to was that numbers for the show were "good but not amazing".
Photo from Willie Johnson.

However, things were about to change, forcing the show to evolve or die.

Partners No More

The central catalyst behind most of the changes between seasons one and two was the departure of Renaissance Atlantic as the show's financial backers. They had been the primary financier of season one, and their departure was a signifigant blow.

> **Renaissance Atlantic decided to pull out. They had their reasons. It was a purely business decision, nothing to do with the content of the show. So we were faced with the reality of having our budget effectively halved.**

Norman Grossfeld
Executive Producer

The loss of this funding could have been a death blow for the show, especially since *WMAC Masters* was already punching above its weight class to get their bang for the budgetary buck. The partnership with Universal Studios, especially, helped them stretch their budget by giving them movie caliber sets for next to nothing.

> *You look at what we were doing, and you look at our budget. You couldn't do that today. Even back then, people wouldn't believe what we were getting made with such a relatively small budget.*

Norman Grossfeld
Executive Producer

With Bandai's financing arm pulling out, the show was faced with the prospect of operating with essentially half of its previous budget.

> *Our production company could put up a certain amount, but that was it. There was no wiggle room. It was basically, "Can you make the show for this amount?"*

Norman Grossfeld
Executive Producer

There was no thought of calling it quits. But, there would have to be changes to the current setup—big ones.

A Change in Focus

The producers had already begun shifting the show's focus away from strictly sport-based storytelling, which focused on the fighters competing for the Dragon Star as the primary through-line of the series, to something more storyline-driven and dramatic, as witnessed by the cliffhanger ending of the first season. However, the radical budget cuts took this shift from a decision to a necessity.

The focus would become an over-arching story of JuKiDo, a martial art that splintered away from the WMAC over disagreements in philosophy. This group would become the prime antagonists of season two (and, ideally, beyond, but we'll get there...).

This story would take the show in a more dramatic, cinematic direction. Instead of the vignettes that populated season one, the second season would feature more backstage segments in the Inner Sanctum, exploring the interactions between the Masters.

Everyone loved the vignettes. We loved shooting them, we loved the stories and the lessons they taught, but on a practical level, we just couldn't afford it.

Dan Hubp
Production Designer, Editor

The cast all had different opinions when it came to the change. Everyone I spoke to understood the necessity, though Norman Grossfeld did tell me the producers did their best to keep the extent of the budget cuts from the majority of cast and crew. "We didn't cut anyone's pay," he told me. Some of the cast disliked moving away from the "life lessons" aspect of the show. However, some went so far as to say that the show "abandoned its original mission."

(After my injury) when I saw the direction they were going, I was like, shoo. Dodged that bullet.

Erik Betts
Panther

Others felt that the quality of the writing, combined with the more focused storytelling allowed by a straight-on good versus evil dynamic, made season two better than season one. Norman Grossfeld, perhaps understandably, shares this view.

The producers were adamant that none of the talent take a pay cut, despite their budgetary concerns. Norman Grossfeld explained that the fighters were all paid at the same rate, but their eventual payday was dependent on how much time they spent shooting. Fighters who didn't want to perform "ninja duty" wouldn't be on set for as long, for example.

I thought the writing was better (in season two). I thought the fights were better. I thought the show was just better. It's not a knock on season one at all. I'm very proud of what we did in both seasons. I just thought season two was stronger.

Norman Grossfeld
Executive Producer

Other cast members liked the more dramatic turn as well, noting that they were able to show more of their personalities, while others felt less restricted in what they could do in the fight scenes.

Departures and New Faces

This change in focus, dictated by the budgetary cuts, is one of the catalysts for several high-profile departures from the show in between seasons.

Shannon Lee, the host of the show, was a casualty of the new direction.

Shannon was great, but we had to decide not to bring her back for season two. There were two reasons, really. With the change in focus, she didn't really 'fit' anymore. She was great as the host, but every minute we were (watching) her, we weren't showing the actual characters, and we only have so much screen time each episode. The second reason was financial. Not that paying her was the problem. It was more the money to shoot all of her stuff- we always shot her separately. It was just a cost we didn't really need anymore with the change of focus. She understood completely and wished us well.

Norman Grossfeld
Executive Producer

I was unable to schedule an interview with Ms. Lee for this book, but she spoke positively of the show in a 2015 Reddit Ask Me Anything, calling it a "fun experience."

There were also a pair of high-profile cast departures, though they were under very different circumstances.

Bridgett Riley, one of the cornerstones of the WMAC Women's Division, second only to Lady Lightning, departed the show between seasons.

I was offered a really great movie part. Like, a dream part. It was a movie called "The Glimmer Man." I'd get to fight Steven Segal. I couldn't pass it up. I went to the producers to tell them and try to work out a way to do both (the show and the movie), and it just wasn't possible. So I had to choose. It was such a huge opportunity to advance my career- as much as I loved the show, I couldn't pass it up.

Bridgett Riley
Babydoll

It was, all things considered, a mostly amicable departure. Riley expressed disappointment that a solution couldn't be found with the scheduling allowing her to do both, but she didn't feel treated unfairly at all.

It's unfortunate, though, as there was still a lot of story left to tell with Babydoll, especially regarding her second attempt to win the Dragon Star. Some fans have speculated that her character would have been an addition to the JuKiDo group, perhaps feeling spurned by her loss.

I have no idea (where the character was going). They didn't really tell me anything like that. I think we were going to build up another fight with Christine (Rodrigues, Lady Lightning), but I don't really remember specifics.

Bridgett Riley
Babydoll

Babydoll was not the only major departure, however. Erik "Panther" Betts would also leave the show under much more dramatic circumstances.

How Things Change- A look at an early S2 Story Outline

According to a season two Story outline provided to me by lighting crew member Robert Tuscani, Babydoll would have played much of the part Chameleon wound up playing in season two. In this early document, written between filming the fight scenes and the Inner Sanctum shots, Chameleon is with JuKiDo from the beginning and it is not ambiguous.

According to the document, Babydoll was to shine in the few women's matches scheduled for season two, making a full comeback from her Dragon Star loss. The story of Black Widow stepping down plays out much the same way, but it's Babydoll vs. Chameleon as the Dragon Star match for the vacant trophy, their Ki Symbol counts being highest among the women in competition, according to the document. Babydoll wins the fight and is the one to have her "Scream Queen" moment as the JuKiDo symbol appears.

There are other differences, as well, mainly regarding the involvement of Panther (see below). There are also a few subplots that made their way into season two that are lacking in the outline, namely the extended nature of the Turbo and Star Warrior rivalry. The document also lacks the wrap-up of "Vision of Evil Part II," ending the season with Babydoll's shocked expression.

Betts suffered an injury early during filming for season two. He played a ninja at the Pressure Pit Battle Zone, participating in a Ninja Challenge fight against Olympus. His injury was severe, a broken femur and hip enough to put him out of action for the remainder of the show's run. Those who were there recall it well, for all the wrong reasons.

When I got the footage, it was... it was a sickening moment.

Dan Hubp
Production Designer, Editor

I was actually at craft services with the set medic when the injury happened. It was a bad, bad scene.

Robert Tuscani
Lighting Department

Erik over-rotated on a flip. It was an unfortunate accident.

Isaac Florentine
Director

He took a fall on one of my kicks and over-rotated, catching his leg in the ground awkwardly.

Herb Perez
Olympus

We were all torn up about it. Just a terrible accident. He just over-did it on a flip.

Norman Grossfeld
Executive Producer

Betts himself disagrees with their diagnosis of events.

Their story is coming from what they saw- what they understand and what they know about acrobatics. From an educated place, the pad (they used) specifically allows you to put your foot on it. As your foot lands, you can slide and pivot; you can still move. So we rehearsed on those pads, we were shooting on them, but one of the cameramen said, "this isn't really working. I can see the pad." We've already rehearsed like crazy. Let's get something more aesthetically pleasing. They brought out what's called a jigsaw non-skid surface. The problem was we didn't rehearse on it. You don't know how it will react due to temperature, or smoke machines, or wardrobe, things like that. Basically, Herb throws the inside crescent kick, I turn and start throwing a front-flip, and he does another move, and I start doing a full twist. As I'm doing the full twist, I land on the pad. But the way I landed, my body was trying to continue to rotate, and it could not rotate because the pad was a non-skid pad against the fabric of the ninja suit. Had it been on a vinyl pad, my leg would've continued to slide right through. But because it's on a non-skid pad, it stopped immediately.

Erik Betts
Panther

David Morizot was near Betts when the injury occured.

I rushed over to him when it happened to try to get the mask off of him. The masks on that set were these weird gas mask looking things. When I got close to him, he yelled, "Get the EXPLETIVE away from me!" so I backed off. He was in extreme pain.

David Morizot
Ninja

They rushed Betts to the hospital, where he was diagnosed with a broken hip and femur. There were further complications, however—dire ones.

The doctor sat myself down, my mother down, also informed production that I had developed a hematoma in my right leg, which is a huge blood clot. And that there was no way they were going to probably be able to remove the entire blood clot. And so he wanted to give me time to get my affairs in order. So he called my agent, he called my mom, and he notified production (and told them) that this guy has a 85% chance of dying.

Erik Betts
Panther

Thankfully, he survived. The recovery process was long and arduous.

I didn't know you could die from something so simple. I had something called an intramedullary steel rod, a full steel rod placed in my leg, from the top of my hip to the bottom of my femur, just above my kneecap. I had something called a distal pin, which is about a 4-inch pin, put horizontally just above the knee, sideways, perpendicular to the rod to keep the rod from dropping further into the femur. And then, two number-2 sized pencils, two screws, 8-inch screws, placed into the hip to protect the doorknob handle of the hip. Because there's an artery that goes in there, so apparently inside your bone, there's an artery that I didn't know, that goes inside that neck, and comes out the end of the ball, and goes into your pelvis. When the ball goes flat, you need a whole hip replacement. So I'm on the table, and they're putting all this hardware in, and they find the hematoma, so they have to take it all back out again. It was an ordeal.

Erik Betts
Panther

The severity of the situation was a shock to all involved.

We were all devastated. We were all worried for Erik, both mentally and physically

Norman Grossfeld
Executive Producer

The injury was only the beginning of the issues for Betts and the show.

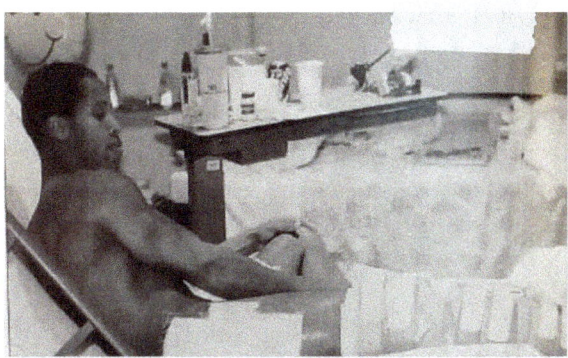

Erik Betts recovering in hospital.
Photo from Erik Betts.

So Norman, he wanted to bring a camera crew in and film my recovery. And of course, I'm already pissed off about the injury, about the pad, and then Norman wants to bring in a camera crew. For me, that was really it, as far as I was concerned.

Erik Betts
Panther

Grossfeld's perspective on the situation was, naturally, different.

Like many of the other cast members, being on the series was important to Erik. When he got hurt, we proposed featuring, in a small way, his rehabilitation and recovery on the show so that he could still feel that he was a part of it all. We felt it was important to let him know how much he was missed and that we were there for him. At some point, Erik sought out legal advice, which was certainly understandable and his prerogative. After all, WMAC Masters was just a TV show—but this was Erik's life. But that's when the relationship turned from being one of camaraderie to adversarial. And it was best to then let the lawyers and insurance company handle it all moving forward. It was an unfortunate incident all around.

Norman Grossfeld
Executive Producer

The lawsuit that followed ended Betts' time on the show and nixed the Panther action figure that was going to be a part of the second wave of figures. Unfortunately, it also put a serious wedge between him and his fellow cast members and crew, many of whom he had known for years.

Front and back of canceled Panther action figure. Photo from Erik Betts.

I was pissed off. Pissed off at the situation, the injury, and then at (the producers) wanting to film my recovery. I wasn't in the best state. I sank into a massive depression. So I'm in the hospital, and Isaac Florentine and a bunch of them come by. And I'm on major drugs, I'm being told I'm gonna be killed, you know, I could die. And it wasn't a sad thing for me. It was an 'I was pissed off at the world' thing. And it's ironic because a lot of my relationships with people then, that's where there was a huge separation for me.

Erik Betts
Panther

The lawsuit would name the show, the producers, Herb Perez, and even Universal Studios as defendants.

I was actually pissed with Herb as well... My attorney said, "Who is this guy?" talking about Herb. And I was like, "A friend of mine. He plays Olympus," you know, gave the whole spiel, "Won the '92 golden medal, blah blah blah". And he goes, "I'll tell you what, you'd be better off with enemies. Because look at... "We kept playing the footage, and when I got hurt, Herb stepped back, stepped away, and just stood there. He didn't come in and see if I was okay or help out. He just stepped back and kinda froze up a little bit. And so every attorney who ever saw that, which there were three of them, they all made the comment about, "Who is this guy, and why wasn't he- Is that a friend of yours?"

Erik Betts
Panther

Herb Perez never commented on being named in the lawsuit. Instead, he remembers how worried he was for his friend.

I rode to the hospital with him, and he was leaning on my shoulder as they drilled through the bone because they don't give you anesthetic.

Herb Perez
Olympus

Ultimately, however, the passage of time healed the emotional wounds between Betts and his fellow Masters.

I was very close to Isaac (Florentine) and his family, but that relationship was kind of lost for a while (with the injury). When his wife died, though, I sent a huge bouquet of flowers. Because it just... it's perspective. For me, all of (the relationships) have mended... These guys are definitely my brothers and sisters. We have gone through it all and then some. There's an old saying, 'monumental moments, critical choices, and pivotal people equal who we are.' It was a monumental, pivotal time in my life. It was life-changing.

Erik Betts
Panther

New Faces

The Producers were some additions to the cast in season two as well. However, none of the newcomers were brought in to replace the departing Babydoll or Panther, each having unique storylines and impact on the show.

They brought in Michael Foley to play Tracy "Tracer" Swedom, one of the primary antagonists of the second season.

I had done a movie (Desert Kickboxer) a year or two earlier with Isaac Florentine. He gave me a call and invited me to California to meet the producers. They hired me on the spot.

Michael Foley
Tracer

Foley had no prior knowledge of the show before meeting with the producers but had acted in several martial arts action films. However, upon arriving for the meeting, he was shown a concept for the Tracer character and was shocked.

I thought they were pulling my leg. (The drawing) looked just like me. One of the producers was really taken aback by the similarities. They had me pegged from the start. Me being an Army officer with combat experience was just icing on the cake.

Michael Foley
Tracer

Foley was a mountain of a man, barrel-chested with a military presence that was not just for the cameras. He was the perfect foil for the heroic, colorful cast of Masters, a more gritty, action-movie-villain-looking antagonist.

Unlike the rest of the cast, Foley's character was given a new name by the writers. As a result, he would not be playing himself. This was partially due to storyline reasons (we'll come to see Tracy Swedom is a very significant anagram) but partially for more mundane concerns.

No one wants to be cast as a villain under their real name. :laughs:

Norman Grossfeld
Executive Producer

The concern was not overblown, as ninja David Morizot remembers.

Someone, I think it was Larry Lam, told me that during season two, as people saw his character go evil, his school started suffering for it. People weren't able to separate the fiction from reality.

David Morizot
Ninja

Sophia Crawford would also join the cast at the start of the second season, playing "Chameleon." Another cog in the *Mighty Morphin Power Rangers* to *WMAC Masters* pipeline, Crawford was a highly touted stunt-woman and was the first "Western" woman to work for a major Hong Kong studio. She would go on to work on numerous high-profile projects after her brief run on Masters, including *Buffy: The Vampire Slayer* and *Charmed*.

The casting process was simple and quick, considering Chameleon's significant role in season two.

It was a whirlwind. It all happened very quickly. First, I was meeting the producers, and the next thing I know, I'm being offered the part, then I'm being flown to Orlando for costume fittings. There was no real time to think.

Sophia Crawford
Chameleon

Being friends with several cast members thanks to her *Mighty Morphin Power Rangers* work Crawford had an idea of what the show was like but hadn't seen any of the episodes.

The producers didn't give me any footage or anything. They explained the show, the character, that I'd be this bad girl, and then when I got to Orlando, it was right into the thick of it.

Sophia Crawford
Chameleon

Also joining the show after a couple of episodes in season two was Akihiro "Cyclone" Noguchi. Another *Mighty Morphin Power Rangers* veteran, he was initially brought in to help with fight choreography, filling the void left by Pat Johnson, but they asked him to be a face character as well.

Isaac (Florentine) asked my teammate Koichi Sakamoto to be the action director of WMAC Masters, but his schedule wouldn't allow it. So I stepped in. When I received the request, I was told I'd be taking part as an action director. I didn't know anything about Cyclone.

Akihiro Noguchi
Cyclone

WMAC Masters was his first time as a director, not simply a performer. He recalls being nervous, unsure if he was up for it.

At Isaac's home, I filmed my teammates' fights for him to watch, kind of like an audition to see if I would be a good action director.

Akihiro Noguchi
Cyclone

How did he become Cyclone if he was just supposed to be a fight director?

One of the actors couldn't make it to the shoot, so they asked me to step in and play Cyclone. Since it was my first job as a director, I told the producer I had too many things to do to also play a character, but he asked me three or four times. There wasn't much explanation of the character. It was all very rushed because of time (constraints).

Akihiro Noguchi
Cyclone

Norman Grossfeld, the executive producer, does not remember casting Noguchi as Cyclone due to another actor failing to appear, nor does Dan Hubp. Instead, both indicated that Noguchi was the original and only choice for Cyclone.

Producer Norman Grossfeld in production office between seasons. On wall behind him you can see alternate color schemes for JuKiDo symbol. Photo from Kathy Pilon.

Newcomer Mike Chat poses with Carmichael Simon on set. Photo from Carmichael Simon.

Unfortunately, Cyclone didn't feature much in the series due to events we'll get to later. However, one character that featured prominently in season two was Wizard, played by Mike Chaturantabut (now known professionally as Mike Chat). Another veteran of the martial arts tournament circuit, Chat had "everything we were looking for," according to Grossfeld.

> *We always wanted there to be more characters, new people coming and others going. The story we went with was a vehicle for that. We liked the idea of having a 'is he good or is he evil' sort of character.*

Norman Grossfeld
Executive Producer

The show would be Chat's first television role.

> *I had just made the jump from the junior circuit to the senior circuit the year before. I was eighteen, nineteen years old. I'd seen (the producers) scouting, and since I knew a lot of the cast, I knew they had looked at me. It was actually Larry (Lam, Warlock) who was my biggest cheerleader. I was staying with him in California, teaching at his school while I attended college. He was a real mentor to me. He called me and said, "They want to bring you in, and they want you to play my brother!" I was blown away.*

Mike Chat
Wizard

The final new character to debut in season two is Black Widow, portrayed by Tiana Noguchi. As season two starts, she is the Dragon Star Champion on the ladies' side, having unseated Lady Lightning in the time between seasons. We will dive deeper into the strange story of Black Widow in Chapter 31.

New Focus

With new faces in the cast and a revamp of the creative direction, *WMAC Masters* was poised to strike out into new ground with their second season. There was a buzz among the cast as filming got underway.

I think everybody was really excited. We kind of got in our groove as the first season went on, so everyone was really ready for season two.

Jamie Webster
Great Wolf

I don't think anyone had an issue with (the new direction). We were all just happy to be involved—we all just kind of wondered where we fit in.

Herb Perez
Olympus

Keeping that buzz was essential to the producers. Having successfully fostered a "we're all in this together" mentality in season one, they were careful to keep morale as high as possible, even in the face of the new challenges imposed by the slashed budget.

We did our best to make sure no one knew that things were tight. We tried to make it as smooth as possible. Not that we felt the cast needed to be in the dark or anything, it was just important to us that we kept that spirit up. The shoots were hard and long, and we wanted to keep everyone as "up" as possible.

Norman Grossfeld
Executive Producer

Their efforts were successful. No one I spoke to recalled any knowledge or gossip about the show's budget changing. Some, particularly the crew, remembered an increase in stress related to production needing to get things shot and wrapped quickly, but it was "typical show stress," not anything unexpected.

The second season of *WMAC Masters* would present new challenges and lows for the cast and crew but also some spectacular highs. As filming began, however, there was only one focus: the resolution of season one's cliffhanger.

CHAPTER 20

S2E01: Showdown Part II

Yin Yang Man

Turbo

Great Wolf

Star Warrior

The Bam

Olympus

"The ninja challenges were always fun"

With changes afoot and a new direction, the season two opener is a bit of a curveball for fans expecting an immediate conclusion to the title fight, but one that sets the stage perfectly for the season to come.

Season two begins with a previously on *WMAC Masters* recap of the shocking conclusion to The Machine versus Superstar Dragon Star Match. It's voiced not by Shannon Lee, who no longer is on the show (see the previous chapter), but an unnamed, heavily processed voice associated with the WMAC Council.

That was usually me. We'd just add an effect and use it.

Norman Grossfeld
Executive Producer

The recap video highlights the Masters who were missing from the Inner Sanctum during the fight. This included Turbo, Star Warrior, and The Bam. We also get a few previously unseen reaction shots of the Masters as the saga unfolded on the Inner Sanctum's big screen. In addition, we get reactions from Lady Lightning, Red Dragon, Tsunami, and even Kid Carmichael.

That may be the only scene where I'm in the Inner Sanctum. I didn't really act at the time, so I wasn't usually called on for those scenes.

Carmichael Simon
Kid Carmichael

We then see extended scenes of the Mysterious Ninja (Not to be confused with the Stupid Ninja. See Chapter 5.) celebrating atop the platform. He waits for the Dragon Star to rise as guard ninjas block the exits, but it doesn't appear. Ninjas cannot win the Dragon Star. A riot begins to break out, the recruits seemingly panicking and trying to rush the platform. The Mysterious Ninja pulls the old smoke bomb trick and disappears, which sends the riot into overdrive. The recruits charge the platform, overwhelming the guards. The Voice of the Council (known as the Cyberdude or Cyberman in the scripts) instructs them to seal the exits. The Mysterious Ninja must be found!

We then get the opening credits, which have been updated for season two. We will see a couple of versions of them this season, changed slightly depending on who is competing in the episode.

We return to some clips of the previous Ninja Challenge episode, voiced over by a female Council Representative (known as the Cyberbabe in the scripts), explaining the rules. This is one spot where the show definitely missed Shannon. The Council voiceovers were fine, but they seemed jarring after a season of Shannon. Plus, the lack of explanation as to just who was talking to us and why could confuse new or irregular viewers. Also, for reasons never explained (and no longer remembered by the crew I spoke to), this concept is now known as the "Super Challenge" as opposed to the "Ninja Challenge." The crew referred to them as "Ninja Bash" episodes, which likely didn't sound formal enough for use on the show itself.

One moment featured in the season two storyline overview (see the previous chapter) but was cut before making air was a brief conversation in the Inner Sanctum where Tsunami mentions that Shannon Lee stepped away from the competition after the masked ninja incident. He says she found it disgraceful and troubling. I have been unable to determine if this was filmed and *then* cut or nixed before filming, but I find the latter to be more likely. As it aired the show offered no explanation for Lee's departure.

Super Challenge Contestant One: Yin Yang Man ⬡⬡⬡⬡⬡⬡ ✦
Battle Zone: Mayan Mystery
Ninjas: Black

Yin Yang Man gets this second Super Challenge started, and a few things are immediately apparent. First, the shooting style is less straightforward, with slow-motion shots throughout the fight. It's also apparent to anyone who watched the first Super Challenge episode that the scoring system, which was absolutely ridiculous the first time around, has been much more evenly implemented. As in, there was at least an attempt to make the scores seem realistic.

Yin Yang brings his typical Wushu "Whirlwind" flips and kicks to the fight, ending up with a 79.

Back in the Inner Sanctum, The Machine rants about the Mysterious Ninja, saying someone sabotaged their fight. He says the ninja couldn't have been from the WMAC 'Academy. The kick he threw to knock himself and Superstar off was too good. The Masters talk about who wasn't in the Inner Sanctum with them during the fight. The Bam saying he was with his son, giving him a credible alibi. They keep referring to the Mysterious Ninja as "he," prompting Lady Lightning to chime in, "What if it's not a he?" Warlock says he knows who the Ninja was, pointing to the big screen where Turbo is getting ready for his turn with the ninjas.

Super Challenge Contestant Two: Turbo ⬡ ⬡ ⬡ ✧
Battle Zone: Mayan Mystery
Ninjas: Black

The ninjas score a couple of strikes on the former Dragon Star champ early, but this only serves to fire him up. He kicks the ninja into next week before throwing another ninja halfway across the Battle Zone.

> *The ninja challenges were always fun. I liked getting to show my stuff a little.*

Mike Bernardo
Turbo

He finishes with 77 points, a much more reasonable score than he would have likely had in the first iteration of this concept.

In the Inner Sanctum, Warlock asks Superstar if any of Turbo's kicks looked familiar. Olympus says Warlock is accusing the wrong man, and the Mysterious Ninja is about to enter the room, but first we get a commercial, the oldest trick in the TV drama book.

It's a great piece of character work to have Olympus, of all people, be the voice doubting Turbo's guilt. It shows that Olympus values competitive spirit above any personal animosity. He battled Turbo for the Dragon Star, and knowing what it means to the man, he can't see Turbo doing something so obviously against the Code of the Dragon Star, even though Turbo is probably the least-liked Master in the eyes of his fellow competitors (at least for now...).

Back from the conveniently timed commercial, Star Warrior walks into the Inner Sanctum. Olympus seems convinced that Star Warrior was the Mysterious Ninja, and Star Warrior doesn't give an alibi, playing dumb. It's not exactly a sterling defense, leading to his brother admitting he doesn't know what to think anymore. Tiger Claw says they want the truth, and Star Warrior says, "It wasn't me. That's all I have to say."

The Council calls over the loudspeaker, requesting The Machine and Superstar to join them. They've decided on the future of the Dragon Star!

Super Challenge Contestant Three: Great Wolf ⬡⬡⬡⬡⬡⬡⬡
Battle Zone: Ghost Town
Ninjas: Ghost

Great Wolf becomes the first Master to participate in a second Super Challenge here. Last time out, he scored a whopping 126 points but finishes with a much more realistic 73 here. The coolest technique in the match is a big series of spin kicks he mows down ninjas with, never stopping to reset. He finishes in last place out of those who have gone so far. So his odds of making his second straight four-man Dome are not looking good!

Back in the Inner Sanctum, Turbo explains that the Dragon Star won't rise out of the Tri-Chamber Cyber-Cell until someone wins the Dragon Star match. The Machine and Superstar emerge from the Council chambers saying they will have their rematch next week at a top-secret location. They won't be told where until later. The Machine, seeing the chance to get inside his opponent's head, needles Superstar about his brother being the Mysterious Ninja.

Super Challenge Contestant Four: Star Warrior ⬡⬡⬡⬡⬡⬡⬡
Battle Zone: Mayan Mystery
Ninjas: Black

Mysterious Ninja or not, Star Warrior gets a chance to shine in this quick battle, executing a series of flashy kicks and twists. He goes to town on the ninjas, posting the highest score of the day so far with a 91!

I loved watching (Ho-Young) perform. His movements were so smooth.

Carmichael Simon
Kid Carmichael

Out of all the characters to get a toy Star Warrior was far and away the least featured in season one. His increased prominence in season two was, perhaps, a reward for his patience in that regard. Screen time was a valuable commodity on the show, and the more quiet and unassuming Pak brother saw his increase dramatically in the second season. This could have caused resentment, but Ho-Young was universally respected by his peers, and no one I spoke to had anything negative to say about the man, his role, or his work.

Back in the Inner Sanctum, we get the debut of Tracy "Tracer" Swedom, saying that Star Warrior is the reason they don't know who the Mysterious Ninja is. According to Tracer, he was in the Arena that day and chased the Mysterious masked man through the underground tunnels the Masters use to get to the Battle Zones. Unfortunately, as he chased the ninja into one of the tunnels, he plowed straight into Star Warrior, giving the ninja time to escape.

In the season two overview, however, it is not Star Warrior but Panther who gets tangled up with Tracer. By the time the scripts were written for the Inner Sanctum pieces, it had been changed to Star Warrior. No doubt due to Panther's injury. According to dialogue in the document, Panther took a tough fall in the tunnels, sending him to the hospital, effectively writing him out of the Inner Sanctum segments for the time being.

This exchange also gives us the first, but far from the last, instance of someone calling Tracer "Tracy." He flips his lid, shouting, "No one calls me Tracy! It's Tracer!" He's so over the top and pompous in his delivery that it's impossible to take him as anything other than a villain, which was precisely the idea.

(That hatred fans felt) was what I was going for when developing the character. I take it as a compliment to my acting skills. It was great fun.

Michael Foley
Tracer

Tracer says he never saw the ninja and Star Warrior at the same time. Superstar is troubled by the implication.

Meanwhile, on the other side of the Sanctum, Red Dragon asks Tsunami who the new girl is. It's Chameleon. Tsunami calls her a loner as we see her cuddling her lizard Baby (not a weird knock on her, that's the lizard's name). Red Dragon says she just hasn't met the right people yet. He approaches her and flirts, and to everyone's surprise, she asks for a "get to know each other kiss!" He happily obliges, only to end up kissing the lizard, to whom Chameleon then apologizes profusely.

> *I was kind of the John Stamos character. They positioned me as this ladies man. I wasn't upset about it! :laughs:*

Chris Casamassa
Red Dragon

Super Challenge Contestant Five: The Bam ⬡⬡⬡⬡⬡
Battle Zone: Ghost Town
Ninjas: Ghost

This is The Bam's first go-round at the Super Challenge. We get more slow-mo shots in this one, which stand out compared to the previous season. The Bam shows off some amazing techniques, but nothing quite as flashy as usual. He does bust out a judo throw, which isn't something we've seen from him before, but it's not enough. He finishes with 72, not enough to make the finals.

> *I didn't care about winning or losing. I was just happy to be there. I came in and did whatever they asked me to do. I was just thrilled to be a part of it.*

Willie Johnson
The Bam

We head straight to the next contestant!

Super Challenge Contestant Six:
Olympus ⬡ ✦
Battle Zone: Pressure Pit
Ninjas: Pit

A note to start, this was the match where Erik Betts, playing a ninja, suffered his injury (see last chapter for details). No footage of the injury is in the episode itself, despite rumors on the internet to the contrary. Dan Hubp, who edited the episode in question, confirmed this to me.

> *No, none of those shots got used. They were locked away.*

Dan Hubp
Production Designer, Editor

This one has quite a bit of action compared to previous fights in this episode. Olympus punches one of the ninjas through one of the barrels decorating the set and manages to hit the flying side kick that cost him the Dragon Star when he missed it on the platform. He finishes with 80 points, enough to send him to the Battle Dome final!

We get shots of the four finalists entering the Arena for the Battle Dome, and it's Olympus, Turbo, Yin Yang Man, and Star Warrior. Then, the Cyberdude explains the rules of the Dome to new viewers as the Dome comes down.

Fun Fact:
According to Willie Johnson, the producers were so impressed with his performance against the ninjas that they scheduled him to take on Great Wolf in the Ghost Town Battle Zone. A fight that would take place in S2E10.

Battle Dome Finals: Olympus ⬡ ✦ vs. Turbo ⬢ ⬢ ⬢ ✦ vs. Yin Yang Man ⬡ ⬡ ⬡ ⬡ ⬡ ⬡ ✦ vs. Star Warrior ⬡ ⬡ ⬡ ⬡ ⬡ ⬡ ⬡

It's rare to have two fighters on their second-degree Dragon Belts in the same fight, let alone three. As in season one, no ninjas will be in the Dome today. Four fighters are enough to deal with.

The four-man fights were a lot of fun, but they were harder to choreograph. Everyone had to hit their marks exactly.

Hien Nguyen
Tsunami

The music to start this fight feels very different from the music in season one. It really changes the atmosphere.

This four-man fight does a great job of telling multiple stories via the action. Olympus and Turbo continue their rivalry, as do Turbo and Yin Yang Man. Star Warrior massively underperforms in the fight, leaving viewers to wonder if it's because of the accusations leveled against him earlier in the episode or maybe guilt over his actions.

Yin Yang Man's performance really stands out, as he demonstrates remarkable athletic ability and agility at various points, using the platforms and rings in the Dome to marvelous effect.

The only downside to this fight is the lack of Shannon Lee. Without her commentary, there is no one to explain to new viewers the history between the fighters, which features heavily here.

In the end, it goes to sudden death, with Turbo picking up the win over Yin Yang Man and claiming three more Ki Symbols!

In the Inner Sanctum, Lady Lightning comments that Turbo is on the fast track back to Dragon Star contention with his big win. The Masters then debate who the Mysterious Ninja might be a little more, with Tiger Claw ominously saying they may never know.

We then get the Dragon Belt ceremony, and Turbo adds three more Ki Symbols to his total. We can spy Red Dragon's symbol already on his belt, making me wish we got to see that particular fight. He poses with his belt and looks ready to wreak havoc on season two!

Conspirators

Somewhere deep in the bowels of the Inner Sanctum, we see Tracer and Warlock engaged in a heated discussion. Tracer takes a mask from Warlock, chewing him out for almost getting caught! Warlock was the Mysterious Ninja! They mention something called JuKiDo, which we will learn far more about as the season goes on, though not as much as most fans would like. We also see their symbol, a strange and ominous red dragon.

Red Dragon... Hmm...

The name JuKiDo (the correct spelling and stylization, according to producer Norman Grossfeld) has long been the subject of rumor amongst fans. One popular rumor is that it is a take on Benny "The Jet" Urquidez's fighting system, Ukidokan. Norman Grossfeld dispelled that.

No, it wasn't based on any existing fighting style. We wanted something that would sound familiar to viewers, like other martial arts, but didn't want it associated with anything actually existing already.

Norman Grossfeld
Executive Producer

This week's post-credits scene is Tsunami talking about not being afraid to try new things and always going after your goals.

Heading in a New Direction

"Showdown Part II" is an effective season opener. It manages to feel coherent with what came before it while still signaling a massive shift in style for the show. It also manages to walk the always difficult tightrope of offering answers to the big cliffhanger mystery while still continuing the story in an engaging, propulsive way. Even in a show aimed at kids, this forward momentum, story-wise, is vital. Had things been wrapped up with a neat bow, the show would have been left with nowhere to go, but had it not been addressed at all, the young viewership would likely have been confused or upset. This episode managed to navigate those pitfalls and deliver a solid episode of action and story. Probably the best of the Super Challenge episodes the series put on.

Superstar and The Machine in the Inner Sanctum. Photo from Bruce Heinsius Photography.

MACHINE
There's no way that Ninja was from the Academy.
That kick had the mark of a Master.

TSUNAMI
Hey, anything is possible. You're forgetting I'm a WMAC
graduate myself.

(He tries to flaunt his skill by demonstrating a KARATE KICK toward RED
DRAGON.)

RED DRAGON
(Reacting to TSUNAMI's showy move with a pregnant pause and a deadpan
delivery. . .)
Like Hakim said, there's no way it was a Ninja from the
Academy.

RED DRAGON cracks up as a few of the OTHER ATHLETES laugh at the
ribbing. TSUNAMI is miffed.

MACHINE
Hey guys -- this is serious. One of you sabotaged our match
and who's to say it won't happen again.

OLYMPUS
Machine's right. It's got to be someone who wasn't around
to watch the match.

SUPERSTAR
(As he speaks, SUPERSTAR moves over to where THE BAM is
working out.)
And that narrows it down to just a couple of people. . .
Turbo. . . and . . . The Bam.

I hear there were a couple of guys missing like Turbo and ... Bam

THE BAM
Hey man, I had nothing to do with it. I was coaching my son
when all this went down.

LADY LIGHTNING
Back off, Hosung, there's no telling who this guy might be.
And who said it has to be a guy?

Script page with Jamie Webster's hand-written additions. Script from Jamie Webster.

CHAPTER 21

S2E02: Dragon Star Rematch

Superstar vs. The Machine

"This was a big moment for the show"

Episode two of the second season contains what is likely the most memorable fight in the entire series, the rematch between Superstar and The Machine on the underground tramway set. It also continues the Mysterious Ninja storyline in a significant way, laying the seeds for the rest of the second season.

We begin in the Inner Sanctum and see that Star Warrior is being put on trial for being the Mysterious Ninja. Olympus, his original accuser, is the prosecution. Tiger Claw is the defense. According to Red Dragon, Turbo is the judge because "he hates all of us equally," a great piece of character work.

Olympus is a lawyer, both in his real life but also within the universe of the show (see his vignette in "Going for the Gold"). It seems a little unfair to Star Warrior to have Olympus handle the accusations, but for a kangaroo court, it's predictable.

We get the opening credits and head to the Arena, where the Cyberbabe from the last episode recaps the previous Dragon Star match between Superstar and The Machine, explaining that today's rematch will be at a classified location.

Back in the Inner Sanctum, Tracer is on the witness stand. Tiger Claw fumbles with legal jargon as he tries to cross-examine the soldier, playing into his country boy stereotype. We see Cyclone, another new Master, watching the proceedings from a wheelchair. Turbo tries his best to hold the proceedings together, only for Red Dragon to throw an old-timey white judge's wig at him. We hear, yet again, that Tracer doesn't like to be called Tracy. It will not be the last time. We even get a "We want the truth," "You can't handle the truth!" moment between Tiger Claw and Tracer because it's 1996, and how could you not, with those two?

That scene (the trial) was really what established me, I think. It was one of my favorite scenes.

Michael Foley
Tracer

He then goes on, in total Bond-villain fashion, to not-answer-answer more questions. His discipline is classified, he says, asking, "didn't you hear about my initiation? It would have been career suicide to try to do what I did." It's totally over the top, pompous, and precisely what a kid's show needs from its first true villain.

Interestingly, this whole scene is lacking in the original story overview for season two. This episode is pegged to have Panther return from the hospital and tell his side of the story. Yes, he did run into Tracer in the tunnels as they both presumably chased the Masked Ninja, but they weren't the only ones down there. Chameleon was as well!

The Classified Weapon

We then see Tracer's initiation, dubbed Army of One. The Council's voiceover guy says Tracer will attempt to demonstrate mastery over all the major martial arts. This, judging by what follows, means punishing a handful of unfortunate ninja recruits.

Highlights include tossing one ninja into a pair of its compatriots, a massive Muay Tai style knee strike, and a Jean-Claude Van Damme style split kick. He then picks up a ninja in a fireman's carry and starts spinning it around, dominating the smaller recruits. The Council's voiceover says that's enough, bestowing Master status on Tracer.

It's a great piece of writing that the Council had to step in and stop him rather than having him end his demonstration on his own. It's not commented on in the show, making it perhaps the only subtle thing in Tracer's entire character arc.

It was just my second day, and we were already working on the choreography for that fight. It was a lot of fun. Since I'm a big guy, they didn't expect me to be able to do things like the split kick.

Michael Foley
Tracer

Back in the Inner Sanctum, Tracer oh-so-humbly declares himself the Master of all Masters because of his mastery of all the disciplines. He then pulls out a glove the Mysterious Ninja dropped during their chase, giving it to the Masters for the trial.

In the Arena, The Machine enters and performs a kata called Body of Steel. A group of ninjas appear to remove The Machine's armor with a rivet gun, an absurd but fun image considering we've seen him casually take it off in previous episodes. Maybe he upgraded between seasons?

He does a brief staff form before throwing the staff, landing it on the bed of nails last used by Panther in his Master Blaster last year. He pulls it out and lays back on the nail bed. A cinder block gets placed on his chest, and a ninja swings a sledgehammer, breaking it. We get multiple camera angles of it, and there are no visible gimmicks, no pyrotechnics, or pre-breaks.

Back in the Inner Sanctum, Olympus, the prosecutor, asks Star Warrior to try on the glove. Tiger Claw tells him to go ahead. It doesn't fit, setting Tiger Claw up for the required "if it doesn't fit, you must acquit" line. Red Dragon dubs him Johnny Lee Cochran. This little back-and-forth has a Pixar-esque joke for the adults watching quality to it, something watching the series again as an adult made me appreciate all the more.

Judge Turbo calls for order. He says that he can explain where Star Warrior was. They were together at the WMAC Academy during the match. No one bothered to ask him, apparently. The Masters, properly chastised, apologize to Star Warrior while Warlock and Tracer exchange a conspiratorial glance.

We then head back to the Arena for Superstar's kata, Balance of Power. It starts on a balance beam with a group of ninjas, followed by some of his usual flashy jumping and kicking.

Michael M. Foley
Tracey "Tracer" Swedom
Discipline: Classified

Without a doubt the most polarizing character on *WMAC Masters*, Tracey Swedom was played by Michael M. Foley. Michael served in the US Army, where he continued his martial arts training, winning the US Army Pacific Rim Heavyweight Kickboxing Championship. He was also a veteran of martial arts action films, once training Jean Claude Van Damme for a role. He now teaches self defense around the world.

T
T
w

Photos from
Bruce Heinsius
Photography.

Script
from Jamie
Webster.

                    OLYMPUS
            Tracy, if we may continue...

                    TRACER
(Interrupting OLYMPUS)
                The name's Tracer. Nobody calls
                me Tracy.

                    OLYMPUS
                Alright, <u>Tracer</u> -- What's your
                discipline?

                    TRACER
                That's classified.

                    OLYMPUS
                Come on soldier, no one's
                discipline is classified.
                How about the truth?

(TRACER bangs his CLENCHED FIST and SHOUTS. . .)

                    TRACER
                You can't handle the truth!
        (He collects his cool. . .)
                    Look, didn't you hear about my
                initiation? It would have been career
                suicide for any of you to try and do
                what I did. But then, you're not
                Tracer Swedom . . .

Dissolve to TRACER Master Blaster Ninja Bash-- he uses tehniques from all the different
disciplines to prove his worthiness before the Council. As the exhibition concludes, we
dissolve back to ...

10   **INNER SANCTUM/TRIAL AREA**   10

TRACER takes his first BITE of the APPLE before he continues.

                    TRACER
                After that, the Council had no
                choice but to let me in as a master
                of all disciplines. I guess that

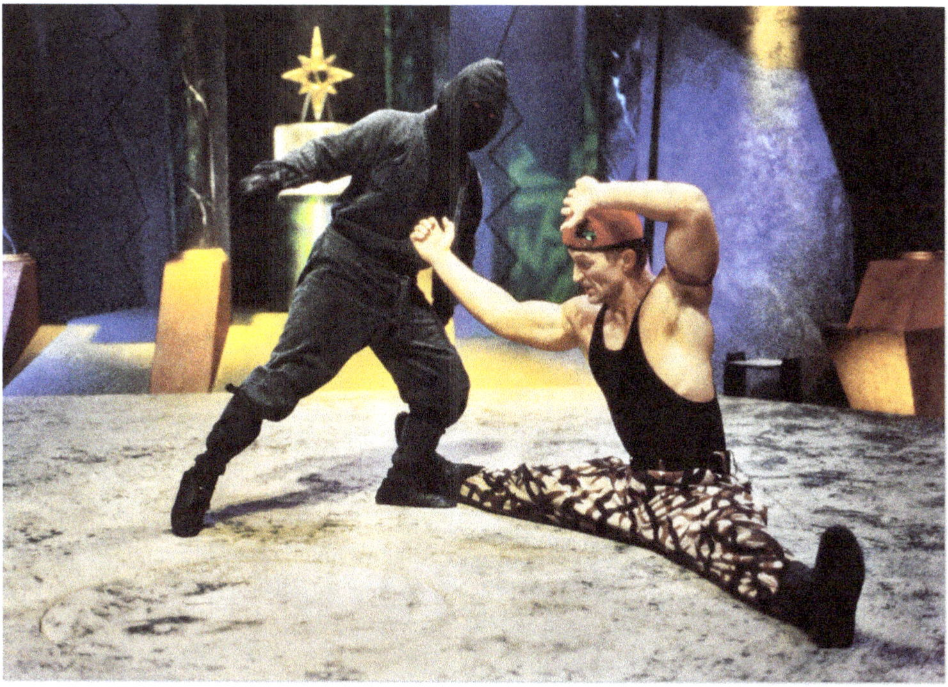

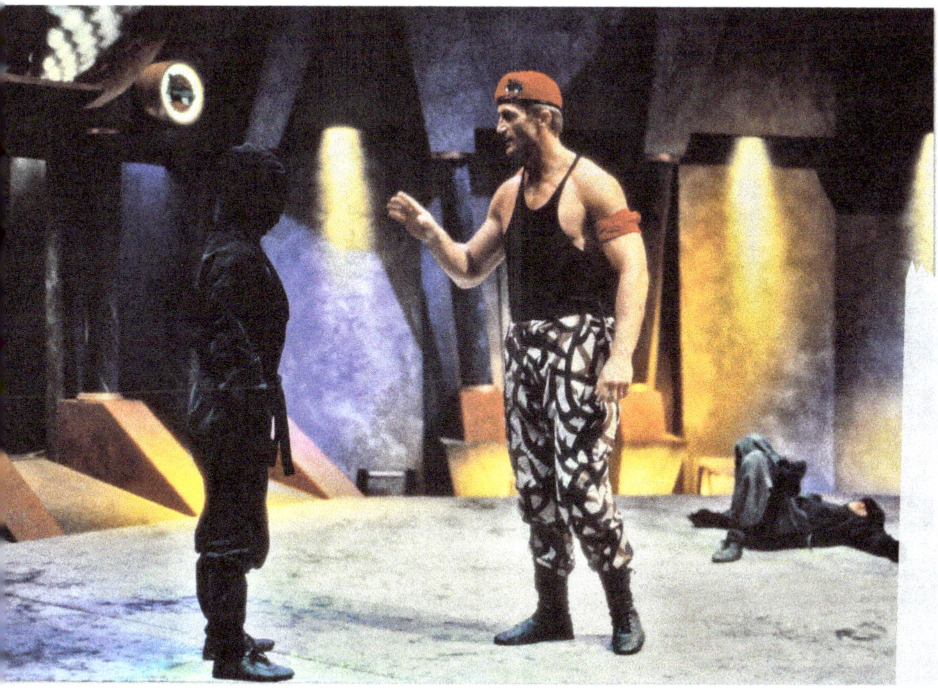

Suddenly he has a strange weapon, like an axe, made out of two handles that press together with a spike on the end. He then turns it inside out for a more pointed/stabby weapon.

(NOTE: I tried to find out what type of weapon this is but was unable to. It's possible it was designed especially for Ho-Sung and the show to sell as a toy.)

He jumps back on the beam, launching a ninja through the air, circus-act style, sending it through a giant The Machine logo. It's obviously a camera trick, but he celebrates, looking hyped up for the match ahead.

Dragon Star Championship:
Superstar (Champion) vs. The Machine (Challenger)

We see Superstar and The Machine emerge from the rapid transit system that takes the Masters to the various Battle Zones. In reality, they are on the earthquake ride at Universal. The voiceover explains the rules for this once-in-a-lifetime match. At the main terminal of the transit system, there is a giant Dragon Star replica (the same one from the unaired pilot that has occasionally been set dressing in season one). To win the fight, a Master must open the replica up and place their Ki Symbol in it. There are no other rules.

This whole battle is incredibly unique, and that begins with this introduction. As the two Masters get off their respective trains, the lighting is different. Red for The Machine and blue for Superstar, matching their Ki Symbol aesthetics. The whole thing has a very cinematic feel, which was far from accidental.

> *I am a big fan of the Western (genre of movies). We wanted this fight to feel epic, important. I tried to bring some of that (Western style) to the direction.*

Isaac Florentine
Director

Ninjas appear almost immediately. Wave after wave of them, and the Masters go to work, treating this fight like a beat-'em-up video game. There are lots of WMAC set dressing and props in these shots, signs pointing the way to the Arena or different Battle Zones, which adds a touch of realism to the setting.

There's no way we could have done something like that without Universal. We couldn't have pulled something of that level of production value off anywhere else, not on our budget.

Norman Grossfeld
Executive Producer

There's a great sequence as Superstar battles ninjas. He sees an opening to jump to the middle platform of the tram system, but as soon as he lands, three ninjas jump up from the next set of tracks to greet him. This is a shot that we'll see used in various intro packages and recaps in the future.

Superstar then hits a wall-run spin-kick, an impressive sight perfect for this style of fight. The angle is great, and the small enclosed space makes it look even more impactful.

While he's doing this, The Machine keeps pace with him, keeping the fighters neck-and-neck for their race to the Dragon Star.

Then, out of nowhere, the ground begins to shake! An earthquake is striking the WMAC! We cut quickly to the Inner Sanctum and see they are feeling it as well. The fight rages on underground, though, with The Machine spinning a ninja into another before scoring with a big punch. He looks to make a move towards the Dragon Star replica, but another tram pulls up, blocking him. The doors open to reveal thirty to forty ninjas spilling out!

As they begin to spill out, another reverberation rocks the Masters, Superstar yelling "Watch out!" to his rival.

That was a tough shoot, but a fun one. It was very physically intense.

Hakim Alston
The Machine

The earthquake absolutely rocks the underground trams. The ground splits open, and ninjas go flying everywhere. We cut to the Arena where the guard-ninjas on the platform go plummeting to the ground below as sparks fly. There's a fire in the underground tramway system, and the Inner Sanctum is shaking to its foundations as pieces of the ceiling fly off! A truck almost falls on The Machine in the underground!

This insanity is filmed wildly different from the rest of the show, with shaky, almost hand-held camera shots. It reminds me of *Cloverfield*, a film that wouldn't come along for over a decade. It's dramatic, engrossing, and above all, cinematic.

This was a big moment for the show. We really wanted it to feel epic.

Isaac Florentine
Director

In the tunnels, both Superstar and The Machine are carrying ninjas, seemingly to safety, when the Council voiceover booms out for them to continue. There must be a winner! The Machine then promptly tosses the ninja he'd been carrying onto the tracks behind him, a shot Norman Grossfeld remains proud of.

There's a shot (in the underground fight) where Hakim has a ninja. And just out of the blue, we had the idea of tossing the ninja. So we shot it with the ninja, then swapped out a dummy, and you can barely tell unless you're looking for it. That's the kind of creativity we had on set, the kind of attitude. The shot ended up looking great.

Norman Grossfeld
Executive Producer

The fighters press on, drawing closer to the Dragon Star replica that is to house their Ki Symbols. As they approach, a water main breaks, flooding the area! The Machine makes it onto a tram to keep his footing as Superstar clings to a pole, trying desperately to hold on! We cut back and forth between them, the drama at a series high, and we see Superstar lose his grip, getting washed away!

Knowing this is his chance, The Machine makes a lunge for the Dragon Star, opens it, and places his symbol inside for the win!

For all intents and purposes, this fight is the high point of the series. While the storyline driven episodes to come provide a lot of dramatic character moments, this episode is the peak of the cinematic, in-fight storytelling. It marks the end of the show's original iteration in my mind. In fact, I'd argue it's the perfect balance of season one's sports-based emphasis and season two's more dramatic inclinations.

After the match, a drenched but otherwise okay Superstar embraces The Machine. Then, back in the Inner Sanctum, we see the reactions of some of their fellow Masters. Red Dragon cheers on his friend while The Bam comments that it was the toughest match he's ever seen. Meanwhile, Tracer and Warlock try to impress Chameleon.

I hung around with Sophia (Crawford, Chameleon) at first since we both started at the same time, and I didn't really know any of the cast coming into the show. She was great to work with.

Michael Foley
Tracer

Michael was a very sweet guy. We kind of gravitated to each other as newbies. He was very kind. Just a sweetheart.

Sophia Crawford
Chameleon

The Machine has made his way back to the Arena and onto the platform, still dripping wet, to claim the Dragon Star. After weeks of being locked in the Cell, it rises as the voiceover narrates the importance of the Star. It is a symbol of being the World's Greatest Martial Artist. He claims the Star and poses.

A Reshuffle in Shooting?
In the Story Outline document for season two, this episode originally included the ladies' fights that are featured in the next episode, complete with different results (which we will cover next chapter). These fights were likely shifted to their own episode in favor of giving the "trial" story more screen time without scraping the fights entirely since they had already been shot.

I was happy to be champion, sure. I wasn't as concerned about it as some others, but it's a good feeling.

Hakim Alston
The Machine

This week's post-credit scene is The Machine talking about adjusting curve balls and expecting the unexpected. Considering how much of season two is a reaction to unforeseen circumstances that are out of the producer's control, this lesson probably was something that hit close to home for the crew of the show.

"Dragon Star Rematch" remains one of the best and most iconic episodes of the series. With a one of a kind fight and major drama and story advancement, it is a real contender for the title of best episode of the show.

Script page showing scene with Chameleon rescuing Baby only a split second was used in the final episode. Script from Jamie Webster.

Greg Hart and Nick Farrell, from the Art Department, standing in front of a giant Dragon Star. Photo from Kathy Pilon.

<u>WMAC MASTERS -- EPISODE #202</u>

          TIGER CLAW
      Forgiveness, Herb -- It's one of the
      eight points of the Dragon Star,
      remember?

CUT TO REACTION of TRACER and WARLOCK who've been SKULKING in a CORNER
of the INNER SANCTUM.

28.   **INNER SANCTUM-- TREMOR**   28

ATHLETES REGAIN THEIR FOOTING after the first TREMOR

      ~~CHI CHROMOSOME~~ *Great Wolf*
    What was that?

         PRINCESS
    Felt like an earthquake.

         THE BAM
    No way, man.

          YIN YANG MAN
    Well, if it was an earthquake, those
    guys better watch out. They're
    fighting underground.

36.   **INNER SANCTUM**

The INNER SANCTUM is SHAKING VIOLENTLY from the earthquake.
The DEMI-DOME is in its season one position, over the yin-yang floor, shaking
violently, about to fall over. Just as it's about to crash on the iguana, Chameleon ru
snatches "Baby." The dome immediately comes crashing down. TRACER and WA
WITNESS this incredible rescue.

Must come out of this with 2 shots!

The Machine and Superstar surrounded by Ninjas in their Dragon Star Rematch.
Photo from Bruce Heinsius Photography.

CHAPTER 22

S2E03:
Ladies Night

Chameleon vs. Babydoll

Princess vs. Lady Lightning

"It was a very welcoming cast"

After the iconic and dramatic "Dragon Star Rematch", the show switches pace, focusing on the ladies of the WMAC for an episode. This serves not only to give some well-deserved screentime to the likes of Lady Lightning but also lets the story breathe. Rather than feeling like a sprint from plot point to plot point, the show allows room to move naturally along the narrative, a sophisticated choice for a kid's show.

We start with another previously on *WMAC Masters* segment, then head to the Inner Sanctum where Tsunami is at a fish tank, of all things. This seems random, but his presence there makes more sense in the script's original draft: he challenges Tracer to a contest of catching fish. Tracer believes the unspoken rule is that they must use their bare hands, but Tsunami never said that and produces a net to win. This is a version of the contest we will see develop between Star Warrior and Turbo and was cut in favor of the latter.

Lady Lightning emerges on a staircase wearing a black robe, throwing away her old, multi-colored gear. "Getting rid of bad memories," she says. Apparently, between seasons (or some other time off-camera), she lost the Dragon Star to Black Widow (who is *not* Tarantula). She says showtime is coming up.

Preliminary Match One
Competitors:
Chameleon vs. Babydoll ⊙ ⊙ ⊙ ✧
Battle Zone: Dark City
Ninjas: Unknown

This is little more than clips. Babydoll had already moved on by this point (see Chapter 19), so this was likely just repurposing footage. There really isn't much to dig into here. It's kind of sad, especially considering it's the debut for Chameleon, who will be a major player this season. Her role was even larger than Babydoll's was the previous year.

However, in the original Storyline Overview document, Babydoll is slated to win this fight, beginning her ascent throughout the season towards another chance at the brass ring.

I'd have loved to fight Bridgett. I just love her. I admired her so much.

Sophia Crawford
Chameleon

That would have been a dream fight for me, too!

Bridgett Riley
Babydoll

Back in the Inner Sanctum, Cyclone tells Lady Lightning she better get ready. Tsunami and Olympus help her disrobe, showing off her new, black gear. She's prepared to strike, she says.

That was something the producers came up with between seasons. It was part of the story of me losing the (Dragon Star) title. I liked the second outfit better. It felt more me.

Christine Rodrigues
Lady Lightning

We then get the opening credits, this time with Chameleon, Lady Lightning, and Princess included! We will see this iteration a few times this season, usually when the women of the WMAC are featured in fights.

After the opening, we are back in the Inner Sanctum and see Olympus clowning around, acting like an old-timey sports announcer, asking, "Will lady luck change for Lady Lightning?" Meanwhile, Superstar and Star Warrior bicker about Superstar not standing up for his brother when he was accused of being the Mysterious Ninja. Cyclone again pipes in, leading Great Wolf and Tiger Claw to joke about how he got hurt, which seems a little mean.

We then get entrances for the second preliminary match. Princess enters and performs a kata with her three-part staff, an impressive demonstration.

Mer Mer made me fall in love with Wushu. Her movements were so beautiful.

Shannon "Irish" Stewart
Script Supervisor

We also get our first look at Black Widow on the throne, looking mysterious and ominous. We hardly get to know her in the series, and as you will see in Chapter 31, she remains mysterious all these years later.

Lady Lightning then makes her re-debut, performing a kata with a pair of swords.

Preliminary Match Two

Competitors:
Princess ○○○○○ vs. **Lady Lightning**
Battle Zone: Dark City
Ninjas: Kabuki Warriors

The voiceover explains the rules of the fights to new viewers. The power bars are also along the bottom of the screen as opposed to on the sides as they were in the first season.

The fight starts with both ladies kicking copious amounts of ninja butt. Princess gets a chance to shine here, something she didn't really get in season one, executing a big double kick that looks very impressive.

> *Mer Mer was so great. We worked together on Power Rangers. She was really talented.*

Bridgett Riley
Babydoll

This fight sees Princess use a trash can lid to block a strike from a ninja, then tosses it at another ninja, taking it out. She's not disqualified, so one can assume that it's only a DQ if you strike another Master with an object. Ninjas are fair game.

Sophia Crawford
Chameleon
Discipline: Not Named In Series

Born in Hammersmith, England, Sophia Crawford has the distinction of being the only WMAC cast member to master the mystical art of mid-fight costume changes. A talented martial artist and stunt-woman, Sophia acted as stunt-double in many famous films and TV shows, including *Anchorman*, *Buffy: The Vampire Slayer*, and *Mighty Morphin Power Rangers*. She now owns and operates a coffee shop in Georgia.

The finish of this fight is particularly remarkable, making fantastic use of the Battle Zone. Both women trade moves that involve leaping off the hood of one of the abandoned cars that make up the set, with Lady Lightning scoring the big victory in the first match of her rebrand!

We then get a voiceover saying Chameleon won the previous match, so she'll take on Lady Lightning in the Battle Dome. That's how big of a throwaway match one was.

Back in the Inner Sanctum, Yin Yang Man is sad Princess didn't win. His Master Blaster is today, and they're both Wushu fighters. Tracer comes over, more or less just to be a jerk. Yin Yang Man calls him Tracy, with the expected result. Yin Yang Man smirks, saying, "Yeah, I know," clearly giving the bigger man a taste of his own medicine.

"He was just that good."

In Chapter 15 the cast and crew of the show shared their memories of the late, great Richard Branden. Perhaps no other scene in the series showcases his talents more than this one, his Master Blaster demonstration, The Historical Weapons of Wushu.

I remember being outside and watching (Richard) rehearse the segment. It was just wild. He'd do his form with one weapon, then just shout for the next one to be thrown to him, and he just wouldn't miss a beat. He'd go straight into the next weapon.

Jamie Webster
Great Wolf

The demonstration is one of the most impressive in the series. Yin Yang Man cycles through a succession of weapon forms. He demonstrates a sword, staff, double broadswords, a three-part staff, spear, some sort of long spear with a dagger-type attachment on the end, and a monkey stick.

To conclude his demonstration, he does a huge flip as a giant Yin Yang symbol lights up. The whole segment is one of possibly the best of the Master Blaster demonstrations.

Richard made it all look easy. He was just that good.

Jamie Webster
Great Wolf

The voiceover explains that martial artists using the Monkey Stick had to move like a monkey, apparently a historical Wushu technique.

Back in the Inner Sanctum, the Masters rightfully applaud his performance, and Princess delivers one of her only lines in the series. Meanwhile, Star Warrior is still angry at his brother for thinking he was the Mysterious Ninja. Cyclone yells at them in Japanese, and The Bam translates. Why was The Bam chosen to be the translator?

I think it was just to finally get me some lines. :laughs:

Willie Johnson
The Bam

We get one more commercial, then come back for the Battle Dome Final!

Battle Dome Final Competitors:
Chameleon vs. Lady Lightning

Both women are looking to start their Dragon Belts here, with Lady Lightning's comeback trail beginning in earnest. Chameleon starts the fight in green. This is our first real chance to see her in action, and she certainly looks up to par with the other ladies based on this fight.

This fight is an even, back-and-forth affair. Perhaps the most interesting aspect of the fight is it debuts Chameleon's palate-swap gimmick. A take on both the Chameleon's natural ability to blend with its surroundings and the idea of a ninja character switching colors, popularized by the *Mortal Kombat* video game series. She starts in green, moves to pink, then finally blue.

> *That was something the producers told me from the very beginning. The color change, and the lizard, Baby. It was always a part of it.*

Sophia Crawford
Chameleon

Chameleon ends up winning her first trip to the Battle Dome in a close-fought contest, narrowly beating the veteran Lady Lightning.

Before the ceremony of the Dragon Belt, they bring Baby the Lizard out to celebrate with Chameleon. Which is either very sweet or very weird, depending on how you look at it. The Dragon Belt ceremony commences without any drama.

> *That poor creature. It wasn't the easiest to work with, but it wasn't its fault. I think the hairspray they had me in, I think it irritated the poor guy. It was always trying to climb away and scratching my neck and shoulder.*

Sophia Crawford
Chameleon

Back in the Inner Sanctum, the Masters discuss the result. Most are impressed the newest combatant could take down the veteran Lady Lightning. Tracer and Warlock, however, whisper about possibly recruiting Chameleon to JuKiDo's cause. Tracer calls Cyclone a broken-down midget, a line you could never get away with today, especially on a kid's show, then mocks Cyclone's lack of English. Cyclone responds, "Get out of my face, Tracy!" Drawing a hearty laugh from everyone except Tracer and Warlock.

Cyclone's lack of English was not an invention of the show. He told me that he spoke very little English at the time and would often rely on an interpreter. This scene was a way to show he was, in fact, a part of the team, language barrier or not.

"Integrating new members into an established cast can be difficult," one member of the crew told me. "It definitely seemed like there was a little divide at times."

I'd say that there was some aloofness from some of the newer faces. Tracer in particular. I don't know if that was just his personality or if it was part of his acting since he was there to destroy the WMAC, but it's fair to say there was some separation.

Hakim Alston
The Machine

It should be noted that in my interviews with Michael Foley, who played Tracer, he never mentioned any sort of divide or tension between the actors. Though in retrospect, the following quote could be viewed in that light.

My first day on set was a lot of fun. I had a mini-reunion with Isaac (Florentine), and he introduced me to the cast. Chameleon was new, too. So we hung out a bit and became friends. For some reason, Great Wolf and Tiger Claw were also pretty open and friendly towards us.

Michael Foley
Tracer

It is possible that any sort of tension or aloofness was due to Foley and Crawford coming from outside the NASKA circuit. Therefore they didn't know as many (or any) of their fellow castmates coming in. Mike Chat, having performed on the circuit even at his young age, didn't recall any sort of tension.

No, it was a very welcoming cast. I was intimidated, sure, because those guys were some of my heroes, but that was just on me.

Mike Chat
Wizard

I think whatever tension there was went away after they saw me perform, got to know me and my heart. That's how martial arts is. You just put it out there, and it connects people. I never had any trouble with egos or any of the cast, anything like that.

Sophia Crawford
Chameleon

Our post-credits scene is Lady Lightning talking about how it's what is on the inside that counts, not the outside. A change in costume isn't going to change your luck around.

This was a fun episode, both from a character and action standpoint. The new faces in the cast really start to shine, and the show's new direction has taken root and is clicking. The only real downside to this episode is the short shrift that Bridgett Riley gets. It's such a shame that she departed the show when she did, as she would have excelled in the second season. That gripe aside, "Ladies Night" is definitely an episode to never skip.

Mer Mer Chen demonstrating a staff form. Photo from Bruce Heinsius Photography.

Chameleon and Baby. Photo from Sophia Crawford.

Promotional photo of Chameleon. Photo from Bruce Heinsius Photography.

Lady Lightning kicks into action. Photo from Bruce Heinsius Photography.

CHAPTER 23

Interlude: They're Not Dolls, They're Action Figures

The Toys of WMAC Masters

"It didn't seem like real life"

Bandai's most memorable contribution to the *WMAC Masters* legacy, aside from financing the production of the actual episodes of season one, was the production of the *WMAC Masters* action figures. The first (and, unfortunately, only) line of WMAC Action figures featured Red Dragon, The Machine, Superstar, Star Warrior, Great Wolf, Tsunami, Tiger Claw, Olympus, and Turbo, released as two series. In addition, there were also several play-sets released featuring Battle Zones, as well as a Dragon Belt play-set.

Though these toys were an early consideration, they didn't hit shelves until late 1995, and some parts of the country dragged into 1996 due to distribution.

> *It's a long process (to make the toys). They have to design them, get approvals, then make the molds... It's a long time from conception to toys on shelves.*

Norman Grossfeld
Executive Producer

Each figure came decked out in their full costume, The Machine's even including his armor, most sporting a weapon as well. Each figure had an "action move," usually a kick or punch of some sort, and each was packed with a not-quite-life-sized version of the fighter's Ki Symbol, which could be added to the Dragon Belt (sold separately).

The figures have a good likeness to the characters, especially by mid-90s standards, before the era of real scan technology. The play-sets (Mayan Temple, Stone Forest, Ghost Town, and Arena) didn't quite resemble the Battle Zones as faithfully but were still an exciting addition
to the line.

The cast was excited about the prospect of being turned into action figures, and those chosen to be in the first wave were thrilled.

> *You knew if you were one of the toys, you were going to be one of the featured performers.*

Chris Casamassa
Red Dragon

I was really excited. It didn't seem like real life. I'm a collector. I collect old Star Wars toys, so to have a toy of me? It was unreal.

Jamie Webster
Great Wolf

In fact, Herb Perez cites the action figure as a deciding factor in why he joined the show.

When the producers approached me to do the show, I was on the fence initially. I went out to New York to spend some time with them, and they convinced me, primarily because they told me I'd get to be an action figure. I figured when would I ever get that chance again?

Herb Perez
Olympus

Not all the fighters were collectors, so some coaching was required to teach them the proper way to refer to the toy line.

They were very clear. They're not dolls, they're action figures. :laughs:

Chris Casamassa
Red Dragon

The figures were a key consideration for Bandai. They were the primary way to earn their investment and were a significant metric for the show's success.

At the end of the day, we wanted to sell licenses, we wanted to sell toys. A lot of what we did (on the show) was about how to sell more toys. I wish that wasn't the case because we all believed in the message we were trying to tell, but it was the only way we could make the show.

Norman Grossfeld
Executive Producer

It was an unfortunate reality, and fascinating dichotomy- *WMAC Masters* was a show with a message that the cast and crew believed in deeply, but it was also a not-so-thinly-veiled campaign to sell toys to kids. "Power Rangers meets the WWF" is the easiest way to explain *WMAC Masters* to the uninitiated, but the show's depth and message made it so much more than that, but at the end of the day, that's what Bandai wanted it to be. So was *WMAC Masters* a show with an identity crisis?

It depends on who you ask. To the producers, the commercial aspects of the show remained top of mind. It was their job to make the show, and selling merchandise was the biggest part of that. It wasn't a philosophic quandary to be wrestled with; it was simply the reality of the situation, "the nature of the beast," as one staff member put it. Without the merchandising, there'd be no show- it was as simple as that.

For the cast, however, it was a different story.

I didn't really worry about that stuff. I mean, if you were a toy character, you got more screen time, which everybody wanted, so I was happy to be one, but I didn't really worry about... "the soul of the show" or whatever.

Jamie Webster
Great Wolf

It wasn't my job to think about that stuff. :laughs:

Johnny Lee Smith
Tiger Claw

Significant money was sunk into promoting the toy line as a vital (or most critical, depending) part of the show. Commercials were made, toy fairs were attended, and promotional material appeared in magazines.

I filmed a commercial. They flew me out to California. I was in the full costume. It was a fun time. Basically, kids were playing with the toys, and I walked into the room as a real-life one. It was a day's shoot. I was happy they picked me out of all the characters to do the commercial.

Mike Bernardo
Turbo

While this author could not find that particular commercial archived online, another commercial that featured a child playing with the toys and using them to beat up the camera is still on YouTube. It is very much what you'd expect from a 1995 kids' toy commercial. Another commercial also remains online. This one is a straightforward look at the toys, their action, and the Ki Symbols. There was also a commercial for the three volumes of VHS tapes that were released, which as of this writing, remains online as well.

With at least three, possibly four commercials out in the world, it would be hard to accuse Bandai of not adequately promoting the toy lines. However, whether they could get them on store shelves was another matter.

I know that because of the name, they had a lot more work to do to get it into stores, places like Toys "R" Us, KB Toys. It was a new property, which is hard enough, but they had to explain what it really was.

Norman Grossfeld
Executive Producer

While I was unable to reach anyone at Bandai to discuss the toys (their response stated that they had no records of the toy line), the memories of the people involved were fairly uniform. Distribution was uneven, but sales were good, at least for the level of market impact they were able to achieve.

They always told us the toys sold well. I guess it just wasn't as good as they wanted.

Chris Casamassa
Red Dragon

By 1995 action figure popularity had waned slightly from its peak in the 80s, where *Star Wars*, *GI Joe*, and *Transformers* toys dominated store shelves. However, it was still big business, with IPs like the WWF, Power Rangers, and various Disney properties moving a considerable number of units. In addition, *Star Wars* was about to launch its massively popular Power of the Force line, making space on store shelves even more scarce. Competing with so many established, heavyweight products made Bandai's job even harder.

For the Masters themselves, having an action figure of themselves was a big deal.

Having a figure of yourself, not a character you play on screen, but actually you… it was the first time something like that had happened for martial artists.

Chris Casamassa
Red Dragon

I think my mom bought all of the Tsunami figures. :laughs: As part of Power Rangers, I'd had figures, but it was always a character, so having one of me was special.

Hien Nguyen
Tsunami

I loved it. It was a dream come true.

Jamie Webster
Great Wolf

The Dragon Belt accessory was worth mentioning, which was sold separately and used to house the Ki Symbols each action figure came with. It is notable for featuring four bonus Ki Symbols of fighters who did not get featured in the toy line or, in two cases, in the show at all.

Cyclone and Yin Yang Man were given Ki Symbols, as were two characters called "Hollywood" and "All American." While these two characters were loosely planned, they weren't included in the Dragon Belt to tease their eventual debuts but rather to make the show's universe feel bigger.

We wanted kids to think that there were more fighters out there than just the ones we see every week.

Norman Grossfeld
Executive Producer

The fact that Cyclone and Yin Yang Man were chosen indicates they were likely not in consideration for the "next" line of toys, which would have come out towards the end of season two or the beginning of season three. We will cover this potential toy line, as well as a few other products, later, but first there bears mentioning some other merchandise that made it to shelves, or maybe didn't, depending on who is remembering.

> *There were going to be lots of things, but unfortunately, we just didn't have the backing to make it to market with most of them.*

Norman Grossfeld
Executive Producer

Left to right: Herb Perez, Ho-Sung Pak, Johnny Lee Smith, Kathy (Borland) Pilon, Chris Casamassa, Hakim Alston, Norman Grossfeld, Jamie Webster at New York Toy Fair. Photo from Kathy Pilon.

Sales material for first wave of *WMAC Masters* action figures. Photo from Dan Hubp.

There was to be a second toy line, which would feature Yin Yang Man along with several other characters that never got the full toy treatment. The line never saw the light of day, despite promo material being printed for them. This line was a set of 3-inch collectibles, two inches smaller than the main action figures, and not pose-able, instead featuring the fighters in "exciting action poses." The line featured twelve figures, seven of which were featured in the main figure line (Red Dragon, Olympus, The Machine, Superstar, Tsunami, Great Wolf, and Tiger Claw), and five new figures (Yin Yang Man, Babydoll, Lady Lightning, the Red Ninja Warrior, and the Kabuki Warrior).

These figures never made it to market, despite printed promotional order forms (to be sent to stores). Herb Perez speculated it was canceled due to the frayed relationship with the toy company after the end of the first season when they pulled funding.

This was a particular disappointment for the ladies of the show, who were not represented in the main toy line.

I remember them doing art, you know, mock-ups for an action figure, but none ever came out. It was disappointing. It would have been super cool to have a toy, not just like, you in a costume (on Power Rangers).

Bridgett Riley
Babydoll

I remember there was supposed to be a toy, but it never came out. I guess they didn't think (the ladies) would sell well enough.

Christine Rodrigues
Lady Lightning

In addition to action figures, there was a planned line of Halloween costumes that is the subject of considerable debate. Herb Perez can't remember if his ever made it to stores. However,there are photos of a child Olympus costume on the internet, so odds are at least a few squeaked out. Red Dragon, Tiger Claw, and Great Wolf all vaguely recalled potential Halloween costumes of their outfits, but there has been no evidence of them found. A reseller site has Olympus listed as "out of stock" as of this writing, with the costume manufacturers listed as Disguise Masters. Research was unable to confirm if this was just a strange way of listing *WMAC Masters*, but that is the conclusion I lean toward, as no listings for Disguise Masters costumes popped up in my research.

In addition to the Olympus costume, there were other *WMAC Masters* releases. Four books for young readers were released during the show's run, two by Michael Eng ("The Ultimate Challenge" and "Power of the Ninja") and two by Charles Hoffman ("Quest for the Dragon Star" and "Enter the Battle Dome"). Unfortunately, like everything associated with WMAC Masters, they are long out of print and go for excessive amounts of money on the secondary market.

There were other products in development that never saw the light of day due to the impending cancellation of the show, which we will dive into in the chapter "All That Could Have Been." It is a sad testament to the show's failure to convince licensees and stores that we do not have more WMAC merchandise to discuss. It's a paltry picking for a show that was, supposedly, all about moving merchandise. This failure to connect with merchandisers and stores is in no way a condemnation of the show's quality, but perhaps one of the efforts of Bandai to market it, or possibly their failure to understand it. Carlin West, the concept's creator, thought that lack of understanding might have been a bit more sinister.

> *Think about it. What was their biggest IP at the time? Power Rangers. A show about martial arts. Aimed at kids. They didn't want to cut into their own margins, take attention and money away from their main product, so of course, we never got the support.*

Carlin West
Series Creator

Others weren't so sure.

Asst.	Description	Individual Package			Std. Pack	Master Carton			Cube	Weight	UPC
		H	W	D		H	W	D			
2801	3" Collectible Figures (12)	8	6	1.5	24	9	15.25	5.125	0.5	3 lbs.	1 00 45557 02801 2
2810	5" Action Figures (6)	10	8	2	12	11	9.5	20	2.0	5 lbs.	0 00 45557 02810 7
2805	Dragon Belt Set	12	8	2	12	12.5	10	12.5	1.0	6 lbs.	1 00 45557 02805 0

Sales material for unreleased scond *WMAC Masters* toy line. Photo from Dan Hubp.

I don't think they (Bandai) ever really "got" the show, even though they were financing it. There was one point where they wanted us to work in thumb wrestling into the show because they had an idea to sell thumb wrestling rings. They had mock-ups and everything designed. We fought on that one and won, thankfully. But that was the kind of stuff we'd have to deal with.

Dan Hubp
Production Designer, Editor

That story, more than any other, encapsulates the challenges *WMAC Masters* faced on the merchandising side. Its partner company could not envision toys that fit the show's direction, and what toys they could agree on ended up never making it to market. *WMAC Masters* may have lasted much longer had things been different, but it wasn't to be.

The 1996 New York Toy Fair. Photos from Jamie Webster.

CHAPTER 24

S2E04:
Fired Up

Great Wolf vs. Tsunami

Star Warrior vs. Red Dragon

"They kind of gave it to him and said, "figure it out!""

Inside the Inner Sanctum, we see Turbo and Yin Yang Man gossip about what is in the briefcase Olympus is carrying around. Their rivalry seems to have led to a budding friendship based in the heat of combat. This is actually another indicator of Turbo's evolving character. He's no longer the lone wolf that everyone else dislikes. He's still the same person, but his competitiveness, skill, and straightforward attitude have started to earn the respect of his fellow Masters, however begrudgingly. As the season continues, so will this storyline, setting him up as almost an anti-hero. I equated him to the Punisher in Marvel Comics.

> *Yeah, that was what we were going for. I was never sure how much it came across, but that transformation was definitely part of the plan. I was still the same guy I was before, but now that there were really villainous characters, I wasn't so bad.*

Mike Bernardo
Turbo

Olympus overhears them and decides to show them, doing a Pulp Fiction style reveal, complete with surprised reactions. Tiger Claw and Tsunami come over to look as well and are suitably impressed, everyone geeking out over whatever Olympus is hiding. Red Dragon, however, isn't interested. He's going for full Dragon Belt today, and he is focused.

Back in the Inner Sanctum, Olympus reveals what's in the briefcase. It's a disc shooter of his own design. Everyone handles it, showering him with praise. Just about everyone, anyway, as Turbo snarkily asks what it has to do with martial arts. Olympus explains it requires calm and concentration, just like any other martial arts technique. Tracer pipes in that he used something like it when he was deployed. Olympus says he doubts it since he invented it himself.

In the Inner Sanctum, Chameleon and Tiger Claw talk about Red Dragon going for his full Dragon Belt today. Tiger Claw says The Machine and Red Dragon are best friends, so it could be challenging for him. If anyone would know about taking on your best friend, it'd be Tiger Claw!

Preliminary Match One
Competitors:
Great Wolf ⬡⬡⬡⬡⬡⬡⬡ vs. Tsunami ⬡⬡⬡⬡⬡
Battle Zone: Ghost Town
Ninjas: Ghost

We get a goofy tease of a storm as Great Wolf warms up, and the referee warns Tsunami about using any debris around the Battle Zone as a weapon, a nice bit of continuity. Also of note, Tsunami has picked up two more Ki Symbols in off-screen competition, which seems like a big jump.

This fight features the typical back and forth, evenly matched action you would expect, as well as a few gags that always seem to pop up when the Masters visit Ghost Town. The highlight is a Buster Keaton style gag where a building falls down around Tsunami after dealing with a couple of ninjas.

We head straight into the entrances for the second match!

Star Warrior enters the Arena and performs a weapon kata, which is always impressive. Red Dragon enters next and has a sword, doing a kata of his own. We also see The Machine on the throne, clad in his full armor, which is a funny sight. Finally, they head to the Battle Zone, so it's time for Red Dragon to take his next step towards full Dragon Belt!

Before the match starts, we get a shot of the Masters chatting in the Inner Sanctum. The Bam appears to be taking notes, and no explanation is given for this.

Preliminary Match Two
Competitors:
Star Warrior ⬡⬡⬡⬡⬡⬡⬡ vs. Red Dragon ●●●●●●●●●●●
Battle Zone: Mayan Mystery
Ninjas: Camouflage

Red Dragon sure was in this Battle Zone a lot.

This fight has an unusual cadence to it. The ninja warriors are called in, and then sent away very quickly, only to be called back after a few moments. Most of the other preliminary fights have a more routine timing to them, something the staff wanted to change up.

> *We really tried to keep the fights fresh. We didn't want every fight to have the same rhythm.*

Isaac Florentine
Director

Star Warrior controls the power bars for a good portion of the fight, but Red Dragon makes a big comeback to pick up the win and head to the Battle Dome!

This was a very even and exciting match. On an interesting note, Star Warrior is once again poised to play gatekeeper for someone looking for their full Dragon Belt, as he was against The Machine, but again doesn't get the job done.

Back in the Inner Sanctum, the Masters' clap for the efforts of both men. Then, Olympus gets on the magical WMAC mainframe computer and plays his weapon video before the Battle Dome.

Master Blaster- Olympus's New Toy

Olympus's invention is a disc launcher. He shoots it at some flash paper, which ignites as the disc passes through. There is a swinging target suspended in the Arena with three different rings to shoot through. He hesitates and looks down, seemingly defeated. He then swings up and nails the shot, all three targets exploding as the crowd goes wild!

This was a short and to the point Master Blaster. It didn't add anything to Olympus's character but got him some screen time. Something he could use, considering he was one of the main characters of season one.

> *We used (the Master Blaster segments) as a way to keep guys involved even if they weren't front and center of the storyline. As we got to season two especially.*

Norman Grossfeld
Executive Producer

Despite the odd nature of the disc shooter, Perez enjoyed working with it.

I loved it. That was a huge prop. One of the challenges was I wasn't a weapons guy. I was a one-on-one fighter. So they had to find something that would make sense for me to do. That thing was not cheap. They spent a lot of money to make all that stuff.

Herb Perez
Olympus

According to Dan Hubp, who directed some of the Master Blaster segments, there wasn't really a plan for the prop.

They kind of gave it to him and said, "figure it out!"

Dan Hubp
Production Designer, Editor

It was a lot of fun. The show was always about a lot of people not knowing exactly how it would play out, so you had to kind of figure it out.

Herb Perez
Olympus

In the end, Olympus's disc shooter Master Blaster, goes down as the strangest of the series. My research has led me to believe that the disc shooter gimmick was likely a demand from Bandai for toy purposes. Though it's impossible to prove that. One of the documents I was given described Red Dragon's weapons that shot sparks as being slated for toy production, so it is not a stretch. In the end, the crew, and especially Perez, deserve credit for making lemonade out of some strange, borderline silly lemons.

Back in the Inner Sanctum, everyone gives Olympus his props for a cool demonstration, even Turbo, his arch-rival. Turbo accidentally launches a disc at Chameleon, but thankfully it's a non-exploding kind, pinging harmlessly off her shoulder. She flips out on him, worried he could have hurt Baby, and he is appropriately apologetic. Warlock snickers behind Olympus's back, scheming. He and Tracer whisper off to the side. Tracer wants a gun like Olympus's, showing his bravado from earlier was false. Warlock says you can't shoot your way to the Dragon Star.

Battle Dome Final
Competitors:
Red Dragon ●●●●●●●●●● vs. Great Wolf ⬡⬡⬡⬡⬡⬡⬡

This fight is one of my favorite of the series and, as such, is getting a more in-depth breakdown than the others because I'm the author here, and I feel like gushing about it.

The match starts hot and heavy, with Great Wolf nailing a big throw. However, he's not about to lay down and let Red Dragon have an easy route to his full Dragon Belt. Ninjas come in quickly for this one. Great Wolf throws the dreaded knockout kick that felled Tiger Claw, but Red Dragon has done his homework. He does the splits to avoid it, and it's a really cool visual.

Great Wolf scores first, nailing a solid kick and sending Red Dragon into the cage. His lead is short-lived, as, a triple-kick combo scores for Red Dragon, equalizing the points at one.

We get several slow-motion shots in this fight, which seems weird considering the fast-paced nature of the match-up.

Red Dragon takes the lead with a smooth counter strike, nailing a back kick after avoiding a kick from Great Wolf. Great Wolf fires back with an amazing combo. He does a cartwheel, but instead of throwing a high kick like Red Dragon expects, he goes low with a leg sweep, knocking Red Dragon into the cage. He follows it up by smashing a pair of ninjas with a super flashy kick. The rest of the ninjas take that as their cue to get out of the Dome, leaving it one-on-one for the rest of the fight.

Both guys trade strikes, neither scoring. It's still tied up as we make our way into the home stretch, then Red Dragon scores with a wicked shotei (palm strike) with ten seconds left! Great Wolf fires back with a big back kick as time expires, but it's too late! The point doesn't count! Red Dragon wins!

This was possibly the best, most exciting Battle Dome in the series. It had everything a great Dome needs, excellent techniques, drama, and an overarching story. Even the twist ending came across well, the slight confusion of 'did it or didn't it count?' playing into Red Dragon's title chase.

I loved that fight. It really came together in the cage. We always rehearsed, but the directors always left us room to do our own thing, just giving us the outline. It was good in rehearsal, but once we were in there, it was one of my favorites.

Chris Casamassa
Red Dragon

That fight was a lot of fun. Our styles meshed really well together. We really clicked.

Jamie Webster
Great Wolf

Back in the Inner Sanctum, the Masters applaud the incredible fight. Then, Warlock says something suspicious, getting him weird looks from his fellow fighters and a glare from Tracer.

Red Dragon then claims his last Ki Symbol needed for full Dragon Belt in the Dragon Belt Ceremony. Nothing of note here except the strange freeze-frame ending that no one I spoke to could explain. They were probably just trying something different, but whatever their reasoning, it didn't come across well.

In the post-credits scene Olympus recaps the points of the Dragon Star for new fans.

"Fired Up" was light on story advancement but heavy on action and featured one of the best Battle Domes of the entire series. For fans of the more sports style of season one, focusing more on the tournament than JuKiDo, this will likely be your favorite episode of season two. It's definitely worth a re-watch regardless on the strength of Great Wolf versus Red Dragon alone.

Robert Tuscani taking a hit from Star Warrior. Photo from Robert Tuscani.

Tags from costume department for wardrobe continuity. Photo from Jamie Webster.

Promotional photo of Great Wolf. Photo from Bruce Heinsius Photography.

GREAT WOLF
- LEATHER / BEADS IN HAIR
- NECKLACE - BUGLE BEAD 2 STRANDS (2 ROWS)
- VEST, LOINCLOTH, PANTS - LT. TAN LEATHER W/ BRN. FUR ON SHOULDER, WHITE TASSELS (2) DOWN CF, FRINGE ON HEM, TURQ. TRIM
- SHOES - HI-TOP, LT. TAN MOCASSINS W/FRINGE (HIS)
- SOX - WHT
- WRIST CUFFS - LT. TAN W/ CONCHO, 2 FRINGE PIECES

GREAT WOLF

CHAPTER 25

S2E05: Wizard and Warlock

Wizard vs. Tiger Claw

Warlock vs. Kid Carmichael

"It was a dream come true. The whole thing"

After last week's more action-oriented episode this week's offering, "Wizard and Warlock," is a return to more story driven episodes, with the added bonus of a Dragon Star match! This episode is one of the best balances between the story advancement and on-screen action in the series and could be held up as one of the show's best episodes if not for some slight misfires in one of the fights.

The episode begins with The Machine entering the Arena with the Dragon Star. He will defend his championship today against his best friend, Red Dragon. First, though, we'll have two previously scheduled preliminary matches!

We get the typical show intro, then see Tsunami and Tracer bicker in the Inner Sanctum. Tracer says that "friends only get in the way" and that the only Dragon Star fight he will be excited for is his own.

We then head to the Arena, where Wizard makes his debut. The voiceover says Wizard was chosen by the Karate Grand Master (presumably the Council member) to represent karate, explaining why he isn't a WMAC recruit and doesn't have to do an initiation. Why the karate Grand Master would feel the need to do this, considering Red Dragon is going for the Dragon Star later and is, in fact, a karate fighter, isn't explained. It's a kid's show, after all. Most kids probably didn't worry about that stuff.

Wizard does his first kata, which includes a nice touch as he does a very similar kick technique to Warlock, which will take on greater meaning in just a few minutes.

In the Inner Sanctum, we see the Masters gossiping about Wizard. No one seems to know much about him, Lady Lightning comments he has a mysterious past. The Masters gossip idly until Warlock appears and says he can tell them all about Wizard because they're brothers.

It was one of those things where it was like, "Okay, yeah, cool." Mike worked for me at my school, and I'd known him since he was a kid (on the competitive circuit). I knew how amazing he was, I was excited for him to get this opportunity.

Larry Lam
Warlock

It was a dream come true, the whole thing. To come in and work with these amazing martial artists who I'd looked up to on the circuit for so long, and then to work closely with Larry, who had already kind of taken me under his wing. For a 19-year-old kid, it was just a dream.

Mike Chat
Wizard

The Masters interrogate Warlock. He says he no longer considers Wizard his brother because Wizard joined JuKiDo, then goes on to explain what, exactly, JuKiDo is. As Warlock explains it, JuKiDo was kicked out of the WMAC for not following the code of the Dragon Star and using martial arts for personal gain.

This is our introduction to JuKiDo, who we will come to know as the Big Bad of the show. It's the evil force conspiring to destroy the WMAC, or steal the Dragon Star, or something. We've seen Tracer and Warlock working together to try to get the Dragon Star and had clues that something bigger was afoot, and now it's revealed what, exactly, that is.

We wanted JuKiDo to be really the antithesis of the WMAC. They were the bad guys. They used martial arts for all the wrong reasons.

Norman Grossfeld
Executive Producer

While the introduction of JuKiDo is dramatic, it's not necessarily clear what their goals are. Early scripts for this episode indicate Superstar was originally going to provide the information about JuKiDo being kicked out of the WMAC, as well as some further detail. He was to point out an empty chair in the upper left of the Arena. This is supposedly where JuKiDo's council representative would sit, which has been left empty as a reminder of their betrayal.

With all that in mind, viewers then get Wizard's debut match, where he'll take on a WMAC veteran!

Preliminary Match One
Competitors:
Wizard vs. Tiger Claw ⬡⬡⬡⬡⬡⬡⬡
Battle Zone: Dark Alley
Ninjas: Black

As the fight begins, Tiger Claw busies himself with beating up some ninjas on a loading dock. He chucks a few off the dock, then does a fun pole-slide down to the street below to continue the beatings.

It was always fun to find new stuff to do. The directors gave us a lot of freedom.

Johnny Lee Smith
Tiger Claw

Meanwhile, Wizard gets his first taste of the WMAC recruits, showing off a markedly similar style to Warlock, despite (nominally) representing a different discipline. He shows off a variety of kicks, many with lots of extensions, just like Warlock.

As the one-versus-one portion begins, and we see a few shots of Wizard hitting techniques that seem to be missing pretty clearly, but are still being sold by Tiger Claw. This is likely just new fighter growing pains. A few seconds later, the same thing happens with a Tiger Claw move.

That was my first time doing camera fighting. Neither Johnny nor I were trained in it. We were real, full-contact karate sort of guys, so we were just doing what we knew how to do. We were really blocking each other's techniques. It felt like getting hit with a baseball bat.

Mike Chat
Wizard

Mike is such a talented guy. He was so good even though he was so young. And we were both laying it in that fight.

Johnny Lee Smith
Tiger Claw

Wizard and Tiger Claw prepare for battle. Photo from Bruce Heinsius Photography.

The ninjas come back in to save us from more not-clicking. Ninjas score a direct hit on Tiger Claw, and Wizard flies in behind them to nail him, emphasizing the power-vs-speed dynamic. This is another spot where Shannon Lee is missed. I don't know if kids would necessarily pick up on the story they're trying to tell in the fight.

I was maybe 150 pounds. He was probably 225 at the time. He was so much bigger than me. On camera, it really showed.

Mike Chat
Wizard

Tiger Claw nails Wizard with the knockout kick, but Wizard stays standing. Tiger Claw must not have hit it cleanly. Wizard replies by leaping over Tiger Claw and nailing a spin kick to book his place in his first Battle Dome final!

This was an effective, though not quite perfect, debut for Wizard. While there were moments when the fight didn't click, it still served its purpose, introducing the new character and making him look good. Having the fight end with a jaw-dropping moment like the flip and spin kick only helped to cement that status. This fight made Wizard seem important, not just another new face in a season full of them.

Back in the Arena, Kid Carmichael is making his entrance, followed by Warlock. They head to the Battle Zone, and we head back to the Inner Sanctum, where Wizard returns from his fight, pleased as punch. The Bam congratulates him.

"It's like a dream come true," Wizard says.

Superstar, Yin Yang Man, and Olympus all come over and are much less welcoming, giving him flak over Warlock's allegations. Wizard asks what, exactly, Warlock told them. He denies having no respect for the Dragon Star, telling the Masters the Warlock they've known is a lie!

On that note, we get a commercial break, then come back for match number two!

Michael Chaturantabut
Wizard
Discipline: Karate

Better known professionally by the much easier to spell Mike Chat, Wizard is a World Martial Arts Hall of Fame member. Sporting an absurdly long braid and sparkling outfit, he plays the half-brother of Larry "Warlock" Lam, although they are no relation. After *WMAC Masters* he would take the Masters to Power Rangers connection to a new level- starring as the Blue Ranger in *Power Rangers: Lightspeed Rescue*, and would go on to a multi-faceted career including MMA commentary.

Preliminary Match Two
Competitors:
Kid Carmichael ⬡ vs. Warlock ⬡⬡⬡⬡⬡⬡⬡
Battle Zone: Doom City
Ninjas: Kabuki Warriors

Kid Carmichael apparently picked up his first Battle Dome win sometime off-screen. Since it was never officially established in cannon who he beat, I asked Carmichael Simon who he thought he should have picked up his first win against.

Oh man, they never told us anything like that. I didn't even know they gave me the win. I'd say Yuji (Noguchi, Cyclone). I would have loved to fight him. He choreographed this fight. He was just so good.

Carmichael Simon
Kid Carmichael

This fight is wild. It's non-stop action from beginning to end, probably both men's best showing in the entire series. It's a total Hong Kong action bonanza, miles away from the style of season one.

They called (this fight) the fastest fight in the series, as far as how much stuff we packed into it. It definitely was my favorite fight. I wasn't getting brought in that much, I knew I wouldn't really have any more fights, so I really went all out.

Carmichael Simon
Kid Carmichael

That was a great fight. Carmichael had such great timing. We clicked really well. Definitely one of the most fun fights. It's always better when everything gels.

Larry Lam
Warlock

It's a match full of wild action and fantastic moves, where both guys come out looking great. Warlock picks up the victory, sending him to a battle with his brother in the next Battle Dome!

This match was the total opposite of the first. This is a perfect example of what kind of magic can happen when fighters click. Whereas the first fight seemed off despite the fact that both guys were obviously working hard, this fight fired on every cylinder, hitting all the right notes. The difference? Chemistry.

Larry and I had great chemistry. He was just so great to work with. I loved working with him, always did. I learned so much from him every time we worked together. I love that guy. He's like my big brother, still to this day.

Carmichael Simon
Kid Carmichael

That Battle Dome will have to wait, as tonight's main event is for a bigger prize, The Dragon Star! We see ninjas guarding the Tri-Chamber Cyber-Cell, the Council on high alert after the issues surrounding the last Dragon Star Match the platform hosted.

Back in the Inner Sanctum, the Masters collectively don't know who to believe. Great Wolf says both Wizard and Warlock are likely exaggerating. Yin Yang Man defends Warlock, a man he's known for quite some time.

On the platform in the Arena, we see Red Dragon perform a kata, complete with Chinese Dragon dancers and a voiceover telling the "Legend of the Red Dragon." It's quite the spectacle, very different from other pre-Dragon Star routines.

He then relinquishes his Dragon Belt, doing a kata with a spark-throwing set of weapons as the dragons dance around him.

Those were actually my competition weapons the prop department tricked out for the show. We were all worried they were going to light me on fire or something!

Chris Casamassa
Red Dragon

Notes attached to the storyline overview indicate that these weapons were in consideration to be made into toys, ala the *Mighty Morphin Power Rangers* weapons that were put out around that time. I doubt they would have thrown fire or sparklers, though.

There's no demonstration from the reigning champion this time. Instead, The Machine places the Dragon Star in the cell, and the fight begins!

Dragon Star Championship
Competitors: The Machine (Champion) vs. Red Dragon (Challenger)

As the fight begins, we get a very clear shot of what is obviously a mannequin in the Council area atop the Arena.

They tried not to make it obvious they were mannequins. Every once in a while, one of the staff would be up there and kind of puppet them, moving an arm or something to make it look like they were moving.

Shannon "Irish" Stewart
Script Supervisor

This fight is exactly what you'd expect from two of the most charismatic, exciting fighters on the show, big moves, drama, and excitement.

Perhaps the most memorable moment in the fight is a gag that Casamassa improvised.

That was improved. I just did a little "oh, I like this" face. That was all me.

Chris Casamassa
Red Dragon

In the end, the first defense curse strikes The Machine, just as it felled Olympus and Superstar before him, as Red Dragon takes the win with a big spinning kick!

I did not enjoy falling off that platform. I was not a fan.

Hakim Alston
The Machine

He did it once and said that was it! :laughs:

Chris Casamassa
Red Dragon

Alston and Casamassa were good friends in real life, and that friendship helped inspire their performances. As two of the main characters of the show, they faced off often, this match obviously being the pinnacle of that rivalry.

I loved working with Hakim. He's one of my best friends. The fights were always great, the energy was always great.

Chris Casamassa
Red Dragon

Chris was a joy to work with. It was like fighting my brother. Everyone talks about my rivalry with Ho-Sung, but to me, the one with Chris was better.

Hakim Alston
The Machine

We see Red Dragon claim his prize and celebrate atop the platform. No controversy in sight.

We fade from that sight to a shot of the empty arena, Battle Dome lowered. For some reason Wizard appears in the area usually reserved for the Council Members. He's apparently there to meet Warlock, who appears across from him. They snipe back and forth, obviously not on the best of terms. Out of nowhere, JuKiDo ninjas appear!

"Welcome to the Battle Dome, Wizard," Warlock says ominously, ending the show!

The only thing that keeps this episode from earnestly contending for the title of best episode in the series is the awkwardness in Tiger Claw versus Wizard. Everything else in this episode fires on all cylinders, and it remains a must-see during any re-watches.

Chris Casamassa
Red Dragon
Discipline: Karate

American karate royalty, clad in his trademark bright red gi, Chris Casamassa possesses a dorky charisma that often makes him the comic relief of the show. Don't let that silliness (or his babyfaced good looks) fool you- Red Dragon has fangs. A member of the American Karate Hall of Fame, Casamassa won several national titles in the late 80s and early 90s before retiring to focus on acting- playing the role of Scorpion in the *Mortal Kombat* film franchise.

Photos from Bruce Heinsius Photography.

CHAPTER 26

S2E06: Battle of the Brothers

"It wasn't a macho thing... you do your job"

After the last episode, "Battle of the Brothers" can feel like a real slowdown, but it's one the show needs. This episode features some much needed backstory and character development, and a tantalizing glimpse into the pre-history of the show.

The show opens with another Previously On... segment, reminding viewers of the cliffhanger from last week. We then pick up where that episode left off, with Warlock and his JuKiDo ninjas ambushing Wizard!

Wizard tries to escape by jumping from the balcony to the top of the Battle Dome. It's an amazing sight showcasing his agility and skill far better than the previous episode's fight with Tiger Claw. Warlock follows, and the two 'brothers' battle in the Dome. The first unsanctioned fight in the series!

The not-actually-a-Battle-Dome fight is very even, as you'd expect from two 'brothers.' Warlock, however, has an advantage because he's willing to fight dirty.

That scene was so much fun, but also a great learning experience for me. Not having any experience in acting or fighting on camera, Larry really took care of me. He'd explain between shots where I should move when the camera moves a certain way or how to make the technique look better for the camera.

Mike Chat
Wizard

There's also a strange, ominous effect on his voice as Warlock delivers some dialogue. Which was incredibly creepy to hear as a kid.

I didn't know they were going to do that, but it worked so well. Really made (the scene) feel different.

Larry Lam
Warlock

Despite Warlock's dastardly ways, Wizard begins to take control of the fight. He knocks Warlock into the cage, showing that the electricity is still on in the Dome. Warlock angrily calls in his ninja cohorts for assistance before leaving the cage himself so he won't be found at the scene of the crime.

Reference shot for the rarely seen JuKiDo ninja. Photo from Bruce Heinsius Photography.

                         I don't understand.

                         WARLOCK
               When we were young, Wizard left my
               family and became a member of the
               Jukido.

                         TSUNAMI
               Jukido?

                         GREAT WOLF
               I've heard of them. They're some
               sort of underground martial arts
               organization.

                         OLYMPUS
               I never thought they really
               existed.

SUPERSTAR knows something. He steps forward.

                         SUPERSTAR
               They exist, in fact, they were
               once part of the WMAC.

                         TSUNAMI
               What happened?

                         SUPERSTAR
               They were thrown out because they
               don't follow the code of the
               Dragon Code.

                         LADY LIGHTNING
               The code of the Dragon Star is
               the most important part of the WMAC.

                         SUPERSTAR
               Did you ever wonder about that
               empty council seat on the left
               side of the arena? That was
               Jukido, so they just leave it
               empty to this day.

                         TSUNAMI
               Jukido would probably do
               anything to get back at the WMAC

                         OLYMPUS
               Maybe they've already started.
               Maybe that's why Wizard is here.

                                        CUT TO:

Script page from "Wizard and Warlock" showing cut dialogue about JuKiDo. Script from Jamie Webster.

The ninjas infiltrate the cage and try to beat Wizard to a pulp. The Arena lighting goes absolutely crazy, adding to this scene's unique, nightmarish look. The ninjas are doing an absolute beat down on Wizard, but Tiger Claw ends up entering the Dome and saving the newest Master from further injury. He ends up ripping the mask off of JuKiDo ninja and seeing the strange red dragon symbol we saw previously tattooed on the man's head. The ninjas retreat, leaving Tiger Claw to help a badly battered Wizard out of the cage.

This scene stands out in the show as the most adult of any of the fights. It's a moment where the show's dynamic (good versus evil in a structured, tournament setting) is completely broken. As a kid, it was jarring and unsettling. Watching as an adult, it's a great moment of tonal shifting. The stakes have truly been raised by JuKiDo. The scene works on an action, dramatic, and emotional level, and it instills a sense of "bad things can happen" to the Masters, something any dramatic show needs to be successful. After all, if there's no doubt that good will triumph, what keeps people watching?

Sadly there was one major negative to come out of this scene, the injury of Akihiro "Cyclone" Noguchi in a stunt accident involving a misplaced trampoline. According to one stunt team member, the trampoline was at a bad angle, so when he made the jump, his leg planted into the ground, breaking.

The injury was unfortunate. I remember it well. He had been sitting on this rail while they rehearsed. He hopped down and jumped on the trampoline. When it was time to shoot, though, he stood up on the rail before jumping off. I never understood why.

Robert Tuscani
Electrician

It was an unfortunate accident that impacted Cyclone's character greatly. Consigning him to a background commentator rather than a competitor due to how the show was shot.

We didn't shoot episodes sequentially. We shot in blocks. So we shot all the Arena stuff (like Battle Domes), then shot the Inner Sanctum scenes. So we didn't have to set up and tear down sets multiple times.

Shannon "Irish" Stewart
Script Supervisor

The next day in the Inner Sanctum, we see Great Wolf and Yin Yang Man returning from the hospital, where they were checking on Wizard. They say he's in "bad shape" and that police are investigating. They ask Tiger Claw if Wizard said anything about who attacked him. Tiger Claw responds that Wizard told him, "You have to get my brother," right before passing out. Warlock, however, was nowhere to be found.

This makes Superstar and Chameleon suspicious, but Great Wolf defends Warlock. Superstar sulks off.

With the attack on Wizard, the day's competition has been suspended, leaving The Machine feeling the need to do something aggressive. He decides to do a breaking demonstration, bantering with Olympus while he sets up.

Tiger Claw describes the tattoo he saw on the JuKiDo ninja's head. We see Tracer has the same tattoo on the palm of his hand, a perfectly normal and not at all conspicuous place to get a secret society tattoo. Tiger Claw also pulls out a Ki Symbol, saying he found it after the attack. Great Wolf and Yin Yang Man both say they recognize it but can't quite place it. Chameleon says they should scan it into the WMAC computer. Lady Lightning says she'll scan it for them after Tsunami's demonstration.

Master Blaster Demo- Martial Arts Extreme!

No, Tsunami is not doing a kata on a skateboard, unfortunately. Extreme, in this instance, refers to extreme heat and extreme cold—fire and ice. He starts his demo with one of his patented back-flip kicks on a balloon, then walks on flaming hot coals on his bare feet. The voiceover says not to try this at home because this is a kid's show!

The ninjas then pour water into a Tsunami-branded bucket (not for sale, big missed merchandise opportunity!), and then an Arctic Chamber lowers from the rafters of the Arena. The water is chilled to a nice and frigid negative fifty-one degrees. A temperature that's squarely in the "danger" area of the meter on the front of the chamber. The chamber rises, showing that the water froze around a chain, forming a massive block of ice for Tsunami to break.

He delivers a version of Bruce Lee's famous one-inch punch, shattering the ice! He celebrates, and we cut to the Inner Sanctum, where everyone claps for him, except for Tracer, of course, who is busy carrying his own pile of bricks and setting them up next to The Machine, whistling the whole time.

They banter a bit. The Machine is obviously annoyed despite trying to ignore him. They decide to get into a breaking contest.

Lady Lightning then pulls up the WMAC Archives and scans in the Ki Symbol. It belongs to Striking Eagle, better known as Taimak! She tells Great Wolf, "it's a blast from your past." Superstar remembered their match "a long time ago," and Great Wolf recalls exposing him. He claimed to be Native American but wasn't. This was enough to get him kicked out of the WMAC, apparently.

Lady Lightning pulls up his match with Superstar, the WMAC computer showing the pilot's intro as it loads the file. We see Striking Eagle beat on some ninjas as the voiceover says his current status is inactive and ineligible. The computer says he had three total matches, and no Ki Symbol's won. We then see some of his fight with Superstar, complete with the season two style power bar graphics. We see Superstar hit the wall kick, pausing to let Striking Eagle get up. Unlike in the pilot, this is the end of the fight. We then get a shot of Striking Eagle watching Yin Yang Man warming up, which isn't explained.

The computer voiceover goes on to say Striking Eagle was last seen on tour in Europe with a fighter known as "The Ratt," another ex-WMAC Master.

This is the only appearance of The Ratt in *WMAC Masters*, and there is no information on him available online. The actor is not even listed on IMDB. Neither series Executive Producer Norman Grossfeld nor Production Designer/Editor Dan Hubp remembered the actor involved, noting that the part was not meant to be anything major, instead "something to make the show feel bigger, wider."

Tom Laskowski, a camera operator on the show, remembered a night shoot for a character that closely matched The Ratt, however. He described "A big, Eastern European guy in all red and gold" who could "take out five guys at once." He told me the shoot was atop a roof somewhere near Universal, with a unique neighbor.

It was right next to a garbage dump. It wasn't the most pleasant experience for any of us. And the actor (who played The Ratt) took forever to get to set.

Tom Laskowski
Camera Crew

His lateness put the shoot behind schedule, and with daylight approaching, it had to be abandoned. Due to the fact that The Ratt was a one-off character, they never returned to finish the shoot, which could be why the character only appeared briefly.

Jamie Webster recalled the Inner Sanctum segment well. It was one of the only times he was uncomfortable with what he was asked to say on the show. He recalled The Ratt being called Ratt Johnson as a knock on former director Pat Johnson. While no one associated with production remembered this, early drafts of the script do, in fact, refer to the fighter as "Rat Johnson." When shown the script, one production member speculated that the name was an attempt at an in-joke and was never intended to make air. Whatever the motivation, Webster recalled it none too fondly. He was also uncomfortable with his role as the one to call out Striking Eagle.

It was... it wasn't my favorite. I did it because I wasn't going to question the producers, but I felt weird about it. I didn't know (Taimak). I didn't want him thinking it was me saying all that stuff.

Jamie Webster
Great Wolf

This Striking Eagle slander was purely story-motivated, however. It allowed the producers and writers to use existing footage they otherwise would have left on a shelf to deepen the backstory of JuKiDo and their attempts to bring down the WMAC.

Anything we could do to deepen (the universe) without breaking the budget we tried to do.

Norman Grossfeld
Executive Producer

Red Dragon and Turbo, two long-time Masters who presumably would have known Striking Eagle and The Ratt, pipe up and say they didn't have anything to do with Wizard's attack. The Ki Symbol was a plant, a red herring designed to throw them off. Great Wolf reluctantly agrees, saying that "something's not right at the WMAC." Just as he says this, Tracer shows back up and does his Ricky Ricardo impression, brandishing a butane torch.

We then get an introduction to one of the more outlandish concepts of the show. Great Wolf explains to Tiger Claw that his father used to tell him about visions he would have that supposedly ran in their bloodline. Great Wolf has been having a recurring vision about something "really big and really bad" about to happen at the WMAC. Tiger Claw replies that he can't shake Wizard's last words to him the previous night. He thinks Wizard was accusing his brother, not calling for him.

Meanwhile, it's time for Tracer and The Machine's breaking contest. Tracer lights The Machine's stack of bricks. Everyone watches on, concerned. He then breaks them cleanly in half, earning a round of applause. The Machine then lights Tracer's stack on fire, which he breaks in kind (though, it should be noted, with a more noticeable pyro explosion). Everyone claps politely, despite their obvious distaste for him. He then plays with the fire on his fingers for some reason. Tracer and The Machine shake hands after their demonstration as Olympus jumps in with a fire extinguisher. Several masters congratulate The Machine as Great Wolf stares off into space, clearly distracted.

> *(Michael Foley) did the bit with the fire-gel on his fingers. Now that stuff will keep you from burning your skin off, but it's still really hot, really uncomfortable after more than a few seconds. He did two or three takes of it and didn't bat an eyelash.*

Jamie Webster
Great Wolf

Hakim Alston injured his hand during the breaking contest. Still, in our interview, he described it as "not a big deal," citing a similar situation during filming the *Mortal Kombat* film, where he was in a motorcycle accident shortly before filming his big scene.

> *It wasn't a macho thing. It was just, you do your job.*

Hakim Alston
The Machine

We fade to a shot of Great Wolf outside of the WMAC Headquarters. He lights a fire and does a "traditional dance" around it. He says, "As the smoke rises, so may my prayer rise to the heavens." It's an ancient ritual to protect the WMAC, heal Wizard, and preserve the code of the Dragon Star from evil. Chameleon hides in the bushes and watches.

In the current, more socially conscious times, this portrayal of his Native American heritage could be considered problematic, but Webster never took issue with it, then or now.

I'm about the hardest guy to offend in the world. I never thought (the portrayal) was exploitative or in bad taste or anything like that. I was proud that I was getting to represent my heritage on national TV. Historically there hadn't been much of that, and most of what there was was bad. It meant a lot to me and to my family that I was putting a positive image out there for our people. I'd go with my father to functions, onto reservations, and people would be really excited to see me because I was on TV, representing our culture. They were proud of me. So no, I never had any issue with anything they asked me to do with my heritage.

Jamie Webster
Great Wolf

Back in the underbelly of the Inner Sanctum, Tracer again berates Warlock, this time for his attack on Wizard. He calls him an idiot, leading Warlock to snipe back, "it's none of your business" what goes on between him and his brother. Tracer threateningly says, "Keep a low profile. We wouldn't want what happened to Panther to happen to you."

This was the show's way of writing Panther out of the storyline, implying that he had been some sort of sleeper agent for JuKiDo, but had somehow met their wrath. This was an on-the-fly change after his unfortunate injury, not something Erik Betts knew about in advance.

I had no idea about the story, where they were going with it, or what role I'd play. After the injury, I didn't keep watching the show, so I didn't know about (the allusion to Panther being bad) for a long time.

Erik Betts
Panther

The post-credits scene has Turbo talking about how it's sometimes hard to tell "the good guys" from "the bad guys," but all martial artists agree that doing drugs is wrong. He was not wearing a D.A.R.E. t-shirt but easily could have been. In fact, several *WMAC Masters* would tour local high schools to give demos and talks in tandem with D.A.R.E. programs as part of the show's continuing efforts to make a difference in the lives of young people.

"Battle of the Brothers" is one of the most story-driven episodes of the series and can, to fans who care more about the action than backstory, come across as a little boring or skip-able. For those fans doing a re-watch, however, it's vital to the lore of the show and really shouldn't be missed.

One of the several takes of Michael Foley lighting his fingers on fire. Photo from Bruce Heinsius Photography.

D.A.R.E. stood for Drug Abuse Resistance Education, and was a widespread program in the US in the 90s to teach elementary school age children about the dangers of drug use.

Tracer and Warlock conspiring in the Inner Sanctum. Photo from Bruce Heinsius Photography.

Early of draft of script showing The Ratt as Ratt Johnson. Script from Jamie Webster.

<u>WMAC MASTERS -- EPISODE #206</u>

                    YIN YANG
          Maybe that's why he was here-- attacking
          the Masters as some sort of revenge.

                    GREAT WOLF
          Yeah, but why Wizard of all people?

OLYMPUS AND RED DRAGON walk over to join the group

                    RED DRAGON
          C'mon, it's obvious Striking Eagle wasn't
          here. Somebody just planted the ki symbol
          to try and confuse us.

                    GREAT WOLF
          I really don't like the sound of this.   *unknown*

                    OLYMPUS
          Y'know, there was one other guy who left
          the WMAC in disgrace.

                    RED DRAGON
          Oh, yeah! The Ratt!

Lady Lightning nods--this is familiar to her. She starts typing away at the keyboard while
at the screen.

                    BAM
          Who?

                    OLYMPUS
          Ratt Johnson! He had one fight, if I can
          recall-- an exhibition match against the
          Machine!

                    LADY LIGHTNING
          I got his file right here! Check it out!

Hits Enter. The athletes all look at the screen.

22.   **LOCK DOWN OF SCREEN**   22

The computer accesses Ratt's file.

23.   **TAPE PACKAGE --THE RATT**   23

Tape package that shows the rooftop fight between the Ratt and The Machine.

24.   **INT. INNER SANCTUM - CONTINUOUS**   24

The Masters finish watching the playback.

                    TIGER CLAW
          He was huge!

CHAPTER 27

S2E07: Bad Blood

Star Warrior vs. The Machine

Turbo vs. The Bam

"We wanted to show martial arts was for everyone"

By this episode, the show was in full swing of its major storyline, and the show's focus had squarely been on the JuKiDo story for a while. In "Bad Blood," the B-Stories take the forefront as Turbo and Star Warrior, two of the toy line characters who have, thus far, had less screen time, take center stage.

This week's episode begins inside the Inner Sanctum. The competition resumes, and Star Warrior is going to be taking part. Superstar is giving him a pep-talk, saying he needs to focus on beating his opening opponent, The Machine, and not making the Dome. The Machine is there to say Star Warrior will not win, showing the Pak brothers versus The Machine rivalry is still going strong.

After the opening credits, Star Warrior enters the Arena. He performs a kata with his three-part staff, looking like a star.

(Ho-Young) always had some of the most impressive form demonstrations.

Norman Grossfeld
Executive Producer

Next, we see the The Machine enter the Arena, flanked by two red ninjas. He extends his staff and takes it apart, which seems a little weird (What can't his staff do?!) before doing a kata with it.

While the fighters make their way to the Battle Zone, viewers are shown inside the Inner Sanctum, where Tiger Claw is chatting with Cyclone (and The Bam, who translates). Cyclone has a funny video to show everyone. It's basically a highlight reel of ninjas getting beaten up with sound effects dubbed over it, akin to sports blooper videos that were popular at the time (forerunners to modern day DVD/Blu-Ray gag reels). The only obviously new footage is of a ghost ninja dancing for the camera.

We wanted to have a moment of levity. We were a kid's show that had just done a really heavy episode. We knew we were doing something a little darker, but we didn't want to be too dark. We wanted that balance.

Norman Grossfeld
Executive Producer

It was also a cost-savings technique. Reusing footage rather than shooting new segments was an easy way to make their slashed budget go further while not detracting from the actual fights.

Preliminary Match One
Competitors:
Star Warrior ⟡ ⟡ ⟡ ⟡ ⟡ ⟡ ⟡ vs. The Machine
Battle Zone: Ghost Town
Ninjas: Ghost

This is The Machine's return to competition after losing the Dragon Star, and he seems intent on making the ninjas pay for his loss, nailing a big spin kick that sends a ninja into a wagon wheel pile. He follows that up with a standing side kick sending another one into a wagon full of hay.

> *I had a lot of fun with the ninjas. This is probably my bad trait of being an oversized guy, but kind of pushing the ninjas around, it was extremely funny. I don't know if they agreed, but I enjoyed it.*

Hakim Alston
The Machine

The ninjas decide they've had enough and head for the hills. The one-on-one portion starts off pretty even on the power bars. As they go at it we get an over the shoulder shot, a particular favorite of Isaac Florentine.

> *Isaac loves spaghetti westerns. If you ever watch his stuff, it's very much in that Sergio Leonne style.*

Herb Perez
Olympus

This is another speed and technique versus power and size fight. It's a classic trope in martial arts carried over into the show. The power bars stay relatively even, but Star Warrior opens up a lead, scoring a rapid pair of front kicks for the win! The Machine, however, keeps trying to fight, having to be restrained. Once he realizes the fight is over, he calms down quickly. They shake hands after the fight, but the Council still calls The Machine to their chambers.

In the Inner Sanctum, the Masters are surprised at The Machine's actions. Tsunami is concerned, as The Machine rarely loses his cool (in fact, the very first vignette in the entire series was about this very topic!). Turbo snarks that maybe The Machine shouldn't be in the WMAC if he can't keep his composure, which seems harsh. Warlock calls it unsportsmanlike, causing Tiger Claw, who is still highly suspicious of Warlock, to get in Warlock's face. Tracer, of all people, calms the situation down, giving Warlock a warning look.

This continues the trend of Tracer being the brains of the operation and Warlock being the fiery young hothead, something that you wouldn't necessarily expect from looking at the two.

> *Everyone expects the big guy to be the dumb muscle. We wanted to do something different, a little more depth.*
>
> Michael Foley
> *Tracer*

We then see Turbo entering the Arena, performing a kata with his trademark staff. The Bam then enters the arena with a pair of swords and performs a kata of his own.

Preliminary Match Two
Competitors:
Turbo ◉ ◉ ◉ ◉ ◉ ◉  vs.
The Bam ⬡ ⬡ ⬡ ⬡ ⬡
Battle Zone: Mayan Mystery
Ninjas: Camouflage

The Bam starts the fight with a back-flip kick, an impressive sight.

Ho-Young Pak
Star Warrior
Discipline: Kung Fu

Superstar's real-life older brother, Star Warrior may have lacked his younger brother's charisma but was every bit the talented martial artist. A specialist in weapons forms, Ho-Young was a stunt double for the *Teenage Mutant Ninja Turtles* films before *WMAC Masters*. After the show he left the entertainment business, teaching martial arts and becoming an engineer, earning his Ph.D.

Isaac (Florentine, Director) made me do that flip so many times. It felt like a hundred times. I was so frustrated that at one point, I walked off set. I ended up calling one of my mentors for advice, and they told me to do my job. I went back and apologized and got the shot.

Willie Johnson
The Bam

Yes, I used to drive everyone crazy until I got the right shot. I remember that incident. It wasn't a big deal (for me). It was fine.

Isaac Florentine
Director

We see Turbo beating on some ninjas, looking absolutely shredded, like he just got out of the gym. For some reason, one of his staffs is planted into the ground near where he is fighting, and he picks it up, presumably to use against The Bam. Inexplicably, he isn't disqualified, and The Bam uses his hair braid to try to wrestle it from Turbo's grasp. It's a completely wild sequence.

I love Kung Fu films. From a young age, I knew I wanted to do (things like that). Those moves, I loved them. I was so happy to work them into the show.

Willie Johnson
The Bam

Turbo counters this hair-whip with a big side kick. It's enough to take the match! The Bam bows to his opponent, always a gracious loser (remember him celebrating his friend Yin Yang Man's victory over him), but Turbo brushes off his attempts to shake hands.

Back in the Inner Sanctum, Olympus, Tsunami, and Superstar complain about Turbo not getting disqualified. Tsunami especially feels hard done by, considering he lost a fight due to illegal object use last season. Superstar, however, is more concerned with getting in his old rival. The Machine's face, demanding to know why he tried to strike Star Warrior after the match was over. The Machine claims it was a mistake. He didn't hear the signal.

The subtext, of course, is that The Machine still thinks that Star Warrior had something to do with being the Mysterious Ninja, despite all evidence to the contrary. This would-be burst of emotion from The Machine goes against his characterization and really hammers home just how thrown off he is (and the rest of the Masters are) by the events surrounding the Mysterious Ninja.

Battle Dome Final Competitors:

Turbo ⊙ ⊙ ⊙ ⊙ ⊙ ⊙ ✦ vs.
Star Warrior ◗ ◗ ◗ ◗ ◗ ◗

This fight pits two of the suspected Mysterious Ninjas against each other and really starts one of the significant B-Stories of season two. Turbo is majorly amped up for this fight, and his moves are even more aggressive than usual, which is saying something. In contrast, Star Warrior is his usual controlled, fluid self. They spend the fight trading points back and forth, eventually going to sudden death overtime!

In the end, the agility and speed of Star Warrior overcome the power and aggression of Turbo, giving Star Warrior the win!

As Star Warrior celebrates, Turbo looks at his hands. He really thought he had the victory.

The ceremony of the Dragon Belt goes off with no drama, despite Turbo being upset he lost.

We head back to the Inner Sanctum, where several Masters congratulate Turbo on the good fight he put up in the Dome. He makes his way over to The Bam to apologize for using the staff in their match. The Bam says "No problem. It made the

Mike Bernardo
Turbo
Discipline: Shorin Ryu

Clad in black denim Michael "Turbo" Bernardo was the inaugural Dragon Star champion. Sporting long black hair and a chip on his shoulder, Turbo was situated as the show's main antagonist in the first season. A weapon forms specialist, having won dozens of titles on the competitive circuit, Turbo would most often be seen with his bo staff. Martial arts film aficionados will recognize him from *Shootfighter*.

Did you notice?
The lights for sudden death change to a unique orange color, a touch not seen in season one.

match interesting." When the exchange is over, they shake hands.

This is a major moment for Turbo's character. Despite the frustration and anger over his loss, Turbo doesn't complain, moan, or even say anything jerkish, as is his usual M.O. Instead, he takes his defeat in stride, even apologizing to The Bam. Despite his attitude, Turbo follows the Code of the Dragon Star, and this little saga cements that fact.

Our post-credits scene this week is Superstar talking about diversity. He is obviously reading off a cue card, which is funny considering he is one of the more trained actors out of the group.

However, diversity was an important consideration for the show from the beginning. From the initial casting stages, back when the show was still *Martial Masters*, there was a concerted effort to bring in as diverse a group of martial artists as possible.

We wanted to show martial arts was for everyone.

Norman Grossfeld
Executive Producer

This episode was the quintessential B-Story episode. The main JuKiDo storyline was hardly mentioned, let alone advanced, but the episode did serve to start (or push forward) other, less important stories. These B-stories or B-arcs are often more character-based, such as The Machine's frustrations. Still, this episode starting the Turbo versus Star Warrior rivalry is the perfect example of the type of story that a show like Masters would need to keep from becoming repetitive. While this B nature theoretically makes this episode skippable, the quality of the Turbo versus Star Warrior dome keeps it squarely in the don't skip category.

IN A HEAD-LOCK WHILE KICKING TWO OTHERS. THE BACK OF THE NINJA'S HEAD IS FACING TIGER CLAW, AND AS HE HOLDS HIM TIGER CLAW YANKS OFF THE HIS HOOD AND MASK. THE NINJA IS BALD, AND TATTOOED ON THE BACK OF HIS HEAD IS THE JUKIDO SYMBOL (A SYMBOL THAT JOHNNY IS UNFAMILIAR WITH). TIGER CLAW IS TAKEN ABACK FOR A MOMENT, AND THE NINJA WRIGGLES FREE. WE DON'T SEE HIS FACE. HE AND THE OTHER NINJAS RUN OUT THROUGH THE ESCAPE HATCH. JOHNNY STARTS TO CHASE, THEN HEARS A GROAN AND TURNS TO WIZARD.

TIGER CLAW PULLS WIZARD AWAY FROM THE DOME, AND THE STROBE EFFECT STOPS. TIGER CLAW IS SEATED ON THE GROUND, HOLDING WIZARD, WHO SEEMS EXHAUSTED AND POSSIBLY INJURED. JOHNNY ASKS: "WHAT HAPPENED MICHAEL? WHO ERE THOSE GUYS?" WIZARD, NEAR PASSING OUT FROM EXHAUSTION, WHISPERS, "MY BROTHER. YOU HAVE TO GET MY BROTHER." -- FADE OUT.

FADE UP ON THE INNER SANCTUM: CU OF TIGER CLAW

TIGER CLAW
AND THEN HE PASSED OUT FROM EXHAUSTION..... I DON'T REALLY KNOW WHAT THAT WAS ALL ABOUT. LUCKY I CAME ALONG WHEN I DID, THAT'S FER SURE!

THE ATHLETES ARE CONFUSED AS TO WHY THIS HAPPENED. SOME THINK THAT WIZARD MIGHT HAVE A PRETTY WICKED PAST, AS WARLOCK SUGGESTED. OTHERS SAY THAT WIZARD WAS CALLING FOR HIS BROTHER FOR HELP -CALLING FOR HIS FAMILY IN TIME OF NEED. BUT TIGER CLAW IS CONVINCED THAT WIZARD WASN'T CALLING FOR HIS BROTHER-- HE WAS ACCUSING HIM! NOBODY KNOWS WHO OR WHAT TO BELIEVE, AND WARLOCK IS NOT AROUND IN THE INNER SANCTUM.

THE COMPETITION
PRELIM MATCH: MACHINE VS. STAR WARRIOR (W)
PRELIM MATCH: BAM VS. TURBO (W)
BATTLE DOME FINAL: STAR WARRIOR (W) VS. TURBO

ATHLETE MESSAGE: TBA

Page from season 2 Storyline Overview. Storyline Overview from Robert Tuscani.

CHAPTER 28

S2E08: Super Challenge III

Great Wolf

Kid Carmichael

The Machine

Tsunami

Warlock

Tiger Claw

"It was very important for me for it to be featured on the show"

This third and final Ninja Bash episode is unique as it plays directly into the larger story of JuKiDo's attempts to claim the Dragon Star. The previous ones essentially operated in a vacuum of their own self-contained stories. This episode also furthers the B-story of the prior episode, making it a great example of how this show can move stories along in different ways.

Unfortunately, some cost-cutting measures also detract heavily from this one, but we'll get to that.

The show opens in the Inner Sanctum, where Warlock is warming up with Tracer. He's going for full Dragon Belt today and needs to be sharp. We also see Turbo warming up with Yin Yang Man. In a rare moment of braggadocio (perhaps a by-product of the recent false accusations against him), Star Warrior mocks Turbo for losing to him last week. Turbo replies he can beat Star Warrior at anything at any time. The Machine calls them all talk, but they ignore him. They're fixated on each other instead. Turbo challenges Star Warrior to a test of strength, and somehow Yin Yang Man decides what the contest will be.

Meanwhile, Tiger Claw and Great Wolf warm up together. Tiger Claw says Warlock will get full Dragon Belt "over his dead body."

Super Challenge Contestant One: Great Wolf ⬡⬡⬡⬡⬡⬡⬡
Battle Zone: Ghost Town
Ninjas: Ghost

Great Wolf becomes the only competitor to participate in all three Ninja/ Super Challenge contests here, but this is far and away the dullest of his three performances. The only real noteworthy spot comes at the very end, where he wails on the same ninja with kicks four times in a row to end up with 75 points.

Back in the Sanctum, Tiger Claw leads the applause for his best friend. Yin Yang Man says Turbo and Star Warrior have to hang upside down by their legs- whoever lasts the longest is the winner. Superstar tries to encourage his brother, and Star Warrior punks Turbo out by telling him his fly is open.

Super Challenge Contestant Two: Kid Carmichael
Battle Zone: Doom City
Ninjas: Kabuki Warriors

This is, unfortunately, one of the major shortcomings of the episode. Kid Carmichael's Ninja Bash fight is just reused footage from S2E05: "Wizard and Warlock." This was likely a cost-savings technique. By this point in the series, the show was feeling the budget crunch. It's disappointing, to say the least, especially considering Carmichael would likely have had a fantastic fight with the ninjas. His style would have suited it perfectly.

Yeah, they just reused footage. They didn't call me back in to shoot more stuff at that point.

Carmichael Simon
Kid Carmichael

Back in the Inner Sanctum, Tiger Claw and Great Wolf discuss his slim lead before giving the stink-eye to Tracer and Warlock. We also get a fun upside-down shot of Yin Yang Man approaching Turbo and Star Warrior. Both guys are still going strong in their contest.

Super Challenge Contestant Three: The Machine
Battle Zone: Ghost Town
Ninjas: Ghost

If there's one thing we know, it's that The Machine loves pummeling ninjas. If there are two things we know, it's that the Ghost Town Battle Zone means someone is going through part of the set. When those two things meet, it is carnage, pure and simple.

The Machine starts his run by punching a ninja through a wagon wheel. Not throwing, punching. He then palm-strikes another through a pile of barrels. He unloads with his bevy of spin-kicks and finishes by side-kicking a ninja through a wall as time expires. He finishes with a whopping 92 points, locking himself into the finals.

Back in the Inner Sanctum, Turbo and Star Warrior, still hanging in their battle of wills, say Tsunami is a shoo-in to reach the finals. Superstar says he doesn't think Tsunami can do it again, nevertheless, a nice call back to the season one Ninja Challenge.

While the cast usually got competitive about nailing their lines in one take, they made an exception for this episode.

The guys kept messing up lines on purpose to keep us hanging up there. It was one of the goofier moments on the show.

Mike Bernardo
Turbo

Super Challenge Contestant Four: Tsunami ⬡ ⬡ ⬡ ⬡ ⬡
Battle Zone: Ghost Town
Ninjas: Ghost

Tsunami starts off in the only way that really makes sense for him in these things, by nailing a back-flip kick on a hapless ninja. He shows off his flashy moves, wracking up the points before a ninja tries to nail him with a barstool! Had Shannon Lee still been commentating, I imagine she'd have a stern word for the ninja on behalf of the Council, but alas, the CYBERMAN/DUDE remains silent. Instead, Tsunami kicks through it, taking out the ninja! He finishes with 88 points, enough for the Dome!

Back in the Inner Sanctum, Tracer warns Warlock not to get over-confident. He can still miss out on the Dome. Tracer thinks Tiger Claw is onto them.

Master Blaster: A Family Affair

The Bam enters the Arena, accompanied by his son, Marco "Little Bam" Johnson, for this father and son Master Blaster called Rite of Passage. Little Bam is the spitting image of his father, down to his outfit and even his hair.

The Rite of Passage involved is the freezing of Little Bam's hair, which is chopped off by his father (as in karate-chopped, not with scissors) and then made into his own Willie Whip. They then do a double kata, first with swords, then their Willie Whips.

Willie "The Bam" Johnson and Marco "Little Bam" Johnson demonstate their form.
Photo from Bruce Heinsius Photography.

We did that kata on the circuit sometimes. Carlin West saw us perform it and said, "you have to do it on the show!" So they worked it in for us. My whole family does martial arts. I was very proud to get to display that on the show.

Willie Johnson
The Bam

Willie Johnson
The Bam
Discipline: Wushu

Willie Johnson is a Wushu practitioner hailing from Baltimore, Maryland. "Professor Bam" as he is known is a 7 time U.M.A.C World Champion and holds a spot in the Black Belt Hall of Fame. After the show ceased airing Professor Bam continued teaching in his school as well as putting out books and movies aimed at continuing to teach young people life lessons through martial arts.

I remember seeing them do it. I was very moved by it. Family is just so important to me, and Willie has such an inspiring story. It was very important for me for it to be featured on the show.

Carlin West
Series Creator

It was very important for Johnson, as well. It was not well known, even to his fellow cast members, but shortly before filming the series, he had been incarcerated.

The show really came along at the perfect time for me. It helped me get my life back on track. I wanted to keep my head down, do my job, and be a good role model for my kid. It was rare then, almost unheard of, to be a black, single father. That's why having him on the show with me, to show us doing martial arts together, was so important.

Willie Jonson
The Bam

This Master Blaster remains one of the most memorable of the show and learning the story behind it only deepened my appreciation for it. Marco "Little Bam" Johnson continues to practice martial arts to this day, although neither he nor his father sport the long braid.

Super Challenge Contestant Five: Warlock ⬡⬡⬡⬡⬡⬡
Battle Zone: Doom City
Ninjas: Black

Much faster fighting from Warlock on this occasion. It's a stark contrast to his previous, more sluggish performance. It really emphasizes how badly he wants to reach full Dragon Belt. He breaks out his usual array of side and roundhouse kicks, putting the ninjas down one after another. He finishes with 86, enough to join the finals.

Super Challenge Contestant Six: Tiger Claw ⬡⬡⬡⬡⬡⬡⬡
Battle Zone: Dark Alley
Ninjas: Black

Unfortunately, this is another reused scene, as the ninja battle here is just Tiger Claw's fight with the ninjas from S2E05: "Wizard and Warlock." One crew member, who asked for anonymity on this point, revealed, "By (that) point of the series, things were getting a little hard, a little hectic and stressful for everyone. There was always a time crunch, I think there were always budget concerns. Norman stepped in more and more to direct and manage to try to get things on task. The ninja episodes were a way to cost cut but still make new content."

With his score, Tiger Claw joins Warlock, The Machine, and Tsunami in the Battle Dome!

Battle Dome Finals: Tiger Claw ⬡⬡⬡⬡⬡⬡⬡ vs.
Warlock ⬡⬡⬡⬡⬡⬡⬡ vs. The Machine ✦ vs. Tsunami ⬡⬡⬡⬡⬡

Tiger Claw locks in on Warlock as the fight starts, completely ignoring the other two fighters. Warlock scores first, hitting a side kick on Tiger Claw, sending him into the cage. Tiger Claw answers him not with a point-scoring move but with a helicopter armbar, a move unique not just in the series but on TV at the time.

Now, I'm not sure of the timing of this, but I might have been the first person to do an armbar like that on American TV. The only other person it could have been was one of the Machado brothers on Walker, Texas Ranger. An episode aired where he did it, but I don't know the timing. So I was either the first or second person to do it on American TV.

Johnny Lee Smith
Tiger Claw

While I couldn't find an air date for this episode, the Walker episode aired the first week of January 1996. Season two of Masters aired in Spring 1996, meaning Tiger Claw likely takes second place to the legendary martial artist, something he's totally fine with. The move was definitely the first armbar on *WMAC Masters* and was, in fact, the only one.

I remember Isaac (Florentine, Director) didn't want him to do it. He didn't think it'd look good. But credit to Isaac, he trusted Johnny and let him do it, and it was one of the coolest moves on the show.

Jamie Webster
Great Wolf

I don't remember that discussion in particular, but grappling as a whole isn't as exciting visually as jumping and kicking. I always went for the visual.

Isaac Florentine
Director

The Machine gets on the scoreboard with a Superman punch followed by a big kick on Warlock.

Every kick Hakim did was big. :laughs:

Jamie Webster
Great Wolf

Tiger Claw and Warlock's rivalry is the main story of this fight, with The Machine and Tsunami mainly just filling out the action. In the end, Tiger Claw's worst fears come true as Warlock wins it! Warlock holds on to reach full Dragon Belt! He and Tiger Claw keep going at it even as time runs out until Tsunami and The Machine break it up, The Machine physically holding back Tiger Claw.

Nobody is getting past Hakim if he's trying to hold you back. :laughs:

Johnny Lee Smith
Tiger Claw

This fight is an excellent example of the storytelling ability within the action we see on the show. Tiger Claw's suspicions of Warlock play out in front of us in visceral form. He focuses on Warlock from the beginning of the fight, seemingly more concerned with taking him out than winning the match. Ultimately it costs him.

Another fun, subtle story detail is the fact that Tsunami didn't score a point. This could, of course, simply be him getting overmatched, but considering revelations to come, I'm inclined to see it as a piece of foreshadowing.

Back in the Inner Sanctum, Tracer is excited Warlock won. A little too excited. The other Masters are obviously suspicious. Star Warrior and Turbo are still hanging upside down in the background.

The Dragon Belt ceremony has some drama to it, as Tiger Claw walks off after handing over his Ki Symbol, something unheard of in the WMAC. The Bam and Yin Yang Man comment on it in the Inner Sanctum, Great Wolf replying, "He has his reasons."

The Bam has the post-credits scene talking about the importance of family. This was not simply a reading assignment for The Bam. It was something he continues to hold near and dear.

I teach martial arts with my wife. All my kids do martial arts. We teach kids how to build a better life through martial arts. (The show) really gave me a platform to spread a message of positivity and try to influence the next generation.

Willie Johnson
The Bam

All in all, this third and final Ninja Challenge is a mixed bag. It excels in the storytelling department, being the first one of the challenges to advance a major storyline, but the reusing of footage really drags down the episode. In short, skip the qualifying matches and stick to the Inner Sanctum, Master Blaster, and Battle Dome segments when doing your re-watch.

WMAC MASTERS -- EPISODE #209 April 25, 1996

> TIGER CLAW
> You're hanging on to first
> place by a thread, buddy boy.
>
> GREAT WOLF
> Hey, a one point lead is still a
> lead.

GREAT WOLF looks over at WARLOCK working out with TRACER.

> GREAT WOLF
> Warlock's looking pretty sure
> of himself.
>
> TIGER CLAW
> He's not smart enough to be
> worried.

TIGER CLAW gives a STERN LOOK over at WARLOCK. WARLOCK senses he's being stared at and LOOKS BACK at TIGER CLAW.

21A. INNER SANCTUM

YIN YANG MAN WALKS OVER to check on TURBO and STAR WARRIOR. CUT TO an upside down POV shot of YIN YANG as he approaches.

> YIN YANG MAN
> How's it going guys?
>
> TURBO
> I feel like a side of beef in a
> meatlocker.
>
> STAR WARRIOR
> You look like an order of
> "Wushu Pork".
>
> TURBO
> So, who's up?

5:33 PM C:\WMAC\WMAC#209.DOC

Script page showing cut dialogue from Star Warrior and Turbo's contest. Script from Jamie Webster.

Carmichael Simon and Hakim Alston behind the scenes. Photo from Carmichael Simon.

CHAPTER 29

S2E09: Mixed Doubles

Superstar and Lady Lightning vs.
Tracer and Chameleon

Red Dragon vs. Warlock

"We had no idea how well it would work"

JuKiDo finally gets their shot at the Dragon Star in this episode as Warlock challenges Red Dragon, who looks to break the first defense curse that has plagued every male Dragon Star champion since Turbo (even Superstar didn't win his defense). With a Dragon Star match on tap we get another special attraction to balance out the remainder of the episode.

We open at the Inner Sanctum. Tracer and Chameleon wish Warlock good luck. Chameleon asks what the two men are always gossiping about, and Tracer, being Tracer, proposes an alliance. She responds none-too-warmly, saying they should focus on their mixed doubles match today and go from there.

We get the show intro, with this week's being the "Ladies Intro" we saw once previously.

We see Team Yellow, which consists of Superstar and Lady Lightning, enter the Arena. They do their own mini-katas back to back, Superstar's including what looks like Liu Kang's fireball motion, a nice little shout-out for those in the know.

I knew Ho-Sung very well. We were both a part of Team Paul Mitchell on the competitive circuit. He was a great competitor. I loved working with him.

Christine Rodrigues
Lady Lightning

We see both Dragon Star champions on the throne. There doesn't quite seem to be enough room for both of them, but they're making it work.

We then see Team Red with Chameleon and Tracer enter the Arena. They each perform a kata, with Tracer holding onto Baby the lizard while Chameleon performs. Tracer's kata features him using sai's. He looks slightly uncomfortable but incredibly intimidating.

Back in the Inner Sanctum, Star Warrior and Turbo continue their rivalry with a game of chess. Turbo takes the battle, making it two games to one. Had the games actually been played for real, however, it likely would have gone very differently for Turbo, considering his opposition.

Tracer gets a rare chance to demonstrate his skills. Photo from Bruce Heinsius Photography.

Ho-Young was one of the smartest people I've ever met. Even back on the show, he either just completed or was about to complete his Ph.D. And he was a champion martial artist. He was just one of those people.

Jamie Webster
Great Wolf

Wizard returns to the Inner Sanctum, and the Masters all welcome him, telling him how worried they were. Warlock pulls him aside, saying they need to talk. Nothing sketchy about that, no way. He tries to threaten his brother into silence, but Wizard is having none of it, saying he's going to the Council.

Mixed Doubles Exhibition:
Team Yellow (Superstar and Lady Lightning) vs.
Team Red (Tracer and Chameleon)
Battle Zone: Dark City
Ninjas: Kabuki Warriors

This fight starts with Superstar going off on some ninjas. It was his first real stretch of showcasing his moves since losing the Dragon Star. The deemphasis of his role is one of the more surprising aspects of season two, considering he came into the year as Dragon Star champion and had acting experience. No one

I spoke to indicated any significant reason for this role reduction, just simply "rotating the face characters." It's reasonable to assume that had season three materialized, Superstar would have had an increased role in the fight against JuKiDo, as would other characters who took a little bit of a back seat in the second season, like Olympus and The Machine.

Lady Lightning takes her turn battering the ninjas, presumably letting off some frustration at losing the Dragon Star herself. However, both ex-champions look to be hitting the ground running in their return to competition, showing no signs of rust.

Meanwhile, Tracer and Chameleon aren't doing as well, presumably due to their lack of previous experience fighting together. While Superstar and Lady Lightning's real-life time as teammates isn't acknowledged on the show, it's fair to assume they'd be at least partially familiar with each other as veterans of the WMAC. The two new recruits wouldn't have that same level of comfort together.

Superstar and Lady Lightning show some great teamwork on the ninjas, which Tracer and Chameleon try to one-up a few moments later, showing some smooth teamwork of their own, and displaying it's not that they're less talented fighters than their opponents, just less comfortable with each other's style.

> *Sophia was a pleasure to team up with. She was trained by members of the Jackie Chan Stunt and Demo team. Our styles meshed well.*
>
> Michael Foley
> *Tracer*

The ninjas leave the Battle Zone, leaving the fight two-on-two. There's no inter-gender fighting here. Instead, the men fight each other, as do the women. Lady Lightning scores the first direct hit on Chameleon, followed by Superstar flashing back to his *Mortal Kombat* days and nailing a bicycle kick on Tracer, yet another awesome nod to his time as Liu Kang.

Chameleon keeps switching costume colors, but nothing indicates if it's on purpose or a continuity mix-up, such as the voiceovers in other fights.

> *(The costume changes) weren't really my department, but we all thought it was a lot of fun. Our team was very good with syncing*

the shots up, so I'd bet they were on purpose.

Shannon "Irish" Stewart
Script Supervisor

The costume wasn't my favorite. It wasn't the wardrobe changes. It just wasn't... it wasn't the best. I know they did what they could with the budget, but if I could have changed some things, I would have.

Sophia Crawford
Chameleon

Tracer clocks Superstar as he tries to help Lady Lightning off the ground because he's a bad guy. Team Yellow gets the last laugh, however, nailing tandem side kicks on their opponents for the win!

Chameleon is irate at the loss. Tracer just looks annoyed. It's a nice little slice of character work, showing their differing priorities.

The tournament was never Tracer's concern.

Michael Foley
Tracer

Tracer's pride would have been hurt at the loss, but he wasn't worried about not getting a Ki Symbol. Especially with his partner in crime Warlock challenging for the Dragon Star later in the show. Chameleon was intent on winning the Dragon Star and the loss of an "easy chance" would have really angered her.

Back in the Inner Sanctum, Tsunami seemingly moved on from his crush on Shannon Lee and says he wants to be paired up with Chameleon next time. So naturally the Masters clown on him for it. Meanwhile, Wizard and Warlock continue to bicker, apparently having paused their intense and dramatic conversation for the duration of the mixed doubles fight. Warlock says the Council will never believe Wizard's accusations once they see his faded JuKiDo tattoo, which he dramatically reveals to the camera.

Back in the Arena, the winners claim the loser's Ki Symbols. Tracer snubs Superstar's handshake offer but stops short of storming off as Tiger Claw did in the last episode.

In the Inner Sanctum, Wizard and Warlock continue to argue. Wizard says his brother doesn't know the difference between right and wrong. Warlock says the Council will never believe him, and if he wants to stay in the WMAC, he needs to keep his mouth shut.

We see Turbo take on another game of chess with Star Warrior. Which, after subsequent viewings, I'm convinced, is a subtle bit of character work. He's smarter than he lets on.

In the Arena, the platform has been raised. Strange, doll-headed ninjas surround Red Dragon. He emerges and does his form—Fight, Fist, and Fire. He breaks some boxes featuring Warlock's logo, each holding one of his special Red Dragon weapons. He does a kata with the weapons, shooting sparks at the end, burning Warlock's symbol, then a portrait of Warlock himself! The head-on shot of him using the weapons is the one we see in the intro for the second season.

Back in the Inner Sanctum, Lady Lightning and Superstar celebrate their win with Tiger Claw. Tsunami made drinks for Chameleon and Tracer as a consolation prize, mainly as an excuse to flirt with Chameleon (or so we're led to believe...). Tracer almost shows his hand tattoo but catches himself. Tracer tries to give Chameleon a weird pep talk, which also serves as a pitch to join his and Warlock's side, but she isn't interested.

On the platform, a strange voice asks, "Do You Believe in Magic?" before Warlock appears out of nowhere, surrounded by ninjas with Fourth of July sparklers, to relinquish his Dragon Belt. He does a kata with his stick weapons, breaking clay orbs with Red Dragon's symbol on them with his signature rapid side kick. We get a shot of him laughing overlaid with a creepy sound effect distorting his voice. It's really hammering home that he is a Bad Guy, in case any kids didn't see the build-up to this episode. He shatters a glass Red Dragon logo while the voiceover says "Magic," replacing it with the portrait of him from Red Dragon's kata. Only this time, it shows him holding the Dragon Star!

That was an interesting shoot. We didn't rehearse with the orbs first. I got there and was like, "Hope this goes well." We had no idea how well it would work.

Larry Lam
Warlock

It was a strange but mostly effective kata. It reinforced Warlock's status as the villain in the story and played into his magical character, which up until now has just been his name (and the fact he carried two little bags with him into the Arena most shots).

Dragon Star Championship
Competitors: Red Dragon (Champion) vs. Warlock (Challenger)

The fight starts off hot, with Warlock looking aggressive. In addition, the background lights change colors more than in previous matches, adding a bit of visual intrigue.

The major story of the match is the completely unprecedented cheating from Warlock and JuKiDo. One of the ninjas who is called in for a violation is in a costume we've only seen once before. He is JuKiDo! This ninja hones in on Red Dragon, ignoring Warlock entirely, effectively making it a two-on-one affair. It somehow goes unnoticed by the other Masters, or presumably by the Council, even though Warlock goes so far as to help the JuKiDo ninja back onto the platform after Red Dragon almost knocks him off!

In the end, the ninja goes for a flying side kick on Red Dragon, apparently, having not seen the Superstar versus Olympus fight, and predictably misses Red Dragon, nailing Warlock and sending him off the platform!

I have a terrible fear of heights. I couldn't do the fall. We had to have a stunt man do it for me.

Larry Lam
Warlock

Red Dragon fires off a spinning back kick and sends the JuKiDo ninja to the ground, retaining the Dragon Star!

I used to tease some of the other guys like Hakim. I was the only guy to defend the Dragon Star in the series. Everyone else lost it in their first defense.

Chris Casamassa
Red Dragon

(NOTE: Lady Lightning defended her Dragon Star against Babydoll, but Red Dragon specified "guy." Turbo defeated Yin Yang Man, but it happened in the show's prehistory, so Red Dragon is technically correct.)

In its context, this is one of the weaker Dragon Star fights. The focus is less on the fight itself and more on the continuing JuKiDo story. The evil ninja cheating to help Warlock is a fun story that definitely makes this fight one to check out, but this one ultimately falls short of some of the previous title fights, which is a testament to the quality of the other match-ups.

There's notably less interest and celebration in the Inner Sanctum than in previous Dragon Star matches. This is possibly a comment on Warlock's recent suspicious activities. Most of the Masters are simply working out. Tiger Claw approaches Wizard and asks about the night he was attacked. Wizard plays dumb, saying he doesn't remember what happened but that he knows Warlock wasn't involved. Tiger Claw doesn't buy it and asks if Wizard is sorry his brother lost his Dragon Star fight. Wizard says no.

This was a strange way to end such a huge episode, but it makes sense from the stance of continuing the drama. Warlock lost his shot at the Dragon Star, leaving JuKiDo in a lurch. So the big question moves from "Will JuKiDo win the Dragon Star?" to "What will happen between Wizard and Warlock next?" A logical progression for the show, considering it wouldn't make much sense, dramatically, for the bad guys to win the Dragon Star. At least not before a season finale.

Larry Lam
Warlock
Discipline: Kung Fu

Wearing a midnight blue ninja outfit and carrying never explained mystical powder bags into the arena, Larry Lam became one of the key villains of the *WMAC Masters* mythos. A Hall of Famer in multiple martial arts organizations, the Kung Fu and Tae Kwon Do Master was the 1989 Rookie of the Year. After attempting to steal the Dragon Star Warlock went on to work as an actor, stunt performer, and stunt coordinator in mega-blockbusters such as *Romeo Must Die*, *The Fast series*, and *I, Robot*.

Photos from Bruce Heinsius Photography.

Photos from Bruce Heinsius Photography.

Photo from Sophia Crawford.

CHAPTER 30

S2E10: Name of the Game

Olympus vs. Tsunami

The Bam vs. Great Wolf

"We didn't have the timing right, and I nailed him in the balls"

After last week's Dragon Star match and Warlock's loss to Red Dragon, the main thrust of the show's story is now at a crossroads. Where does JuKiDo go from here, and will they face any suspicion after their blatant attempt at cheating last week?

We begin in the Inner Sanctum, where we see Star Warrior breaking boards. The Machine and Wizard watch him warming up and we learn Star Warrior and Turbo have a speed-breaking contest to finally settle their rivalry. The Machine mentions their hanging-upside-down contest ended in a tie, as they were both found unconscious the next morning, having fallen asleep and fallen to the ground!

Across the room, Warlock complains about the Council and their decisions, but Tracer advises patience. There's a rumor about Black Widow, the reigning Women's Dragon Star Champion, that may mean good things for JuKiDo. They both do an evil laugh which the rest of the cast apparently doesn't notice.

This may be a reach, but after several rewatches of the series, the storyteller part of my brain wonders if this lack of attention for Warlock and Tracer's obvious evilness is a deeper storytelling device. Could it be that the WMAC is so full of itself, so confident in their position as the supreme ruling body of martial arts, that they fail to see the threat right in front of them, like the Jedi Order in *Star Wars*? Or is it simply that it's a kid's show, and there wasn't much room for the bad guys to act with subtlety?

After the opening credits of the show, we then see Turbo and Star Warrior enter the Arena for their speed-breaking contest. It's pretty straightforward, break as many boards as possible before time expires. Both guys use the demo as a chance to show off their arsenal of kicks, punches, and, of all things, head-butts. It seems like a game of one upmanship. In fact, Star Warrior breaks a board with his head, then Turbo does the same, but Star Warrior takes the metaphorical cake with a back-to-back head-butt breaking.

The Council scores the fighters. One point for each clean break, plus points for technique, originality, and execution. After a moment's pause for drama, Star Warrior is announced as the winner! In a shocking turn of events, Turbo shakes Star Warrior's hand and embraces him as the winner!

This is a significant character moment for Turbo. Sadly, it's one that came too late in the series to truly be followed up on. However, it completed his season-long transformation from the lone-wolf bad guy, which he undeniably was at the end of season one, to more shades of grey sort of good guy, akin to the Punisher in Marvel Comics. He isn't the traditional hero like Olympus, his former arch-rival, but at the end of the day, he stands for the Code of the Dragon Star, despite his cold demeanor and standoffishness.

That was really what we were trying to do, yes. Even in the first season, Pat (Johnson) told me, "don't worry, we're going to redeem you." That kind of journey, going from selfish bad guy to someone on the side of good, but still their own sort of person. It really would have come full circle in season three, I think. It could have went further.

Mike Bernardo
Turbo

That transformation would not have been possible without Star Warrior, the perfect foil for Turbo. Another quiet character (and actor), Ho-Young Pak's Star Warrior was portrayed as heroic in the first season, particularly in regards to his more egotistical younger brother, but fell under suspicion at the start of season two. That slight edge his character took on allowed there to be some room for doubt as to whether he was a good guy or bad guy, letting Turbo's change happen naturally.

Had Turbo been feuding with Olympus or The Machine, he would never have been able to escape the perception of being the bad guy. On the other hand, had it been with Tracer or Warlock, it would have been so obviously a good guy that he lost the shades of grey edge.

Star Warrior and Turbo also worked well together on screen. Their styles complemented each other well, and the two even matched up well visually.

Me and Ho-Young, I liked working with him a lot. He's very quiet as well, so we didn't talk a lot. Doing the fight scene with him was neat. It was nice to talk to him and get to know him. He did have a different style. I liked that it was easy to contrast the two of us that way.

Mike Bernardo
Turbo

Following the breaking, we are back to regular action and the Arena entrances for match one stand out for being unique and slightly out of place. First, Olympus brandishes some Olympic style torches, then Tsunami beats up a ninja with his stick weapons while also painting his logo on him. They're very different from the usual, straightforward pre-match entrances.

We tried to have fun with the shots, especially in season two.

Isaac Florentine
Director

Before the preliminary fight begins, we head to the Inner Sanctum, where some of the Masters are playing with an anagram generator on the WMAC computer. Because in the 90s, it was really wild that you could do something like that. No, really.

Preliminary Match One
Competitors:
Olympus O 🟡 vs. Tsunami O O O O O
Battle Zone: Pressure Pit
Ninjas: Pressure

The ninjas swarm to start, their outfits (gas masks and black-and-neon-striped ninja garb) straddling the line between absurd and creepy. This fight is a fun romp through one of the more absurd Battle Zones. Both fighters use their surroundings in unique ways, including Olympus releasing steam from one of the valves into Tsunami's eyes. Which, for some reason, isn't a disqualification. The finish of this fight is also fantastic, as Tsunami scurries up a ladder, back-flips, and lands behind Olympus before scoring a big dropkick for the win!

This was a fun fight that took advantage of one of the lesser Battle Zones, emphasizing the strengths of the performers, especially Tsunami, who scored one of his bigger wins of the series. Olympus continues his poor run of form since losing the Dragon Star, a plot thread that, like so many others, never got the chance to play out.

Back in the Inner Sanctum, the world's greatest martial artists continue to take great joy from an anagram generator. The 90s were a simpler time. The Machine and Superstar crack jokes on each other over the results (real highbrow stuff), while Chameleon isn't impressed. She walks away and bumps into Tracer, who tries to encourage her, as only Tracer can. Predictably, it does not go well for him.

Black Widow shows up and announces to a bewildered Inner Sanctum (who might be trying to figure out who the heck she is, considering we've seen approximately thirty seconds of her, ever) that she's stepping down as Dragon Star champion and retiring from competition.

Preliminary Match Two
Competitors:
The Bam ⬡⬡⬡⬡⬡ vs. Great Wolf ⬡⬡⬡⬡⬡⬡
Battle Zone: Ghost Town
Ninjas: Ghost

This fight serves as a showcase for Great Wolf, but a large part of the credit for that has to go to The Bam, who seems to specialize in making his opponents look their best. This fight shows Great Wolf's agility, as he pulls off a number of exciting moves, including a perfectly timed double back-flip with The Bam, which is a truly impressive sight.

Jamie is a big guy, but he's so, so agile.

Isaac Florentine
Director

Great Wolf also delivers what he told me was one of his favorite moves of the show.

There was this fight where I hit four or five big spinning kicks in a row, never stopping. That was one of my favorite moves.

Jamie Webster
Great Wolf

It is a wonderful technique that looks fantastic on film. He makes it look easy, a true testament to his skills as an athlete.

As the fight winds down, Great Wolf is ahead on the power bar and hits a leg sweep, taking The Bam down. Great Wolf stays down as well, break-dancing up into a back-fist as they both remain on the ground, scoring and winning the fight!

Post-fight, the two fighters shake hands, as usual for The Bam.

Respect is very important to me. It's one of the building blocks of the Warrior's Mindset. It was very important to me that I was exhibiting respect on the show, even in losses.

Willie Johnson
The Bam

NOTE: The Warrior's Mindset is Johnson's life philosophy he teaches as part of his curriculum.

This grace in losing was also something the producers wanted to demonstrate to the young viewers. While the shift away from flashbacks in season two made the presentation of life lessons less obvious, it was still a key part of the show's mission. There was no one better suited in the cast to demonstrate this quality than Willie "The Bam" Johnson.

I wasn't worried about wins or losses or looking good or anything like that. I was just happy to be there, to be doing the work and living my dream. Whatever they asked of me, as long as it was in keeping with my personal beliefs, and it always was, I was happy to do it.

Willie Johnson
The Bam

Back in the Inner Sanctum, the anagram generator is still creating barrels of laughs. Meanwhile, Lady Lightning asks Black Widow why she's leaving. She doesn't really answer and calls the guys playing with the anagram generator crazy. Tracer shows up and berates the crew playing with the anagram program, saying they should quit playing games. They put his name in and let it run while the Battle Dome Final is on.

In the season two storyline overview, this is where Babydoll rushes in and says that since she and Chameleon have the most Ki Symbols on their Dragon

Belts, they will face off for the Dragon Star once it's vacated. Bearing in mind that Chameleon is much more closely aligned with JuKiDo in that document, this seems like a second chance for the evil-doers to nab the Dragon Star.

> *I think I was originally going to be more of a villain, but as they saw my performance, they made me more shades of grey.*

Sophia Crawford
Chameleon

Battle Dome Final
Competitors: Tsunami ⬡⬡⬡⬡⬡ vs. Great Wolf ⬡⬡⬡⬡⬡⬡⬡

Both of these guys are fantastic fighters who aren't near the top of the pecking order as far as in-universe competition results at this point in the series. This fight delivers big on the action, showing off Tsunami's dazzling flips and Great Wolf's mix of power and agility.

One of the highlights is Great Wolf uppercutting Tsunami out of the air, a move he took from a perhaps not-so-surprising source.

> *I loved to take techniques from all over movies, TV, even video games. (That uppercut) was inspired by Mortal Kombat. In the video games, you could time your uppercut as someone flipped over you and get a special reaction, so I tried to work that in. I thought it was cool.*

Jamie Webster
Great Wolf

Great Wolf follows the video game uppercut with a movie-like leap to one of the platforms in the cage, crouching up there while Tsunami hits a big, multi-rotation spin kick on a ninja. After Tsunami resets, Great Wolf leaps down with a kick, but Tsunami avoids him, instead hitting his rainbow kick for another point, securing the win!

Once again, Great Wolf brings his A-Game in a Battle Dome, and Tsunami more than held up his end of the bargain. This was a great fight showcasing two guys who are usually relied on to make other fighters look better, giving them a chance to shine.

There was also one other moment Great Wolf remembers well, but it didn't visibly make the show's final cut.

So you may not know this, but in the center of the Arena set, there was a circle that was sometimes moved and a trampoline placed there to give us more bounce. So in this fight, there was a moment where he used the trampoline and tried to spring over me, and I was supposed to hit him, but we didn't have the timing right, and I nailed him in the balls. I felt so bad.

Jamie Webster
Great Wolf

The Dragon Belt ceremony follows, with no drama involved because they're both good guys. Right?

Back in the Inner Sanctum, the Masters all sing "For She's a Jolly Good Fellow" for Black Widow, filing out to go to her farewell party, which sadly we don't get to see. Warlock approaches Tracer, who is lagging behind, saying it will be suspicious if they don't show up at Black Widow's party. Tracer says he'll be right there. Tiger Claw walks by and gives Warlock a heaping helping of stink eye. Tracer is the last one left in the Inner Sanctum, so he's the only one there to see the anagram of his name. DESTROY WMAC!

Tracer then loudly sings, "For I'm a Jolly Good Fellow!" as he walks off, capping it with an over the top evil laugh.

It was a lot of fun (playing the villain). It had to be over the top since it was a kid's show.

Michael Foley
Tracer

This ending wasn't exactly a cliffhanger, but the fact that Black Widow is vacating the Dragon Star is a great way to add intrigue and continue the JuKiDo story. Warlock blew his chance to win, but the bad guys still have a shot. It's almost an inverse of the typical formula, which sees the good guys struggling to overcome the odds, they rally, but things take a dark turn once again for one last dramatic twist. Typically the heroes overcome this last hurdle in dramatic fashion. What will happen with the shoe on the other foot?

Photo from Bruce Heinsius Photography.

From left to right: Willie Johnson, Chris Casamassa, Victoria Gay, Mike Chat, Richard Branden, Ho-Sung Pak. Photo from Willie Johnson.

WMAC MASTERS

4 KIDS PRODUCTIONS, INC.
1000 Universal Stdios Plaza, Orlando, FL 32819   DAY: 4   OUT OF: 41
PHONE: (407) 354-6480   FAX: (407) 354-6586
NY OFC: (212) 754-5482   FAX: (212) 754-5480

CALL SHEET

Exec. Produc Norman Grossfeld

Producer: Michael Attanasio

Producer: Kathy Borland

Director: Isaac Florentine

1st Asst Dir: John O'Rourke

DAY/DATE: THURSDAY MARCH 7, 1996

CREW CALL: 6:00PM

SHOOTING: 7:15PM

SUNRISE: 6:44AM   SUNSET: 6:29PM

WEATHER: CHANCE OF SHOWERS & T-STORMS, LOW 60'S, WIND NW 15 MPH

LOCATION: INT. WILD WEST (GHOST TOWN)   UNIVERSAL STUDIOS

INT/EXT SETS	SCENE	CAST	N/D	PAGES	DESCRIPTION
INT. WILD WEST	E #8B	9,19, NINJAS, REF	N	3:00	THE BAMVS GREAT WOLF
(GHOST TOWN)					THE BAM VS NINJAS
					GREAT WOLF VS NINJAS
					WINNER: GREAT WOLF
					INTRO

CAST	NAME	CHARACTER	LEAVE	M/U	SET	REMARKS
9	WILLIE JOHNSON	THE BAM	5:45PM	6:00PM	6:45PM	P/U @ DELTA RESORT
19	JAMIE WEBSTER	GREAT WOLF	5:45PM	6:00PM	6:45PM	P/U @ DELTA RESORT
N	RICHARD BRANDEN	NINJA	5:45PM	6:00PM	6:45PM	P/U @ DELTA RESORT
N	HIEN NGUYEN (UNREHEARSE	NINJA	5:45PM	6:00PM	6:45PM	P/U @ DELTA RESORT
N	YOSHI	NINJA	REPORT	6:00PM	6:45PM	REPORT TO WILD WEST
N	JOHN MEDLEN	NINJA	REPORT	6:00PM	6:45PM	REPORT TO WILD WEST
N	DAVID MORIZOT	NINJA	REPORT	6:00PM	6:45PM	REPORT TO WILD WEST
N	ROB STIO	NINJA	REPORT	6:00PM	6:45PM	REPORT TO WILD WEST
REF	DON DINO	REFEREE	REPORT	7:15PM	7:45PM	REPORT TO WILD WEST

NOTES

DEPARTMENT INSTRUCTIONS

HAIR & MAKE-UP: WORKING ON LOCATION

WARDOBE: NINJA'S BLACK W/ WHITE MASKS, WORKING ON LOCATION

PROPS: SMOKE, 1 BREAKAWAY CRATE, PADS, 1 TRAMPOLINE
               2 SCORED BOARDS

PRODUCTION: LIGHTING STRIKES GOES ON PRODUCTION CUBE

TRANSPORTATION

TRUCKS WILL LIVE ON LOCATION TILL FRIDAY

SPECIAL INSTRUCTIONS

EMERGENCIES: #351-8550   SANDLAKE HOSPITAL
STUNT SITUATION

SEE REVERSE FOR ADVANCE SHOOTING NOTICE

Call sheet from The Bam vs. Great Wolf fight. Call Sheet from Jamie Webster.

CHAPTER 31

Interlude: The Mystery of Black Widow

"Do you know this woman?"

In the course of writing this book, I attempted to contact everyone involved with the show that I could find, no matter how closely or tangentially related they were. Some were easy to get in touch with; others took more digging. Several required introductions from other cast and crew members. Some, sadly, I was unable to make contact with. There was only one, however, that I could find no trace of at all.

Tiana Noguchi is credited as playing Black Widow in season two. Unfortunately, as of this writing, there is no information about this person available online that is not connected to her portrayal of Black Widow. She has no social media accounts, no martial arts schools, and no additional credits on IMDB. Wikipedia, ever the bastion of accurate information, lists her as Akihiro "Yuji" Noguchi's sister, but the man who played Cyclone told me this was, in fact, not the case.

The person who played Black Widow is not my sister. She just had the same surname as me. I'm sorry, I don't know anything more about her.

Yuji Noguchi
Cyclone

This was, without fail, the answer I got from every cast and crew member I asked about the elusive Tiana. Even Pati Robinson, casting director, drew a blank.

I'm sorry, I have no memory of the situation around Black Widow.

Pati Robinson
Casting Director

Dan Hubp, my usual go-to for information, also came back empty-handed.

Black Widow is a mystery. I watched the episode in question but didn't recognize her.

Dan Hubp
Production Designer, Editor

He suggested I try Chris "Red Dragon" Casamassa, who shared a scene or two with her as her fellow Dragon Star Champion, and behind the scenes was considered a ladies man by some. Unfortunately, this didn't prove to be helpful when it came to Black Widow.

Unfortunately, I can be of no help. I vaguely remember her and have had no contact with her.

Chris Casamassa
Red Dragon

I got a similar answer from every cast member I reached out to, from Carmichael Simon to Hien Nguyen. So with my usual avenue of investigation, asking the cast members I'm already in contact with for an introduction, closed to me, I changed tactics.

I am not an investigative reporter; that should be said upfront. However, I have better than average Googling skills, honed over years of researching writing projects, and have been lucky enough to connect with several talented individuals with research skills (and access to tools) I don't possess.

Searching for any lead on Black Widow, I (and my helpers) scoured dozens of databases, from court records to obituaries and marriage filings to the white pages. There were no results for any Tiana Noguchi. Zero. Just like her digital footprint, her paper trail is non-existent.

What does this mean?

While there are several possibilities, the most likely is that Tiana Noguchi was a stage name, not her real name. This would explain why there are no official documents on her, as well as why she has no further IMDB credits. She could have continued acting under her real name (or another stage name). The other leading theory is that she got married and no longer goes by the surname Noguchi, which is possible, but marriage records *should have* pinged in our search.

It's fitting that out of all the actors on the show, Black Widow would be the most elusive. Her character appeared suddenly between seasons, winning the Dragon Star from Lady Lightning off-screen. This new champion would be a mystery. We never see her fight, we learn nothing about her, and we don't even hear her speak until she's announcing her retirement. She is less a character than a plot device, an assessment that initially sounds harsh but one that is shared by the show's lead creative.

We invented the character as a story mechanism.
I don't recall the actress (who portrayed the character).
It was really more of an "extra" role, despite being
Dragon Star Champion.

Norman Grossfeld
Executive Producer

Ultimately, with no one from the show remembering anything of substance about her and the lack of documentation, the search for Black Widow, aka Tiana Noguchi, has gone cold. It is possible, unfortunately, that Ms. Noguchi (or whatever her name ends up being) is no longer with us, in which case I offer my condolences to her friends and family. It is my hope that this book might generate more "leads" (for lack of a better term) about her, possibly even bringing her into the spotlight. If you believe you have some information about her, please email WMACMastersBook@gmail.com.

CHAPTER 32

S2E11: Vision of Evil Part I

Cyclone vs. The Machine

Yin Yang Man vs. Olympus

"Great guy, but fighting him wasn't always the most fun"

Although fans didn't know it at the time, *WMAC Masters* was nearing the end of its run on TV. This is the penultimate new episode and the first of a season-ending two-parter (ignoring the clip show tacked on at the end of the series). With an ominous title and a major storyline to wrap up, things really feel like they're coming to a head.

In the Inner Sanctum, the Masters discuss the Council's solution for the unprecedented vacated Dragon Star. They've chosen the top three female competitors, Lady Lightning, Chameleon, and Princess, and the three of them will have the first ever three-way Dragon Star match! Chameleon boasts that she's going to win it. Olympus plays with his disc shooter and gets told off by Chameleon, who doesn't want a repeat of last time, where she got shot.

Meanwhile, Great Wolf talks with Tsunami and The Bam. He relays to them that he had a vivid nightmare, something he thinks was a vision of the future. Turbo scoffs at him because, despite his recent respect-filled feud with Star Warrior, he's still the same Turbo. Great Wolf says Tsunami was in it, which of course gets Tsunami's attention. He then narrates the dream, which we see play out.

A dream sequence in a show like *WMAC Masters* could easily come off as silly, but this one manages to strike an ominous if confusing chord. It centers around The Machine and Olympus taking part in a Dragon Belt ceremony, an event that could happen if matches today shake out a certain way!

Back in reality, Tsunami says it's cool that he was the hero (an interesting interpretation of events). While Great Wolf says, the weirdest part is that Olympus and The Machine can end up in

This dream sequence also features a creepy set of lines from the WMAC official we see each episode instructing the fighters to head to the Battle Zones. This official was played by David "Fang" Yuen, who unfortunately passed away in 2021.

the Dragon Belt ceremony if they both win their fights today. Yin Yang Man, who had been hovering just out of camera shot, says he'll make sure it doesn't happen. He's going to beat Olympus.

In the season two storyline outline, this is actually set up in the previous episode, Great Wolf is described as being able to enter a trance (thanks to his heritage and some sort of training) and see possible visions of the future. I find the decision to take the agency out of it interesting. He can't do it at will, but it happens in times of need, making him more of a Chosen One figure.

Preliminary Match One
Competitors:
Cyclone ⬡ ⬡ ⬡ ⬡ vs. The Machine ⬣ ⬣ ✦
Battle Zone: Ghost Town
Ninjas: Ghost

First, Cyclone on four Ki Symbols seems ridiculous at first glance, as we have never seen him compete before, but it can be explained.

We wanted it to feel like there were more fighters, lots of fighters, that kind of moved in and out of the competition, ones you didn't always see. Just because you were seeing someone for the first time (on the show) doesn't mean it was their first fight. We wanted the world to feel bigger.

Norman Grossfeld
Executive Producer

Cyclone busts out a big spin kick to start, making an impressive first impression. The Machine continues his tradition of sending ninjas through various parts of the Ghost Town set, palm-striking a ninja through a pile of barrels. He follows that up by doing the same to another ninja, sending it crashing into a wheel. To cap off the destruction, he side-kicks a ninja through one of the sets.

That's enough for the ninjas, the one versus one starting quickly. We get a fun old west style shot as the two men stare each other down. The one against one quickly turns into the power of The Machine versus the agility of Cyclone. The Machine has the early advantage, but a big jump kick sends him through a wagon wheel. Cyclone follows that up with a double rotation spin kick, looking very impressive against the former Dragon Star champion.

> *The Machine was twice as tall as I was and had the power. So (my character) decided to compete with skill and speed (in the fight).*

Akihiro "Yuji" Noguchi
Cyclone

The ninjas are called back in to up the action, and Cyclone does the traditional "run into the saloon and beat up ninjas off screen" spot. He somehow makes it to the second story of the saloon, where he takes on a ninja and is down to one power bar!

The Machine decides to do something dramatic. He kicks the pillar holding up the second level of the saloon, breaking it and sending Cyclone and the hapless ninja crashing to the ground! The impact is enough to drain Cyclone's last power bar, giving The Machine the win! The ninja celebrates like it was his victory, for some reason, while The Machine gloats but then helps Cyclone up.

> *That gag was part of the Wild West Stunt Show (at Universal). We just used it to our advantage.*

Isaac Florentine
Director

This was a wildly fun fight. Cyclone was made to look incredibly strong for a debuting fighter, going toe-to-toe with one of the best in the WMAC, but not at the expense of the The Machine. They had excellent chemistry, as The Machine tended to have with smaller, more agile fighters, and they made use of the Ghost Town Battle Zone in a new, unexpected way, which at this point in the show was very hard to do.

Of the few cast members to only have one fight in the series, Cyclone's is far and away the best performance from an on-screen action perspective, and it was a personal highlight for Noguchi.

> *(Hakim's) personality was excellent. We had no problems with the fight. It was a good memory for me from the show.*

Akihiro "Yuji" Noguchi
Cyclone

Yuji, however, remembers this fight being a one time appearance, not recalling having any other fights pitched for him or scheduled, which is a real shame.

Back in the Inner Sanctum, Great Wolf is disturbed. His vision seems to be coming true. The Bam and Turbo say it's all coincidence. After all, the odds of The Machine winning were fifty-fifty.

Yin Yang Man enters the Arena, and we get a cool but creepy shot of his glass eye which has his Yin Yang symbol on it! He also wears a cape. Capes are cool. He does a kata, which includes a spot where he does a neck-bridge front flip all the way across the set. It's not something that looks phenomenally exciting to a kid, but to someone who has watched any degree of martial arts, wrestling, or other combat sport, it's a staggering show of strength.

Olympus enters next, bringing his disc shooter. He does a few kicks and then fires the gun at a box with Yin Yang Man's symbol on it. There's a fun first person POV shot where it seems like the camera is mounted on the disc, long before GoPro's made it commonplace. The disc ruptures the box, Yin Yang gives Olympus a "what is that it?" sort of look, and Olympus counts down from three with his fingers. As the countdown ends, the box explodes.

Preliminary Match Two
Competitors:
Yin Yang Man ⬢⬢⬢⬢⬢⬢ ✦ vs. **Olympus** ⬢ ✦
Battle Zone: Mayan Mystery
Ninjas: Camouflage

The ninjas start with a bang in this one, scoring a big front kick on Yin Yang Man right from the word go. Both Masters show off an array of kicks while dealing with the ninjas, Yin Yang Man with more variety but Olympus with more power.

Some of those guys (in the cast) had tons of moves since they came from the touring circuit. I didn't come from that world. I came from Olympic Tae Kwon Do, which is very different. I didn't have as many fancy techniques, but I tried to make them look as real as possible.

Herb Perez
Olympus

Yin Yang Man busts out a series of strikes on a ninja that resembles something from a video game, a sort of mega combo of non-stop quick hits. Meanwhile, Olympus fights atop the Battle Zone, near the tops of the statues, something we don't often see, nailing a judo throw on a ninja.

The one versus one portion starts with Olympus going hard for the win early, scoring with his trademark strong kicks.

Herb had the strongest kicks. His legs were just... he was just so powerful.

Jamie Webster
Great Wolf

He loved the nadaban kick. He'd go outside-in. He could clobber you if he wanted to.

Erik Betts
Panther

David Morizot, one of the stuntmen to regularly play a ninja, also remembered the kick.

Herb was a guy who didn't come from (the stunt and acting) world, so choreography wasn't always his strong suit. If he ever forgot a move, he'd start throwing those (nadaban) kicks, and boy, you had to watch out!

David Morizot
Ninja

Akihiro Noguchi
Cyclone
Discipline: Karate

Better known as "Yuji", the man who would have been Cyclone ended up doing more as a stunt coordinator for the show than an actual character thanks to an unfortunate accident that left him with a broken foot. Took part in several iterations of the Power Rangers franchise, and went on to have a prolific career as an action director and stunt coordinator.

The Nadaban kick, also known as the Tornado kick, is a spinning roundhouse kick popular in Tae Kwon Do. Herb Perez used it throughout the series.

The fight is close, but Olympus's powerful kicks end up being too much for Yin Yang's flashy Wushu, and the gold medalist wins!

Back in the Inner Sanctum, the Masters talk about Great Wolf's dream. The Bam points out that Great Wolf already knew who was fighting, so it was easy for his subconscious to put the pieces together. Someone points out that Tsunami is now missing, just like in Great Wolf's dream.

Battle Dome Final
Competitors: The Machine ⬣ ⬣ ✦ vs. Olympus ⬣ ✦

The battle starts very even, as you'd expect from two former Dragon Star champions. The first ninja enters the fray just as the Masters grapple with each other, rappelling right between them, scoring a double kick on both Masters! Quite the feather in the cap for that young recruit, it must be said. The Masters then proceed to pummel the ninjas for a little, once again, making one wonder why anyone would willingly join the WMAC Academy. They've only graduated *two* people, and most of your time is spent getting walloped by the world's greatest martial artists.

Next comes an absolutely wild spot. The Machine throws Olympus up in the air, but Olympus catches himself on the gymnast rings that hang down in the dome. The Machine then lobs a ninja at him, but Olympus kicks it back at The Machine, who avoids the falling foe. By this point in the series, it takes something truly remarkable to really create a wow moment, and this definitely qualifies.

The Masters' exchange punches, neither landing anything heavy, but then The Machine finally opens the scoring with a spinning roundhouse kick, sending Olympus into the dome!

> *Hakim was a heavy hitter. Great guy, but fighting him wasn't always the most fun.*

Herb Perez
Olympus

Olympus manages to tie it up, sending the fight to sudden death. It doesn't last much longer, however, as The Machine's size and strength are too much for

Olympus to handle, giving The Machine the win!

The Machine celebrates by jumping onto one of the platforms lining the cage before hopping down to shake Olympus's hand. Olympus's run of bad luck after losing the Dragon Star continues, while The Machine seems to be getting back on track. Red Dragon applauds his friend and rival from the Dragon Star throne.

Back in the Inner Sanctum, Great Wolf is very nervous before the Dragon Belt ceremony, saying, "This is it." Clearly expecting it to unfold as it did in his dream. Tiger Claw, the voice of reason for a change, tells him to relax.

From the comfort of the Inner Sanctum, Great Wolf watches the ceremony nervously while several other Masters watch him. In the end, the ceremony goes off without a hitch. No drama, no spooky ranting by the WMAC official, and no save by Tsunami. Turbo takes the chance to mock Great Wolf, but Great Wolf still thinks something is very wrong. Tiger Claw asks, "what could go wrong in a Dragon Star match?" which is met with incredulity, Turbo reminding them of the Mysterious Ninja.

The episode then pauses there with a dramatic "To be continued!" freeze frame that is somewhat undercut by the addition of a post-credits scene featuring Tiger Claw. He speaks about honoring your elders and how the knowledge they pass down can be important, be that martial arts, heritage, or even recipes.

This episode is a strange one. It has two fantastic opening fights and a good Dome, but the central storyline of the episode (Great Wolf's dream/vision) doesn't really have a payoff. While the Tsunami involvement is a subtle bit of foreshadowing, the whole thing feels like treading water for the next episode. The end of part one of a two-parter should leave things amped up, full of tension and drama. This simply feels flat. It's not a bad episode by any stretch, but definitely a missed opportunity.

CHAPTER 33

S2E12:
Vision of Evil
Part II

Lady Lightning vs. Princess vs. Chameleon

"I had no idea it would be happening until I got the script"

As expected, this episode starts with a previously on *WMAC Masters* recap of the last episode's events.

After the show's usual intro (not the Ladies Intro, surprisingly), we see Black Widow presenting the Dragon Star to the Council, bowing to them, about to relinquish it once and for all!

Back in the Inner Sanctum, Red Dragon and The Machine play chess while Yin Yang Man watches. Red Dragon says he doesn't understand Black Widow's decision. If he had to give up the Dragon Star, he'd want to go down fighting, just like The Machine did. The Machine says he hopes that Red Dragon is still on the throne when he gets back to full Dragon Belt so he can take the Dragon Star back from him. Their banter is friendly but serious, reflecting their real-life competitiveness and respect.

Chris and I are good friends. We played off each other well.

Hakim Alston
The Machine

Red Dragon quickly jumps up and yells at Turbo to stop messing with his special Red Dragon weapons (which we last saw before his Dragon Star match with Warlock). Turbo says he was just admiring them (a decided non-apology). They snipe back and forth, reinforcing their characterizations. Turbo is still Turbo, full of venom and intensity despite no longer being an outcast, and Red Dragon, despite being a good guy to the core, still has a high opinion of himself.

I was definitely portrayed as having an ego, but we all had egos. We were the best of the best, all of us. We were world champions, Olympic gold medalists. It was friendly, but there was definitely competition there.

Chris Casamassa
Red Dragon

After a break, there is another Inner Sanctum scene with Red Dragon. This time he is speaking into a tape recorder, narrating the legend of the Red Dragon. He explains that there used to be five dragons, each of a different color, the red dragon being the most powerful, the one the others turned to when they needed help. He explains that's why he chose the name.

Next, they ask Turbo to come up with a story. They're working on something for Secrets of the Masters, their new website. Wizard shrinks back, saying he doesn't have any secrets (not suspicious in the slightest). While Turbo snarks that they should stop worrying about the past, history is being made right now in the Arena!

WMAC Masters did have a presence on the nascent World Wide Web at the time, one that was fairly advanced for the era. Their website hosted chats, behind-the-scenes videos, and other planned content had the show continued.

My company, Pangea, was the agency of record for Bandai's digital solutions. We launched their first ever website across multiple platforms such as America Online, Prodigy, and Apple's eWorld called Pangea ToyNet. WMAC Masters was one of the featured properties on the website.

John Schulte
Creative Consultant

While Secrets of the Masters never had time to come to fruition, Schulte remembered they did several narrative segments built around the show, so the concept very well could have ended up on the website had the show continued.

Back in the Arena, we see Lady Lightning, Princess, and Chameleon all make their way onto the Dragon Star platform. Black Widow sits on the throne, holding the Dragon Star for one last time. Each of the challengers approaches her and bows, showing respect for the departing champion. Baby the lizard accompanies Chameleon because of course he does. After she bows to Black Widow, Chameleon gives her fellow challengers the iciest of icy glares.

The Council calls down the Hapkido Council member, an ominous figure clad in a black cloak, their head totally covered, to ceremonially assist Black Widow in surrendering the Dragon Star. As they place the Star in the Tri-Chamber Cyber-Cell, they play an audio message from Black Widow, wishing everyone well, talking about how proud she was to hold the Dragon Star, and telling everyone to live their lives by the Code of the Dragon Star.

This whole ordeal is strange and more than a little suspicious. It immediately set the stage for something being out of the ordinary. Watching as an adult, the resemblance to a sports retirement ceremony was more obvious, but as a kid, it just seemed weird. Nevertheless, the scene works, setting the stage for what's to come by making the whole fight feel unprecedented.

The Council Member and Black Widow leave the platform, leaving it time for the Dragon Star to be decided!

Dragon Star Championship: Lady Lightning vs. Princess vs. Chameleon

The fight starts off fast and furious. First, all three women get a chance to showcase their skills. This is particularly true of Princess, who hasn't had nearly as much screen time as her fellow fighters and deserved the opportunity to show off her talent.

Mer Mer was a total sweetheart. She made me fall in love with Wushu. Her style was just so beautiful.

Shannon "Irish" Stewart
Script Supervisor

Shannon "Irish" Stewart and Mer Mer Chen behind the scenes. Photo from Shannon "Irish" Stewart.

There's a fun moment as Chameleon is knocked onto the side of the platform but manages to hold on. When she re-emerges atop the rotating stage, she's wearing blue, not green.

That fight was difficult. So many people on that platform. And it was even harder because I had to keep jumping off to go change wardrobe to the different color tights.

Sophia Crawford
Chameleon

Lady Lightning scores a big kick on Princess, sending her off the platform and ending her hopes of becoming Dragon Star champion!

Mer Mer was great. Just a really talented, hard-working girl.

Christine Rodrigues
Lady Lightning

The platform fills up with ninjas due to the numerous violations by the fighters. It's a full platform, even without Princess remaining in the fight, probably the most packed of any Dragon Star fights.

The Masters go to work on the ninjas, absolutely hammering them. Chameleon hits a beautiful jumping split kick, a fun camera trick hiding another costume change, leaving her in pink. The kick sends two ninjas off, as well. The Masters work together to kick the last ninja off, but he holds onto the side of the platform, as Chameleon did earlier. He climbs back up and grapples with Lady Lightning. Chameleon seizes her moment, nailing a flying side kick, sending both off the platform and winning the Dragon Star!

We cut to the Inner Sanctum, where everyone celebrates the awesome match. Or at least everyone who is *there* celebrates the awesome match.

Baby the lizard joins Chameleon on the platform through methods unknown to celebrate. The Tri-Chamber Cyber-Cell rises, but instead of the Dragon Star, a giant JuDiKo symbol is revealed!

We get a quick cut to the Inner Sanctum, where all hell breaks loose. Turbo shouts, "What is that!?" while everyone else freaks out. Everyone but Great Wolf, that is, who looks dejected and says, "I knew it."

Back in the Arena, we get a nice pull-back shot of Chameleon freaking out. We even see the Council, definitely not mannequins this time, arguing with each other!

This reveal was far and away the most shocking moment of the series up to that point, only to be eclipsed by the series-ending cliffhanger still to come. Chameleon's reaction, a mixture of confusion and fear, was perfect. After being heavily recruited by Tracer and Warlock for most of the season, fans would naturally wonder if she was in on JuKiDo's plot. Her reaction could either be read as a rebuttal or as playing along.

This episode is really Sophia Crawford's time to shine. Her performance in the Dragon Star match was fantastic, showing off her array of martial arts skills, and her pitch-perfect reaction demonstrated she was one of the better actors on the show.

We head back to the Inner Sanctum, where the strange JuKiDo star sits on a table. Tiger Claw stares at it, saying it's the same as the JuKiDo ninja's tattoo that he saw. He beats himself up about not holding on to the ninja who attacked Wizard, instead choosing to get Wizard medical attention.

The Machine says Tiger Claw did the right thing. They lament having no clue who this group could be, but Olympus appears and says they do have clues. There's been a plot unfolding for quite some time, he says, brandishing a BINDER!

He explains that the Council gave him full access to the WMAC Archives for his investigation and proceeds to lay out a very impressive case against Warlock and Tracer. He points out how the Mysterious Ninja used a smoke bomb, just like Warlock did during his kata before his Dragon Star match, as well as noting how the strange ninja in that fight didn't appear to attack Warlock at all, focusing instead on Red Dragon.

He exonerates Chameleon, however, noting her horrified reaction to the JuKiDo symbol. This gives viewers another shot of it, including, for the first time, its conclusion, where she lets out a horror-movie-worthy scream-queen shriek.

The Masters proceed to talk some serious crap about Tracer and Warlock. Tiger Claw, angry at the whole situation, says there's a lot of stuff Wizard didn't tell them. Wizard appears and says it's time for them to learn the rest. He explains that he knows what they're up against and gives them the backstory on his and Warlock's history with JuKiDo. He shows them the faded tattoo of the JuKiDo symbol, saying he's had to live with that burden most of his life.

The Masters speculate that Warlock's entire career was an attempt to infiltrate the WMAC for JuKiDo. Their plan to steal the Dragon Star was only enacted after Warlock's Dragon Star match. Had he won it, they wouldn't have needed to steal it. Wizard says he doesn't know Tracer at all, but he wants answers just as badly as the others. Now they just have to find Warlock and Tracer.

The show ends with the most shocking cliffhanger imaginable. We get a shot of someone placing the Dragon Star into a briefcase. Then, we see Tracer and Warlock on some sort of flight deck of a naval carrier. Tracer tells Warlock the chopper will be there in five minutes. They celebrate their win, saying the only thing to do now is to figure out what to do with the Dragon Star. Then, in the most shocking reveal of the show, Tsunami, wearing all black, holds the briefcase and asks, "Yeah, what should we do with it?" before laughing!

I had no idea it would be happening until I got the script. We didn't usually get things that far in advance, so it was definitely a surprise. It was cool, though. Just a surprise.

Hien Nguyen
Tsunami

It's impossible to overstate how incredible this reveal was. Tsunami, the everyman character, the underdog, the unquestioned good guy turning out to be part of JuKiDo? It was unthinkable. I distinctly recall conversations at the lunch table of my elementary school about it. One of my friends was in disbelief that his favorite could have gone rogue.

It remains the great, lingering question of the series, but before we can address it, we have one more episode to look at, although it's one the vast majority of *WMAC Masters* fans don't even acknowledge.

In "Vision of Evil Part II" Olympus lays out the evidence against JuKiDo.

Chameleon watches Great Wolf's ritual in "Vision of Evil Part I." Photos from Bruce Heinsius Photography.

CHAPTER 34

S2E13:
The Turning Points
of the Masters

This, the final episode of *WMAC Masters*, is what is known as a clip show, an episode of a series pieced together entirely out of previously seen footage. There is no closure to the shocking Tsunami revelation, no new footage at all. It is an entirely disappointing and unworthy way for such an amazing television show to end. It is not even a particularly convincing recap of the series as a whole, as the clips are entirely from season one, which does nothing to show the massive evolution of the show.

The episode was a necessary evil. They had already wrapped shooting when it was realized they needed one more episode to fulfill their commitments. This need was likely tied to the funding and budget issues that plagued season two, though no one I spoke to remembered the exact circumstances that necessitated this bonus episode. The season two storyline document listed some episodes and stories being "out of place" compared to their final running positions, so a shuffle in production likely produced the gap.

This episode adds nothing new. It is instead simply a re-airing of the flashback vignettes from The Machine, Yin Yang Man, Superstar, and Olympus. There is no reason to make this episode part of your re-watch or your first watch. The vast majority of fans discount this episode having existed at all, considering the end of the previous episode the actual end of the series, with its intense, shocking cliffhanger the much more fitting finale than this sad pile of reused footage.

CHAPTER 35

What Could Have Been

Season Three and Beyond...

"The plan was always to do three seasons..."

WMAC Masters ended its television run on a major cliffhanger, leaving its legion of young fans with burning questions that should have been answered in season three. There was no reason to think that the answers wouldn't be coming. Even the cast didn't see the cancellation looming.

The plan was always to do three seasons so we could hit the episode limit to get into syndication. Then it could be on weekdays after school, Monday through Friday. That's where the real money was. So three seasons was the expectation from the start.

Norman Grossfeld
Executive Producer

I think we were all expecting (a third season). We knew it was the plan to get into syndication, so we were all expecting to be called back for season three. No one thought the last episode was the last episode.

Chris Casamassa
Red Dragon

I definitely thought there was going to be more. I didn't know what was going to happen, but I figured it wouldn't be good for (my character). If you're the focus of a big cliffhanger moment (like the JuKiDo Statue rising), it's rarely a good thing. I've been on enough shows to know that. :laughs:

Sophia Crawford
Chameleon

Before the cancellation, there were definite plans in place for the direction of season three, including full-on set designs. Dan Hubp, the jack of all trades who worked as a Production Designer, Editor, and Second Unit Director, shared some of them with me for this book.

They depict an obstacle course-like structure featuring the rotating platform from Dragon Star fights, like something out of *American Ninja Warrior* or *Ultimate Beastmaster*. The cast would fight on it, he told me, though exact details of how the match would end eluded him, if they had ever been fleshed out, to begin with.

Original sketches for
proposed season 3 sets.
Photos from Dan Hubp.

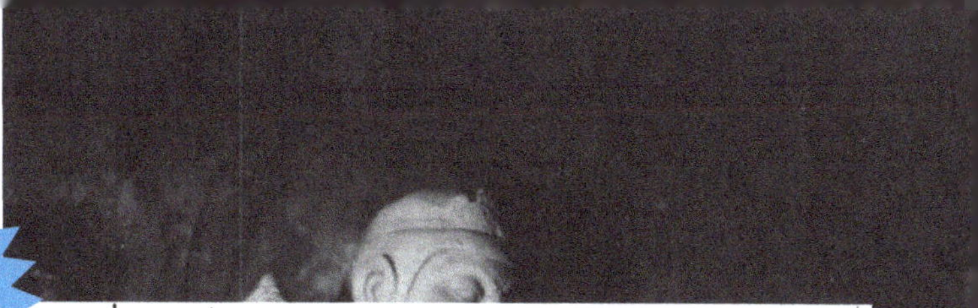

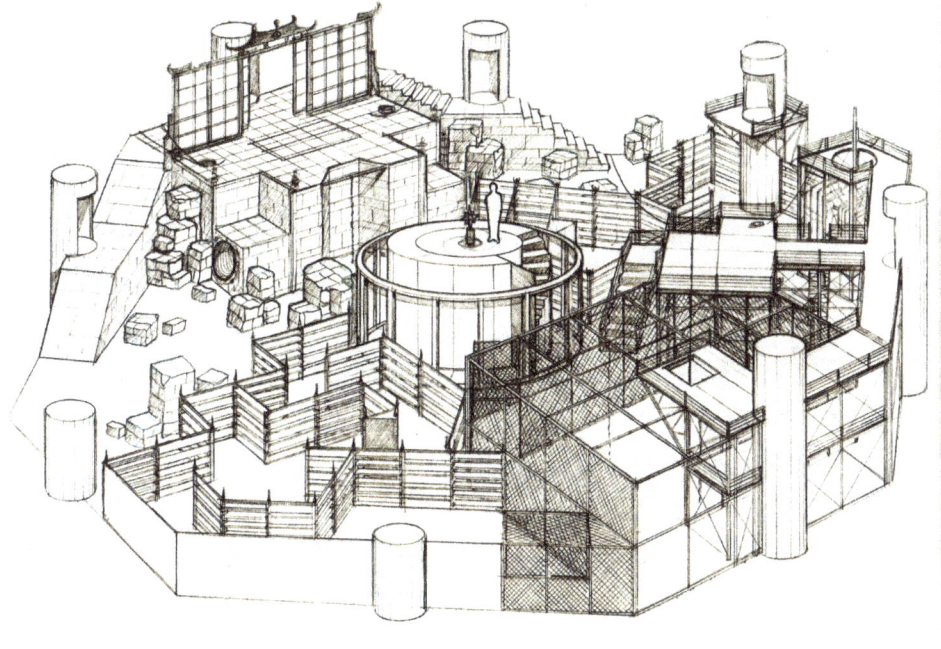

These were all ideas. Nothing was really finalized. A lot of things would have been budget-dependent.

Dan Hubp
Production Designer, Editor

Any plans that were in place were the definition of preliminary, subject to the ever-changing state of the show's funding, which ultimately is why the show never got the third season.

The numbers just weren't there. I think it's fair to say everyone wanted to continue the show, but it came down to a business decision.

Norman Grossfeld
Executive Producer

There were persistent rumors on the internet that there were scripts written for season three. However, this comes from a misinterpreted comment from Herb Perez in the 2000s. Several commenters continue to assert that Herb Perez claimed to have S3 scripts, but the man himself disputes this.

There are never any scripts written for season three. What I said was after the show ended, Dan (Hubp) and I worked on some ideas to continue the legacy of the show, but in its own universe. It wasn't WMAC Masters, just in the same spirit of the show.

Herb Perez
Olympus

Not getting a season three was not necessarily a death knell for the show. Even during season two, there were plans to continue to tell the story of *WMAC Masters* in other, non-television forms.

During season two, there were several conversations that happened about what plans could be. At one point, a movie was discussed.

Hakim Alston
The Machine

It's important to remember that we got our budget slashed for season two. It became pretty apparent (while filming season two) that, barring some sort of miracle, there wouldn't be a third season. So we shifted our focus to trying to set the story up to be finished as a movie, be that a made-for-TV movie or theatrical or whatever. That's why we moved towards the cliffhanger ending, to set that up.

Norman Grossfeld
Executive Producer

WMAC Masters: The Movie

A word of caution before moving into the meat of this particular section is in order. The conversations I had with Norman Grossfeld were 25 years after the show. Memories are fallible. While I have no doubt he gave me his best recollections, he stressed that they were simply his memories, not necessarily the Gospel truth. While he, perhaps more than anyone else, was in a position to know, he wanted to stress that it was possible others might remember things differently, and that didn't mean either one of them was wrong.

The other, perhaps even greater caveat, was that all of what follows was strictly in the conversation stages. Unfortunately, the efforts to make a movie never moved beyond the pitching stages into actual pre-production, so all the information Grossfeld had to give me was strictly hypothetical and, like the talk of season three, entirely budget-dependent.

That said, here is what the man behind the story told me about *WMAC Masters: The Movie.*

The movie wasn't written, but the idea was JuKiDo was set up as this anti-WMAC, anti-Code of the Dragon Star organization, so we were going to introduce who was behind JuKiDo, sort of an uber bad guy that had his own plan.

Norman Grossfeld
Executive Producer

This makes total sense. Neither Warlock nor Tracer screamed evil mastermind. They were soldiers, not commanders. Who would play this big bad? It would have depended entirely on funding, according to Grossfeld. Casting discussions never began, even preliminary ones, so the "big bad" existed only as an abstract. Considering the connections between *WMAC Masters* and martial arts action cinema, it's not unfair to presume that the actor (or actress?) chosen to play the villain would have come from that world.

So this leader of JuKiDo would have orchestrated all this to get control of the Dragon Star. The movie would have been about the Masters trying to get the Dragon Star back, finding out why JuKiDo wanted it. It would have put the show in a much wider world outside of the WMAC Headquarters.

Norman Grossfeld
Executive Producer

When asked about what they had hoped to happen in season three (had it transpired), several of the cast mentioned the idea of taking the series outside the bounds of the tournament (or Universal).

I wanted to see the show go bigger. We were moving that direction with the story. I wanted it to open up outside of the WMAC, the Inner Sanctum, and Arena.

Herb Perez
Olympus

Jamie Webster remembered an idea he wanted to pitch for season three, based on a real-life event transpiring at the time.

In Native American culture, the birth of a white buffalo is a big deal. It's considered an omen of something important happening, a sign of times changing. Back then (at the time that season three would have been shot), a white buffalo had just been born. I wanted to work it into the story as some omen of the battle between JuDiKo and the WMAC. I thought it would be so cool to fly out to the reservation and film with it, show actual Native culture and belief. It would have fit the story so well, but obviously, it didn't happen.

Jamie Webster
Great Wolf

In terms of the movie, the big question would not only have been "Will the Masters get the Dragon Star back?" but also "Why is the Dragon Star so important?" Obviously, the Dragon Star was the trophy of the WMAC, representing that its holder was the "World's Greatest Martial Artist," but according to Norman, its importance ran far deeper than that.

The thought was there'd be more to the Dragon Star than just a symbol of who the Dragon Star Champion was. It was going to fit in; it'd be this sort of ancient thing that somehow connected to the "sun source" of all the martial arts. And the Dragon Star itself was some sort of device that would unlock an amazing secret. What it was going to be, and where it was going, what the power was that would be unlocked wasn't all figured out, but that's why there was value to having the Dragon Star. It would do something, unlock something for this bad guy organization. So we'd introduce the idea that all the martial arts stemmed from one source, but what would that source be? Was it another planet, another dimension? That was all stuff that was going to be revealed.

Norman Grossfeld
Executive Producer

So the Dragon Star was not just a symbol but an ancient artifact connected to the origins of martial arts. It sounds astounding in the context of the show, but with the expressed goal of expanding the scope of Masters to a broader universe, it makes sense.

Interestingly, Michael Foley expressed a similar idea that he pitched to me, supposedly for season three (not a movie follow-up).

I actually pitched an idea of how to combine Star-Gate Atlantis with the WMAC and how the Dragon Star was a key to open up an ancient vault with hidden secrets to put an end to the villains of that show; some kind of life-force sucking aliens of a vampiric bend. The martial art talents would be especially necessary to defeat the highly trained guards of the vault. They liked the idea, but then we were canceled. Keep in mind this was just my idea, not the producers.

Michael Foley
Tracer

While Stargate SG-1 didn't hit the airwaves until 1997, the original Stargate film was released in 1994, and the cross-pollination of ideas was certainly possible (with the ravages of 25 years switching the Stargate iterations around in Mr. Foley's mind). Whether or not Michael Foley's suggestion influenced what Norman and company had planned for the continuation of the show is impossible to say with certainty. Norman didn't indicate that the idea came from outside the creative team. Still, in other conversations, both cast and crew members mentioned that the producers were always "Willing to listen to suggestions."

With the Dragon Star being the key piece of the movie puzzle, not quite a MacGuffin but close, another question near and dear to the hearts of Masters fans was a simple one- what would have happened with Tsunami? Was he really in JuKiDo? Was he a double agent? Even the man himself had questions.

I have no idea what was supposed to happen! :laughs: I didn't know I'd be joining the bad guys until I got the script, and they never gave me any idea what was going to happen next. I was left hanging just like everyone else.

Hien Nguyen
Tsunami

While I initially found this hard to believe, the sentiment was echoed by every member of the cast I spoke to.

Yeah, they didn't really tell us in detail where things were going. They'd give some of us kind of a big picture overview, but it wasn't all laid out.

Chris Casamassa
Red Dragon

We didn't know what would happen until we got the scripts. Then we'd all race to see how many lines we had! :laughs:

Jamie Webster
Great Wolf

MacGuffin
an object or device in a movie or a book that serves merely as a trigger for the plot. The phrase was coined by Alfred Hitchcock.

Back to the traitorous Tsunami, was he really a bad guy all along?

We didn't have all the details worked out, but we knew the character arcs for the major players- where they were, where they were going to end up. We just didn't know in exactly what way we'd end up there. But yes, Tsunami was someone who was going to go through some things and eventually have to decide what side he was on. Ultimately he'd end up rejoining the side of good.

Norman Grossfeld
Executive Producer

It is, of course, the logical conclusion to his storyline. The young fighter the audience connected with, somehow tempted by the allure of JuKiDo, eventually redeems himself, proving that the Code of the Dragon Star was the true path. It's a mini version of the hero's journey.

And what of Warlock, Tracer, and the other supposedly JuKiDo aligned fighters? Norman didn't recall specific plans, but Tracer was not likely to have had a redemptive ark.

Norman did, however, remember the idea for the epic final battle between good and evil.

There was going to be a climactic battle featuring everyone from the series fighting it out to get the Dragon Star. It was going to be huge, epic, far beyond the scope we could do on TV.

Norman Grossfeld
Executive Producer

It's not hard to picture legions of JuKiDo ninjas lining up to be mowed down by the combined forces of the WMAC. Tracer and Warlock doing battle with the main series heroes. Tsunami, coming to his senses, turning the tide of the battle, perhaps even securing the Dragon Star for the good guys. It could easily resemble a scene from *Seven Samurai*.

But it wasn't to be. The funding just couldn't be secured. The same problems that plagued efforts to continue as a TV series were impossible to overcome, either as a theatrical or made for TV film. Despite creating a wildly ahead of its time show on a shoestring budget, in the eyes of many in the entertainment industry, the show was a failure. There would be no movie.

This was not the only possible future for *WMAC Masters*, however. When I showed Norman Grossfeld the designs for season three by Dan Hubp, he speculated that they were from an idea they had to extend the show's shelf life and secure new funding.

We had talks with several potential partners in Las Vegas about making the show an attraction there. This was around the time where Vegas was beginning to market itself as more "family-friendly" and have stage shows and more kid-friendly activities. We thought we might be able to find a partner at one of the major casinos and make WMAC Masters a live event experience in addition to the TV show. These (sketches) could have been part of that.

Norman Grossfeld
Executive Producer

As with the other possible continuations of the show, these talks never advanced, and there were never any set plans in place. In the end, none of the possible scenarios came to fruition, ending the show after two seasons and canceling a slew of other projects that had been on tap...

I Never Got My Action Figure!

As season two was being filmed, there were plans in place to make another series of the main *WMAC Masters* toy line. Unfortunately, the show's cancellation ended these plans, leaving several of the cast with memories of seeing designs or concept art but no toys to show for it.

> *The toy company (Bandai) sent representatives to the set to get photographs of all the new guys, take measurements, and get a "favorite technique" for each of us for use for a toy. If things had gone to a third season, I would have got a toy. I was disappointed in that.*

Michael Foley
Tracer

Bruce Hiensius was a photographer on the *WMAC Masters* set and ended up taking pictures of Wizard for Bandai to use to design a toy, confirming that he was to be included in the next series.

It stands to reason that Warlock, who plays such a prominent role in season two, would have also been included. No women were in the first wave of figures, but Chameleon seems a likely addition to the line due to her importance and Michael Foley's memories of all the new actors being photographed for toys. While Crawford didn't recall any reference photos being taken, she did recall being told she'd be in the line.

> *Yes, I definitely was going to be one of the toys. The producers told me early on that I'd be getting a toy. I was very disappointed it didn't happen.*

Sophia Crawford:
Chameleon

Willie "The Bam" Johnson was not a second-season addition to the show but recalls seeing concept art for a Bam action figure, presumably to be released in the next line. While he was not permitted to keep the art, he described it as comic book-like.

Other Projects

Another wave of action figures was not the only merchandising casualty of the decision to cancel the show. I spoke to John Schulte, whose company Pangea worked as a creative development company for Bandai. They had several different *WMAC Masters* related projects, including building and managing the show's web presence, and several more that never saw the light of day due to the show's cancellation.

The most interesting of these products that never saw the light of day is what he described to me as a "complete CD Rom," a sort of interactive encyclopedia for the show. These hybrid "edutainment" titles were all the rage in the 90s, and a martial arts themed interactive encyclopedia just screams *WMAC Masters*.

There are also persistent rumors of a *WMAC Masters* video game that never got made. Considering that *WMAC Masters* has often been described as "live-action *Mortal Kombat* for kids," a *WMAC Masters* fighting game in that style seems a no-brainer. One early 2000s internet thread claimed that there was a *WMAC Masters* game in "Heavy Development," including footage of the cast being captured *Mortal Kombat* style. Norman Grossfeld debunked this myth.

A WMAC Masters video game was always part of the plan, but it was never realized. I'm sure there were many conversations about it with potential licensees, and there may have been some preliminary planning, but "heavy development" was not done.

Norman Grossfeld
Executive Producer

In addition to a video game and more action figures, there were tentative plans for more books, as well as tie-in toys such as toy versions of the Master Blaster weapons for Red Dragon and Olympus.

We wanted to license everything. That was the goal, to create licensing opportunities. We had talks about all kinds of products. We wanted it to be everywhere like Power Rangers was, or Pokémon would later be.

Norman Grossfeld
Executive Producer

This can be seen from the trademark filing for the *WMAC Masters* dragon logo. The logo was trademarked for use across dozens of different categories, ranging from the expected books and VHS tapes to ice cream treats, debit cards, and plastic cake decorations. This filing is a sort of standard catch-all for licensing-heavy companies and doesn't necessarily mean they were actively creating all of these products, just that they wanted the option to.

In the end, *WMAC Masters* never got the chance to become the global brand its creators envisioned. There would be no *WMAC Masters* lunchboxes, comic books, or bed sheets. Despite its footprint not being as deep as the creators envisioned, the show would still leave a lasting legacy.

Reference photographs for future action figures.
Photos from Bruce Heinsius Photography.

CHAPTER 36

We Changed the Game

WMAC Masters's Lasting Influence

"It meant a lot to me to see that kind of diversity"

One thing mentioned by nearly everyone I spoke to associated with the show was how ahead of its time it was. Not only was the storytelling high level for a mid-90s kid's show, but the actual action sequences were among the best of the decade on TV, let alone on kid's TV.

> *You look at what we were doing. There weren't a lot of guys doing that at the time, especially on TV. In a few years, you'd have a lot of the Hong Kong action guys come over and start taking over the stunt world, but that hadn't happened yet.*

Carmichael Simon
Kid Carmichael

> *We changed the game, man. We were real-life superheroes. We weren't Power Rangers under masks. We were using our real names, doing real martial arts. We influenced a whole generation of kids.*

Willie Johnson
The Bam

This may sound like braggadocio, but it's true. In interviews for this book, people from walks of life as diverse as professional wrestling, stunt work, acting, and traditional martial arts all expressed to me how *WMAC Masters* influenced them.

> *I'd been a martial artist my whole life, but I was thinking about quitting. I was around 14 or so. Then the show aired, and I saw some of the people I was competing with and against, like Richard Branden, who actually mentored me in Wushu, and it made me feel like if they could do it, I could do it, too!*

Jimmy Manfreddy
Martial Artist, Hollywood Stuntman

Manfreddy would go on to do stunts in hit shows like *Ozark* and, most interestingly, *Cobra Kai*, where he worked alongside *Quest For The Dragon Star's* co-host William Zabka.

It came on here after Saturday morning wrestling.
It was just the coolest thing. The moves, the characters, how
diverse it was... all my friends and I were obsessed.

Ophidian
Professional Wrestler

With the close proximity to wrestling programs and the many connections between the show and pro wrestling, it's no surprise the show left a lasting impression on the sports entertainment industry.

A lot of what we did in CHIKARA, especially with the Crucible
storyline, was inspired by Masters. The idea of a company being
invaded by this outside force but having it happen from within.

Ophidian
Professional Wrestler

Like many fans, the show spoke to the young luchador-to-be on a deep level.

I tell you what, as a young Puerto Rican kid, it meant a lot to me
to see that kind of diversity in martial arts on my TV.

Ophidian
Professional Wrestler

There was nothing like it at the time from a diversity standpoint.
Men, women, all races, all martial arts disciplines...

Norman Grossfeld
Executive producer

It was not only the young, impressionable fans of the show who were influenced by the Masters and their skills. In the years that followed the show's end, the cast branched out in numerous directions. In the years and decades that followed, they collectively and individually left a massive mark on several industries.

Several stayed in the entertainment industry, working as actors, stuntpeople, directors, and fight choreographers. It's hard to say who has been the most prolific, as several of the cast have had massively successful careers, particularly in the stunt sphere.

An argument can be made for Larry Lam, who has had an amazing run as a stunt performer, choreographer, and actor. He is still active in the industry (my interview with him for the book coming on his lunch break from filming in Canada) and has worked on mega-hit franchises such as *The Twilight Saga*, *The Mummy* films, and DC's *Shazam*. Despite all of the hit movies on his IMDB page, he told me he's still remembered, for one thing, Warlock.

> *Even with everything I've done the thing people ask me about, I've had people run through airports trying to get my attention to ask me about Masters, about Warlock. It's wild.*

Larry Lam
Warlock

Bridgett Riley was another cast member who went on to have a prolific career in the stunt world. She worked with Lam on *Watchmen*, one of the many high-profile projects on her resume. She also appeared in *Transformers* and *Jumper*, amongst dozens of TV and movie roles.

Other cast members who continued to work as stunt performers or fight choreographers include Ho-Sung Pak, who worked on *Westworld* and *Transformers: Age of the Fallen*, Sophia Crawford, who doubled Sarah Michelle Gellar on the iconic *Buffy: The Vampire Slayer*, and Erik Betts who worked on *24*, *Westworld*, and *The Fate of the Furious*.

Several of the Masters also branched out into less expected directions. Herb Perez, already a

CHIKARA was a Philadelphia-based pro wrestling company that can best be described as a live-action, family-friendly Lucha Libre comic book.

lawyer at the time of the show, continued that path and eventually became mayor of Foster City, California, in addition to continuing to teach Tae Kwon Do, with a particular focus on teaching children.

Ho-Young Pak took a path away from martial arts as well, entering the world of business in the field of logistics. Over the years, he worked his way through the ranks of various major companies, eventually becoming president and CEO of a major Chicago-based logistics firm.

Michael Foley has also had a very colorful post-Masters career. In addition to his work as a martial arts teacher, he has authored several books. He has also worked around the world doing seminars on self-defense to victims (or potential victims, as the case may be) of human trafficking. As we were doing our email correspondence for the book Mr. Foley was asked to go to Kenya for this very reason- a truly noble calling.

Much of the cast continued to be heavily involved in training the next generation of martial artists, passing along the values of the Code of the Dragon Star to their students. Willie Johnson, Jamie Webster, Christine Bannon-Rodrigues, Mike Bernardo, Lynette Love, Hien Nguyen, Carmichael Simon, Herb Perez, Johnny Lee Smith, and Chris Casamassa all own and operate their own martial arts academies.

I know a lot of us tried to kind of... keep the spirit of the show alive.

Herb Perez
Olympus

With all due respect to all of the outstanding cast members, in this author's humble opinion, no one has done more to keep the show's spirit alive through teaching martial arts than Willie "The Bam" Johnson.

Master Bam, or Professor Bam as he's known in some circles, can be described in many ways. To me, however, he is the living personification of the Code of the Dragon Star. In the two and a half decades since the show, he has dedicated his life, both personal and professional, to help improve the lives of children through martial arts.

It's all a part of the same thing. We teach those same lessons, that creed. It's called something different, but the base of it is the same.

Willie Johnson
The Bam

Master Bam teaches "The Warrior Mindset," a creed that preaches several of the same concepts that made up the points of the Dragon Star, including respect, determination, and discipline. His martial arts school services Baltimore, Maryland, one of the toughest cities in the US for youth to grow up in. It's a place that has informed much of Master Bam's work and something near and dear to his heart.

I want kids to see that they don't have to go to the streets. They have options. I don't want kids- my kids, other kids, any kids- to end up doing what I did, end up going to jail. With everything going on in the world, with COVID and all the death and drugs and violence, I want to give kids the chance to take a different path.

Willie Johnson
The Bam

His work, which has grown to include books, music, and movies, all centers around this concept. As of this writing, he is in the midst of a drive to try to fund one million martial arts scholarships for youth across the United States. In the course of working with him on interviews for this book and planning the August 2022 *WMAC Masters* reunion in Washington, DC, we spoke for hours, and every conversation was packed with passion for the youth of America. I can't count the times he told me, "It's all about the kids."

It is impossible to rank, quantify, or even do justice to the myriad accomplishments and influences the cast and crew of *WMAC Masters* have left in the show's wake. I have done my best to shine a light on some of the connections and impacts the show made across martial arts and entertainment, but they're best viewed for yourself. The films, fights, stunts, and other action scenes that live on forever on film (or digital) are only part of the show's legacy. The lessons it taught an entire generation of would-be martial artists and the philosophy it extolled are perhaps its even greater legacy. It is my sincere hope this book did it some small justice.

THANK YOU

There are entirely too many people to thank for me to even know where to begin. When I started this project, I envisioned thanking the cast for their participation and maybe a few people who helped me along the way. Now, one year and hundreds of conversations later, I remain overwhelmed by the number of people who have gone out of their way to help me on this journey.

First and foremost, I must thank the cast and crew of *WMAC Masters* who spoke to me for this book. Every single one, without fail, treated me not as an over-excited fan asking them questions but as a legitimate journalist, an equal, and their encouragement and respect lifted me enormously during times of self-doubt (of which there were many). From the first person I spoke with for the book, the incomparable Chris Casamassa, to the last, the cast and crew were a pleasure to talk to. The fact that these amazing people took time out of their busy schedules, often more than once, to field questions for a book they weren't seeing a cent for remains one of the most amazing, humbling experiences of my life.

I do feel the need to recognize a couple of people from the show for their help above and beyond. First is Dan Hubp, who, in addition to answering dozens of questions about the show after our initial interview, also provided most of the fantastic behind-the-scenes art and documents you see in this book, as well as the drawings for the cover. I have unofficially dubbed him the WMAC Archivist, as he had more info and documentation for me than anyone. This book would be so much less without him.

The second is Isaac Florentine. Interviewing him was a huge boon to the book in its own right. But, in addition to the wonderful stories he shared, he also sent me an email with almost a dozen contacts to reach out to, including executive producer Norman Grossfeld.

Norman is another I want to thank specifically. He has trusted me to tell the story of what could have happened in season three of the show. He didn't have to share that with me, but he did. Not only did he give this book its major "hook" in doing so, but he also fulfilled a long-standing desire to find out the truth.

Last but not least, on the crew side, I owe a huge debt of thanks to Shannon "Irish" Stewart. Despite being a super busy badass writer with a million spinning plates going at all times, she still routinely went out of her way to help me track down and contact crew to interview. Her continued support and enthusiasm were amazing, and her advice was incredibly valuable.

On the cast side, everyone was a joy to speak with, no matter how hard they were to track down. I do want to give special thanks to Jamie Webster, Carmichael Simon, and Willie Johnson, who all went well beyond the typical interviewer-interviewee relationship. Master Webster was a fountain of information. I think I spoke to him about the show longer than anyone else. His stories and memories were amazing, and talking to him felt like talking to a cool uncle. He's just that friendly. In addition to being a great person to interview, Master Bam has become a mentor to me. Sitting under his learning tree has been massively illuminating, and I'm beyond grateful for his advice and guidance. He also allowed me to be a part of the cast reunion he put together at the 2022 US Capitol Classics, something he didn't have to do by any stretch of the imagination. I could not be more grateful. Master Simon has taken on that role as well, helping to give me a broader perspective of where this book fits into the landscape, as well as offering amazing and inspiring advice.

Outside of the cast and crew, I've been helped by innumerable people, fans of the show and martial artists, TV writers and pro wrestlers, and a myriad more.

Rommel Thorpe of the Mel and Smooth podcast was beyond helpful, particularly helping me secure a couple of major names to interview. I am lucky to call him a friend. His show has interviewed most of the cast, and they are all amazing interviews to watch. Anyone looking for more stories after this book should check them out immediately.

Cytonius from the Youtube Channel OMNIFRAME is another creator I connected with who has become not only a supporter but a friend. He is the person who brought the *Martial Masters* sales tape to my attention, and I can't thank him enough for it.

To everyone who has supported the book on social media, and especially on Patreon, you have been a constant encouragement. The enthusiasm you all have had for the book has carried me when my own has started to wane.

Nimrod Zalmanowitz, Nick Nielsen, the staff of Webster Martial Arts, the staff of Bernardo Martial Arts, and Daniel Pesina are all owed a debt of gratitude for their efforts to help me secure interviews, no matter how successful those attempts ultimately were.

Last but furthest from least, I want to thank my team. My amazing wife, Victoria, has supported this crazy endeavor from day one and also designed this book and turned it into the amazing document you now hold. In May of 2021, I told her, "I think I kind of blacked out and did a thing. I might have just started a new project." She is used to me having a million ideas, and neither of us thought it would end up anywhere near this big. She is the best wife, mother to our children, support system, and partner I could ask for. I'm truly lucky to have her.

My editor, Jenny Liedecker, also should be venerated as a saint, if only for having to deal with my erratic sense of punctuation and proclivity for using "air quotes." She makes me a better writer and has made this book immeasurably better.

Laura Marie Bailey-Schmidt and Tristan Strecker also provided vital help in my hour of need, and both deserve a round of thanks.

To everyone who has made this book possible, I love you all and hope this book makes you proud.